William B. Worsfold

South Africa

A study in colonial administration and development. Second Edition

William B. Worsfold

South Africa

A study in colonial administration and development. Second Edition

ISBN/EAN: 9783744755573

Printed in Europe, USA, Canada, Australia, Japan

Cover: Foto ©Andreas Hilbeck / pixelio.de

More available books at **www.hansebooks.com**

SOUTH AFRICA

A STUDY IN COLONIAL ADMINISTRATION AND
DEVELOPMENT.

BY

W. BASIL WORSFOLD, M.A.

OF UNIVERSITY COLLEGE, OXFORD; AND OF THE MIDDLE TEMPLE,
BARRISTER-AT-LAW

SECOND EDITION, REVISED

METHUEN & CO.
36 ESSEX STREET, W.C.
LONDON
1897

PREFACE.

In these pages I have endeavoured to set out in a connected form the most important features in the past history and present circumstances of South Africa.

Additional information, with extracts from authorities somewhat difficult of access, is contained in the Notes; and I have added a Historical Summary, a Statistical Appendix, and the Text of the Convention of London. This latter is given because of its importance (as governing to a large extent the present relationships of England to the Transvaal), and also because the Blue-book which contains it is, I understand, out of print.

I should perhaps say that I have been able to bring information acquired during a residence of nearly two years in the Cape Colony and Natal to bear upon the treatment of this subject.

W. B. W.

LAMB BUILDING,
June 10*th*, 1895.

PREFACE TO SECOND EDITION.

THE rapid march of events in South Africa has made it necessary to increase the original contents of this book by two additional chapters, which deal respectively with the recent disturbances in the Transvaal and the insurrection of the natives under the administration of the Chartered Company.

In connection with these chapters I desire to acknowledge my indebtedness to Mr Henry Hess for his courtesy in permitting me to embody in the text some remarks on the Jameson case and other comments taken from articles which I had contributed to the *African Critic*.

At the same time I have taken the opportunity afforded by the issue of a fresh edition to bring the information contained in the original chapters down to the present date.

I have also added three notes, which refer respectively to the Transvaal Legislation of 1896, the population of Johannesburg, and the Rinderpest.

W. B. W.

LAMB BUILDING, TEMPLE, E.C.,
December 7th, 1896.

TABLE OF CONTENTS.

CHAPTER I.
EARLY HISTORY.

Variety of political and social conditions of South Africa makes its history specially instructive—Connection of South-east Africa with trading nations of antiquity—The discovery of the maritime route to India causes the Cape to be used as a half-way-house by the Portuguese, English, and Dutch traders—A station established in 1652 by the Dutch East India Company—The station becomes a settlement—Huguenot emigration—Relations of the Company to the natives, and to the Franco-Dutch settlers—Review of the period of the Company's government 1

CHAPTER II.
THE KAFIR WARS.

Early British Government. Introduction of English element by Albany Settlement—The expansion of the Cape Colony becomes a record of conflicts between the white settlers and the Kafirs, *i.e.* military Bantu—Emancipation of coloured races within the colony—Colonial frontier policy reversed by Lord Glenelg—Emigration of large section of Franco-Dutch population—The cost of the Kafir wars determines the British Government to allow the dismemberment of the white communities, and to withdraw from the administration of native territories outside the limits of the Cape Colony and Natal—Independence of emigrant farmers in the Transvaal (1852), and in the Orange River Sovereignty (1854), recognised—Grant of Representative Government to the Cape Colony—General progress of the Colony . . 25

CHAPTER III.
SIR BARTLE FRERE AND FEDERATION.

Sir George Grey—Kafir Policy—German immigration—His condemnation of dismemberment of South Africa, and proposals for the introduction of a Federal system—The discovery of diamonds causes the reversal of the policy of non-intervention—Resumption of British authority over Griqualand West (Kimberley district) in 1871—Dissatisfaction of the Free State—Lord Carnarvon's proposal for reuniting the white states in a federal system similar to that of the Canadian Dominion—Mr Froude's mission—The annexation of the Transvaal in April 1877—Sir Bartle Frere appointed to give effect to Lord Carnarvon's policy in 1877. Widespread movement of revolt among the Bantu peoples—The subjugation of the natives becomes a condition precedent to the re-union of the white communities—The revolt of the Kafirs under Kreli crushed—Ketshwayo's "fighting machine" broken up by the Zulu war—Reduction of Sikukuni—Settlement of Zululand by Wolseley—Movement among the Transvaal burghers for the restoration of their independence—Sympathy with them in England and in the Cape Colony—The Federation proposals of the Cape ministry abandoned—Recall of Sir Bartle Frere—Review of his administration (1877-80) 43

CHAPTER IV.

THE BOERS.

Transvaal Revolt—History of the Boers—Their services to South Africa—Defeat of Moselekatse and Dingan—Relations between the emigrant farmers and the Imperial Government—Transvaal Revolt, 1880-81—Attitude of the Free State; of the Africander party at the Cape—Services of Sir Evelyn Wood—Retrocession of Transvaal can only be justified on grounds of political expediency—Position of the Boers in South Africa 61

CHAPTER V.

NATAL AND THE KAFIR PROBLEM.

Constitution of Natal a separate colony in 1848—European emigration — Physical characteristics of the country—Carrying trade—Sugar Industry—Indian labour imported for the plantations—Development of Coal Mines—Grant of Responsible Government in 1893—Smallness of white population (one in ten)—System of native administration—Rapid increase of Kafir population—Question of the growth of the Bantu population in South Africa—The wider question of the ultimate numerical relationship between the white and coloured races of the world raised

CONTENTS ix

PAGE

in Pearson's "National Life and Character" —Native education in the Cape Colony and its results—Mr Pearson's "Forecast" 79

CHAPTER VI.
THE BECHUANALAND SETTLEMENT.

The Hottentots and Bushmen (yellow-skinned) are practically extinct, but the various branches of the Bantu (dark-skinned) race thrive in South Africa—Comparison of military and industrial Bantu—Basutoland : ability displayed by Moshesh —Bechuanaland : the scene of the labours of Moffat and Livingstone—The trade route to Central Africa—Western Border of Transvaal not delimited until 1884—Claim of Boers to Sovereignty over Bechuanas—In 1884 Imperial Government determine to assume control of northward expansion of the white settlers—In defiance of British Protectorate Transvaal freebooters effect settlements in 1884— Importance of maintaining the trade route to the interior recognised—Change of opinion in the Cape Colony— Bechuanaland expedition under Warren—Restoration of British prestige in South Africa—The Bechuanaland settlement is the turning point in British Administration of South Africa 99

CHAPTER VII.
AGRICULTURAL AND PASTORAL RESOURCES.

Sea-borne trade of England—Deficiency of South Africa in grain, cattle and sheep as compared with other new Anglo-Saxon countries—Situation and characteristics of chief agricultura and pastoral districts—Special industries, ostrich farming, angora goat, and wine farming—Deficiency due to uncertain rainfall, and unprogressiveness of Boer—Evidence of travellers unanimous—Man, not nature, at fault—Efforts of Colonial Government—Agricultural department created, and means for (scientific) agricultural education provided throughout the Colony—System of land tenure in British colonies generally, and in the Cape Colony—New countries must not be judged by the same tests as old countries . . 117

CHAPTER VIII.
THE DIAMOND MINES (KIMBERLEY).

Accounts of the discovery of diamonds—Rush to the Vaal in 1870—Kimberley mine opened, July 21, 1871—Small extent of diamondiferous area—Geology of diamond mines : pro-

b

bably volcanic funnels filled with mud—Origin of diamonds a mystery. Difficulties and discomforts of early miners—Formation of "Mining Board" in 1874—Old system: ownership by claim and surface working—Claims gradually converted into companies as difficulty of working increases—Reef (*i.e.* sides of workings) falls in—Crisis in 1883—The problem of sinking shafts for subterranean working solved—Amalgamation of companies: until, in 1888, the De Beers Consolidated Mines practically absorbs the whole industry—Regulation of output and economy of working secured—Description of mines: methods of extracting diamonds from soil raised from mines; housing and payment of European employés; absolute control of natives—Town of Kimberley—Special legislation and extraordinary precautions to prevent the illicit sale of diamonds in the Cape Colony—The story of the diamond industry a remarkable record of commercial enterprise . . . 136

CHAPTER IX.
GOLD-MINING.

Distribution of minerals throughout South Africa—Iron: Copper: Silver: Coal: Gold—History of gold-mining in the Transvaal—Original discovery discountenanced by Government on political grounds—Gold laws—Gold-mining commenced at Leydenburg in 1873; at De Kaap fields in 1882; at Witwatersrandt in 1886—Foundation of Johannesburg in 1886-87, now a town of 70,000 inhabitants—Description of the Randt basin—Estimates of the extent of the auriferous deposits—Comparison and review of gold out-put of North America, Australia, and South Africa—The world's out-put, 1700-1894—Effect of increased gold product upon commerce of the world 152

CHAPTER X.
CONFLICT OF NATIONALITIES AND RACES.

Out of three (main) elements, Bantu, Dutch and English, are formed a variety of governments differently related to the Imperial Government and to each other—An inquiry into the comparative failure of British administration—Divergences of opinion between the Imperial and Colonial Governments—More fatal than special difficulties—Nationality difficulty and native question—Examples of disagreement between "the man in Downing Street" and "the man on the spot"—England never assumed the rôle of para-

CONTENTS

mount power until 1884—In 1884-85 (Bechuanaland) the Imperial Government avoided the mistake of 1854, and determined to control the northward expansion of the whites—Extension of this policy to Mashonaland in 1889—The factor of race is becoming gradually less important—Partial union of parties effected by Mr Rhodes—Amalgamation of the Dutch and English races is being brought about by the spread of education and extension of railway communication—Question of slavery lay at the root of the separation of the Europeans in South Africa—Treatment of natives is still most formidable barrier to reunion—Mr Rhodes deals with the Bantu problem by the Glen Grey Act—The Africander race 166

CHAPTER XI.

SOUTH AFRICAN LITERATURE.

Colonial literature; in what sense it can be distinguished as such; birth of the author in a colony not a sufficient test; knowledge of special locality and of local character not enough; the characteristic quality is the reproduction of the spirit, and not the letter, of colonial life—This "feeling" gives a special value to the poetry of Adam Lindsay Gordon and Rudyard Kipling; to the prose-fiction of Browne (Rolf Boldrewood), and Olive Schreiner—Thomas Pringle is a South African poet, he portrays characteristic incidents in the life of the natives and settlers; his inspiration comes from the desert and the wild uplands of the Eastern frontier—Olive Schreiner: her youth—The "Story of an African Farm" is a book of "thought"; Part i. is a study of child-life in a South African setting; Part ii. an essay on woman's rights. The book is redolent of the Karoo, its incompleteness, its strange gaps, faithfully reflect the physical and moral conditions under which it was written—It is valuable to the student as a picture of typical South African life and of Boer character—Estimate of its literary merit—Political essay-writing at the Cape . . . 186

CHAPTER XII.

THE CHARTERED COMPANY AND MR CECIL RHODES.

Mashonaland identified by Mr Theodore Bent with the land of Ophir—Zimbabwe ruins—Victoria Falls on Zambesi—Conquest of Mashonaland by the Matabele Zulus and devastation of country—Extension of British sphere to the Zambesi

	PAGE
(1885)—Concession granted by Lobengula for exploring and prospecting (1888)—Charter granted to British South Africa Company (1889)—The Occupation of Mashonaland by the Company—The Pioneer expedition, conducted by Selous, reaches Salisbury, Sept. 12, 1890—Colquhoun administrator, 1890-91 ; Jameson, 1891—Anglo-Portuguese Convention (1891) opens east coast—Lobengula attacks Mashonas in Victoria—Matabele war, 1893—Extension of railway and telegraph systems northward—Development of Mashonaland plateau—Growth of Buluwayo—Commercial basis of Charterland—Shareholders' profits from minerals only—Mr Rhodes' "Patent"—Prospects of gold-mining—Buluwayo in Autumn 1895	204

CHAPTER XIII.

THE REVOLT OF THE UITLANDERS.

Terms of Transvaal Independence in 1881—Alteration of position of British population by successive enactments of the Raad—The admitted grievances of the Uitlanders—Lord Loch's action in 1894—Dr Jameson's incursion—Mr Chamberlain's action—Lord Rosmead (Sir H. Robinson) at Pretoria—Position of Mr Rhodes—Trial of Reformers at Pretoria—of Dr Jameson in London—Responsibility for the Raid 223

CHAPTER XIV.

THE INSURRECTION OF THE NATIVES IN RHODESIA.

Immediate changes in the Chartered Company consequent upon the Raid—South Africa Committee—Causes of Native Insurrection—Action of local government and settlers—Measures taken by High Commissioner and Imperial Government to relieve whites—Colonel Plumer's force—General Carrington appointed to command—Course of military operations—Shooting of M'Limo—Mr Rhodes's *Indaba*—Reforms proposed by Chartered Company—The future of Rhodesia 245

NOTES 265
HISTORICAL SUMMARY 291
STATISTICAL APPENDIX 295
TEXT OF CONVENTION OF LONDON 300

CHAPTER I

The Early History and Occupation by the Dutch East India Company.

IN one of those reflections which delight us by their simplicity and astonish us by their profundity, Pascal remarks that the first object of a man's study is his own person, that is to say, that portion of matter which is immediately under his own control. But he adds that a man can never attain to a full knowledge of himself until he has mastered the science of the universe. And the same thought occurs in a somewhat different form in that defiant line in the opening stanza of Mr Rudyard Kipling's ballad of " The English Flag "—

" And what should they know of England, who only England know ? "

Somewhat on this principle I am going to commence the study of South Africa by a review of the leading characteristics of the other three great provinces of the Empire —Australasia, Canada, and India ; and by a comparison of South Africa with these provinces.

South Africa—which means for us Africa south of the Zambesi, omitting the German territory on the west, and the Portuguese territory on the east, coasts—has an area (in round numbers) of one and a quarter million square miles, and a population of four millions. It resembles Australia to some extent in physical characteristics, for in both countries there are central and western desert lands, and mountainous and more fertile eastern and southern littorals. In both countries the land requires to be irrigated and fertilised, and the task of turning the desert into the garden is the primary labour which engrosses the inhabitants of both alike. The area of Australasia—that is, Australia and New Zealand—is more than twice as large as that of South Africa, but its population is the same—four millions. There is a circumstance, however, which makes the character of these two provinces of the Empire entirely different: whereas the population of South Africa is composed of Europeans and natives in the proportion of one to seven or eight, the four million people of Australasia are almost exclusively of Anglo-Saxon origin.

The area of Canada, or British North America, is nearly three times as extensive as that of South Africa; and its population, which is composed almost entirely of persons of European origin, is five millions. In physical characteristics the two countries are absolutely diverse. Canada is well supplied with navigable rivers and inlets of the sea. South Africa is peculiarly deficient in this respect. In the "barren ground" of Northern Canada is the haunt of the musk-ox; the Kalihari desert is the home of the lion. But there is a point of resemblance between Canada and South Africa. In both countries the European population is divided into two sections. In Canada there are a million and a half French people and three and a half millions of English; and in South Africa the Dutch population exceeds the English in the proportion of five to four. In both countries, therefore, there is the "nationality" difficulty, the difficulty of making two diverse peoples pull together in the work of civilisation.

Lastly there is India. The area of the two countries [*] is much the same, but their respective physical characteristics are absolutely unlike. With its deficient rainfall and its useless rivers, South Africa grows barely enough food

[*] Including Burmah in the area of "India."

EARLY HISTORY AND OCCUPATION 3

for its small population, but India is a very garden for fertility, and supports a population of little less than *three hundred* millions. But here, again, there is a point of contact. In both India and South Africa the basis of the population is formed by the native races. In certain districts of South Africa there is an overwhelming majority of dark-skinned people, and in these districts the social and political conditions are those of India. That is to say, the coloured races are controlled and administered by the handful of Europeans resident among them.

From the political point of view, South Africa exhibits a bewildering variety. Unlike Canada, the several states are not yet united under a Central Government; unlike Australia, these states are by no means equally advanced in the path of civilisation. The two colonies, the Cape of Good Hope (with which Southern Bechuanaland is now incorporated) and Natal, enjoy the freedom of "responsible government." The Free State and the South African Republic, or the Transvaal, are two Dutch Republics possessing full internal freedom. Of the native territories, some are administered by Imperial, and some by colonial officers. Finally, there is the British South Africa Company, which exercises a civil administration over territories as extensive as the combined areas of France, Germany, Italy, and Austria. In certain territories the "regulations" * of the Company's Administrator have the force of law by virtue of their Charter and subsequent Agreements with the Imperial Government.

But if the political conditions of South Africa are characterised by variety, an equally well-marked note of uniformity runs through its physical features. Great ranges of mountains run down the eastern coast, along the southern coast, and more brokenly up the western coast, at varying distances from the coast-line which they thus approximately follow. Behind these barrier

* Clause 10, Agreement of May 1894.

ranges are high plateaux declining into the western and central deserts; between the ranges and the sea the land falls rapidly either in terraces, or in a succession of lesser ranges, or in both. There are two facts then which the briefest survey of the physical characteristics of South Africa reveals. In the first place, owing to the great elevation of the central regions, the climate improves as we advance from the coast inland; and, in the second, the spasmodic character of the rainfall (due in part to the disposition of the great mountain ranges), acting in combination with the rapid fall of the land from the high plateaux or mountain ranges to the coast, renders the rivers of South Africa singularly inefficient for purposes both of irrigation and of navigation.

The history of South Africa does not begin with the station which Van Riebeck planted in 1652, in the south-western corner of the Continent, but on the low-lying land of the south-east coast. It is unnecessary to recapitulate the interesting chain of evidence by which the identity of Mashonaland with the "Ophir" of antiquity is practically established by Mr Theodore Bent. It is sufficient to know the result of this evidence as it is summed up in a single sentence by the explorer.*

"Here, near the east coast of Africa, far nearer to Arabia than India and China and other places, which they were accustomed to visit, not only is there evidence of the extensive production of gold, but also evidence of a cult, known to Arabia and Phœnicia alike, temples built on accurate mathematical principles, containing kindred objects of art, methods of producing gold known only to have been employed in the ancient world, and evidence of a vast population devoted to the mining of gold."

This, then, was the most fruitful source from which was drawn that supply of the precious metals with which

* "Ruined Cities of Mashonaland," pp. 193-4.

EARLY HISTORY AND OCCUPATION 5

Phœnicia was enriched at the period when Zechariah said of her principal city, "Tyre heaped up silver as the dust, and fine gold as the mire of the streets." Here, too, was the storehouse of that profusion of wealth of which Horace spoke when he taunted the Roman millionaire with the thought that "the undivided possession of all the treasures of Arabia and the sumptuous Orient"* could not case the heart of the dread of death.

And now a difficulty arises. How was it that the inquisitive Greek and the ubiquitous Roman remained in ignorance of the region from which their supplies of this precious metal came? Because, says Mr Theodore Bent, it was part of the recognised policy of the Semitic nations to rigorously conceal the knowledge of their trading routes—whether those routes led westward beyond the pillars of Hercules to the White Island of the Atlantic, or eastward to India, China, and the east coast of Africa. The secret was kept so well that it was not until the end of the fifteenth century that the nations of Europe were brought into direct trading connection with the East.

At this period the Mohammedans had succeeded the Phœnicians as the commercial intermediaries between the East and West, and in order to understand the political significance of the discovery of the maritime route to India, we must regard that discovery as part of the great political duel between the East and the West which runs through the whole course of history. In that duel the chief antagonists were Greece and Persia, Rome and Parthia, Christendom and Islam. The merit of opening up the maritime route to the East belongs to the Infante Henry of Portugal. This prince, it is pleasant for Englishmen to reflect, was very closely connected with our own royal family. His mother was Philippa of Lancaster; Henry IV. was his uncle, and

* "Intactis opulentior
  Thesauris Arabum et divitis Indiae."—'Odes,' III. 24.

Henry V., the conqueror of Agincourt, his cousin. In his youth he was engaged in the wars with the Moors in Africa; and, as a result of this experience, he appears to have added a passion for geographical research to the enmity which he inherited against that people. He founded a naval college and an observatory, and, in spite of failures and discouragements, sent out a succession of navigators to explore the western coast of Africa and find an ocean pathway to the East. In fact, he seems to have grasped this central fact—that, so long as the trade of Europe with the East remained in the hands of the Mohammedans, the merchants of Europe were undoing the work of her captains and men-at-arms. For although the Moors had been driven from the Iberian Peninsula, the Turks were securely seated at Constantinople, and threatened to advance into the heart of Europe: and it was the profits of a world-wide trade which supplied the treasure by which this formidable military power was supported.

Henry the Navigator died in 1460. He died, therefore, without seeing the fruition of his plans. In 1486, in the reign of John II. of Portugal—the brother of the Infante Henry—Bartholomew Diaz, while engaged in this work of exploring the western coast of Africa, was carried by a storm to the southward. At first he steered in an easterly direction, but when he failed to make the land, he altered his course, and eventually struck the southern coast of the continent at a point slightly westward of Cape Agulhas. On his return to Portugal he proposed to name the terrible promontory where he had been overtaken by the storm, the "Cape of Tempests." But John, realising the importance of the discovery, changed the name to one of happier augury—the "Cape of Good Hope." At the same time the king sent to Cairo and to Aden, at that time the centres of geographical knowledge, to collect information respecting the routes to the East.

EARLY HISTORY AND OCCUPATION 7

Ten years later, in the reign of Emanuel the Fortunate, Vasco da Gama started on his memorable voyage. He left Portugal in July 1497, reached the Cape in November, touched at Natal on Christmas Day, and finally presented his credentials at Calicut, on the west coast of Hindostan, early in the following year. Only six years previously Columbus had discovered America in his endeavour to achieve a similar purpose; and so it happened that two events so pregnant with change as the discovery of the " new world " of America, and the establishment of direct maritime communication between the western nations of Europe and the East, were almost contemporaneous.

From this time onwards Portuguese, Spanish, Dutch, English and French ships made the Cape of Good Hope, or rather Table Bay, a port of call on the voyage to and from the East; but it was not until a hundred and fifty years later that a permanent station was established there.

By this time the East India trade had to a large extent fallen into the hands of the Dutch and English. It had been organised by the establishment of two great trading corporations, the Dutch and English East India Companies, which were chartered almost simultaneously in the opening years of the seventeenth century.

The event which immediately led to the foundation of a naval station at the Cape by the Dutch East India Company was the wreck of the *Haarlem* in Table Bay in 1648. The crew of the unfortunate East Indiaman remained on the shore of Table Bay for five months before they were carried back to Holland by the homeward bound fleet. On their return, two of the shipwrecked crew, Janssen and Proot, drew up a "remonstrance," which they presented to the Chamber XVII., the directory of the Company. In this memorial they set out the advantages which, in their opinion, would arise from the establishment of a station there, and enlarged upon the suitability of the place for this purpose. Ultimately the directors decided to carry out the proposal, and the command of the expedition was given to Jan Antony van Riebeck, a surgeon in the Company's service.

The scope of the Company's operations was exceedingly limited. Their object was entirely practical, and excluded any motives of political ambition, or religious or scientific enthusiasm. Van Riebeck was instructed to erect a wooden building for the accommodation of invalided sailors and soldiers; to construct a fort with accommodation for a garrison of seventy or eighty men; to form a garden where vegetables could be grown—this was a matter of great importance, for at that period scurvy was a terrible scourge; and to treat the natives kindly. He carried out with him materials for the wooden building, and four iron culverins to arm the fort: and he was further bidden to keep a diary for the information of the directors. The expedition was conveyed in three ships, the *Dromedary*, the *Heron*, and the sloop *Good Hope*, and it was composed exclusively of persons in the civil or military employment of the Company, who, with a few female relatives, amounted to a total of less than two hundred in all. Van Riebeck embarked on the *Dromedary* on the 16th December 1651, and set sail from the Texel on the 24th; and all three ships were lying at anchor in Table Bay on the morning of Sunday, the 7th April 1652.

The period of the Dutch occupation dates from the arrival of Van Riebeck. At this time what is now the Cape Colony was as much an uninhabited country as Australia was a century ago. There was a fringe of Hottentots and Bushmen inhabiting the western and southern coast districts and the banks of the Orange River, but that was all. This population, amounting to a probable total of only 150,000 degraded and miserable yellow-skinned people, were the aborigines of South Africa. The dark-skinned race—the Bantu—a people far higher in the scale of humanity—had as little claim to the title

EARLY HISTORY AND OCCUPATION

of "natives" as the Europeans; but they had already passed down the eastern coast between the Drakensberg and the Indian Ocean, and penetrated southwards as far as the Kei River. And so the southern extremity of the continent came to be occupied almost contemporaneously by the Europeans and the Bantu.

The station at Table Bay was a very small affair. As a unit in the system of the Dutch East India Company (Note 1), it was simply a dependency of the third rank of the Council of India, which sat at Batavia, in Java, then, as now, the centre of the Dutch possessions in the East. Van Riebeck was styled only a "Commander," and he was liable to be superseded whenever an admiral or a high official came into Table Bay. Some of the most important of the early measures of the Cape Government are due to the presence and action of these visiting authorities. The Commander was assisted in the government by a "Council of Policy." The first council was formed by Van Riebeck, the sergeant, and the "bookkeeper": but when it sat as a court of justice, the constable of the fortress, and the two corporals, were admitted to the board. The only religious functionary was the "sick-comforter." Marriages were performed in the presence of the Secretary of the Council, after the banns had been published by the "sick-comforter."

For the first few years this handful of Europeans lived the sort of life which is described in those imaginary accounts of persons wrecked on uninhabited or savage coasts so dear to our boyhood. A picture of almost photographic exactness is presented to us in the "Diary" which Van Riebeck was ordered to keep, and of which a great part has been fortunately preserved.* Under the date October 1652, we read that Herman Van Vogslaar was convicted of "wishing the purser at the devil for

* "The Record," a collection of original documents made by Donald Moodie, Lieut. R.N. : published at Capetown in 1838.

serving out penguins instead of pork," and sentenced "to receive one hundred blows from the butt-end of a musket." On January 1st, 1653, the first cabbage was cut. On the 15th of the same month a galiot, or despatch boat, arrived from Europe. Among the items of news which she brought were accounts of the execution of Charles I., and of the declaration of war between the Commonwealth and Holland. On Sunday, October 19th, David Janssen, a herdsman, was assegaied to death during service-time by the Hottentots, and the cattle under his charge were stolen. On March 6th, 1854, a dead "basmanneken," or baboon, was found and eaten. The animal is described as being "as large as a small calf," and was evidently regarded as a welcome accession to the larder. On the 6th of April, the second anniversary of the foundation of the settlement was celebrated. "Owing to scarcity of bread and meat," it was impossible for the little community to have a feast; but, "we abstained from labour," the diary says, "and listened to a long sermon, and thus made the most we could of the occasion." June 29th, 1656, was observed as "a day of prayer and humiliation." The community were reproved for their carelessness shown in the omission of prayer before partaking of food; and the Council ordered that the neglect of this religious duty should be punished by a fine amounting to 1s. for the first offence, and 2s. for the second, *beside* " arbitrary correction "

Five years after the arrival of the expedition, a step was taken by the Directors which changed the establishment at the Cape from a mere naval station to a permanent European settlement. At this time the residents in and around the fort on the shores of Table Bay amounted to 134 white persons and a few slaves. In April 1657, nine soldiers and sailors were discharged and established as market-gardeners or farmers on the banks of the Liesbeck, the small stream which traverses the Cape Peninsula, at a place called then, as now, Rondebosch, and situated

EARLY HISTORY AND OCCUPATION 11

about three miles from the fort. They were allowed to occupy holdings of twenty-six acres in extent, and they were provided with tools and seeds from the Company's stores. They were also exempted from taxation for a period of years. In return for these benefits, the settlers, euphemistically termed "free burghers," were required to bring their produce to the Company's stores, and sell it at prices fixed by the Company's officers. After the Company's requirements had been satisfied, they were at liberty to dispose of their surplus produce to the crews of foreign ships in the Bay; but they were not allowed to go on board these ships until three days after arrival—that is to say, until the Company had itself sold all that it desired to sell. Similarly, in regard to cattle, they were compelled to purchase from the Hottentots at the same prices as the Company paid, and to sell only to the Company.

These arrangements are characteristic of the principles and methods of colonisation pursued by the Dutch East India Company during the whole period of their occupation of the Cape. The colony was regarded merely as an estate belonging to the Company, and the settlers as the agents of the Company employed in the cultivation of this estate, and entitled, therefore, to only such profits as were recognised by the terms of their employment. Under the name of the "Culture" system, these principles may be seen in partial operation to-day in Java. Even in that country the system has become discredited; and it is one which is wholly unsuited to a settlement of Europeans which is in any sense a "colony" according to the modern acceptance of the term.

This essay in colonisation was the occasion of the first serious conflict between the Europeans and the Hottentots. One of the migratory clans had been accustomed to resort periodically to the banks of the Liesbeck for pasturage. Access to these pastures was now hindered by the enclosures of the settlers; and, therefore, as a Hottentot prisoner, "who spoke tolerable Dutch," explained, the "Caepmans" resolved to "dishearten" the settlers by taking away their cattle (Note 2). The policy which the Company had at first pursued towards the Hottentots was one of "peace at any price." The cattle with which the garrison and the Company's fleets were supplied came from these nomad clans, and it was essential, therefore, that they should not be frightened away by harsh treatment. After the murder of David Janssen, Van Riebeck applied to the directors for instructions. He was ordered to put to death only the actual murderer or murderers of the dead man, and to take in reprisal only the same amount of cattle as had been stolen. These instructions were both humane and politic, but it was impossible to carry them out. In his reply Van Riebeck points out two fatal objections. In the first place, he had no means of identifying the individual evil-doers, and, in the second, private property was an institution not yet established among these tribes. The only way to punish the actual evil-doers under these circumstances was to punish the tribe *en bloc;* and he proposed, therefore, to capture the whole tribe and all their cattle. But the directors would not consent to this course, and in the end nothing was done. In this incident we have an excellent illustration of the respective attitudes of the Home and Local Authorities in questions of native policy. What the former proposes is nearly always just, and generally sound in theory; but it fails from a want of knowledge of the special circumstances of the case. That knowledge is possessed by the local authority, but he is rarely allowed to adopt the course which the local conditions require, because, without a knowledge of these conditions, such a course naturally appears at variance with the principles of conduct recognised by civilised peoples.

Van Riebeck first communicated the intelligence of the Hottentots' attack upon the Liesbeck settlement to the Indian Government. In a somewhat cool reply they advise him "to stand up stoutly to his own defence," and at the same time authorise him provisionally to increase the strength of the Cape garrison by drafts from passing ships. The attack occurred in July 1659. Peace was ultimately concluded at the Fort on April 6th, 1660, between Van Riebeck and "the captain and chief of the Caepmans" and various lesser personages. The Hottentots made many complaints, and required that free access to the pastures should be granted. In reply to the argument that "there was not grass enough for their cattle and for the settlers' cattle also," they enquired, "Have we then no cause to prevent you from procuring any cattle? for if you get many cattle, you come and occupy our pasture with them, and then say the land is not wide enough for us both! Who then can be required with the greatest degree of justice to give way, the natural owner or the foreign invader?" Worsted in argument, Van Riebeck had, at last, frankly asserted that he "would not restore the land, as it had now become the property of the Company by the sword and the laws of war." The whole of these negotiations were fully recorded in the diary, and transmitted to the directors.*

These latter admit that the "discontent" shown by the Hottentots is "neither surprising nor groundless," and suggest that the land should be purchased from them, or that they should be otherwise satisfied.

For some reason or other this politic suggestion was not carried out until twelve years later. Van Riebeck had been removed at his own request after ten years' command at the Cape, and his fidelity and capacity was rewarded by the governorship of Malacca. He subsequently became secretary to the Council of India, and his son, born at the Cape, was Governor-General of India. Other lesser men had followed him; a strong castle—of which part is still in existence — had replaced the original fort, and the

* The "Record," p. 205.

settlement had grown in numbers and in importance, when a high official, Aernout Van Overbeke, arrived on his way home from Batavia. Under his direction formal agreements were concluded with two native chiefs, by which the districts of the Cape and Hottentots Holland were respectively ceded to the Company in return for certain "goods and articles of merchandise." The actual value of the "tobacco, beads, brandy, bread and other trifles," which constituted the consideration in both cases, was extremely small—it amounted in fact to little more than a hundred florins "prime cost"—and on this account the transaction is generally represented as a mere trick. It appears, however, that at this time the directors made a serious endeavour to legalise their *de facto* possession of the Cape Peninsula and the districts beyond, by the purchase of territorial rights from the native chiefs. In the first place, they persistently pursued such a policy in Java, the centre of the operations of the Company, where they ultimately acquired possession of territorial rights over the whole island : next, although the goods were trivial to the Dutch, they had a far higher value to the Hottentot purchasers. What that value was can only be seen by comparing this transaction with other commercial dealings at the same period between the Dutch and the Hottentots. Soon after Van Riebeck's arrival "three elephants' teeth" were sold for some copper and tobacco, worth two stivers and three pennings, or $2\frac{1}{4}$d.; a sheep for a yard of thin copper wire; and three young ostriches for 2 oz. of tobacco. Obviously ten pounds worth of goods would represent a large consideration on such a scale as this. Moreover, the native chiefs did not surrender entire possession of these territories ; they were to be allowed to come with their herds to such districts as were not occupied by the farms and cattle of the Company, or by those of the "freemen" (Note 3).

It may be asked, however, why the Company did not continue this policy, and make further purchases of terri-

EARLY HISTORY AND OCCUPATION 15

torial rights? The answer appears to be this. As the Dutch advanced inland they found the country practically uninhabited, and there was, therefore, no necessity to acquire further deeds of cession. The inland districts were traversed by nomad clans of Bushmen and Hottentots, but these people, with their migratory habits, could establish no right of possession sufficient to bar the occupation of the Europeans.

It was during the governorship of Simon Van der Stell (the first official so styled), and that of his son Adrian, covering a period of nearly twenty years, from 1679 to 1707, that the material foundations of the colony were laid. Up to this time only a few persons had been induced to leave Holland for the Cape: but in 1679 a party of fifty emigrants arrived. A few years later a town was founded thirty miles in the interior to which the name of Stellenbosch was given; and the first " landdrost," or district magistrate, was appointed. In this same year, 1685, an event happened in Europe which was destined to have an important effect upon the fortunes of the Cape Settlement. By the revocation of the Edict of Nantes, the Huguenots were driven from France; and large numbers took refuge in England and Holland. The Dutch East India Company offered to provide a home for some of these French refugees at their new settlement, and, during the years 1688-90, as many as two hundred Huguenots arrived at the Cape (Note 4). This was an important accession to the population of the settlement, for these French settlers were not only numerous—relatively, that is—but they were drawn from classes higher in the social scale than the Dutch emigrants. There were farmers, shop-keepers, and even members of the French nobility among them,* and they were accom-

* Among the emigrants were members of the houses of Du Plessis, De Mornay, Roubaix de la Fontaine, De Villiers, Le Sueur, Du Pré, and Rousseau.

panied by their pastor, Pierre Simond. A few were settled on lands near Capetown and Stellenbosch, but the majority found a home in the Berg River valley.

Van der Stell was instructed to take all necessary measures for incorporating the French emigrants into the community. The settlers of both nationalities were carefully intermingled, and the French children were at once taught the Dutch language. More than one attempt was made by the French to preserve their identity, but these "French impertinences" were vigorously restrained. In 1709 the use of the French language in official communications was forbidden, and in 1724 the Bible was publicly read in French for the last time.

By these means the French element at the Cape was absolutely absorbed into the Dutch. This policy was undoubtedly harsh; but if we look at the circumstances of the settlement, we must admit that it was not only justifiable but necessary. Twenty-five years after the Huguenot emigration the whole population of the settlement amounted to only some two thousand persons, of whom nearly one-half were children. It would have been obviously most disastrous to have allowed this small community to be divided into two distinct sections, speaking different languages, and having different customs and modes of life.

The Company's administration of the Cape Settlement from its foundation to the middle of the eighteenth century appears to have been both just and politic. We cannot reasonably complain either of the policy the directors pursued towards the Hottentots or towards the French emigrants. Moreover, there was as yet no manifestation of that harsh attitude towards the coloured races which has since characterised the Franco-Dutch population in South Africa. In the seventeenth century the Dutch regarded the inferiority of the native races as a question not of colour but of faith. A profession of

EARLY HISTORY AND OCCUPATION 17

Christianity placed the coloured person on the same level as the European. In the instructions issued to Van der Stell in 1685, by Commissioner H. A. Van Rheede, directions are given for the training of the slaves* in the Company's possession. These slaves were mainly Asiatics brought from the Indian possessions of the Company.

"The labour of the Company's slaves also [*i.e.* as well as the free settlers previously discussed] produces much profit, and holds out equal hopes for the future; but these poor men must be looked upon with other eyes, for they are the Company's own people, not hirelings; they cannot quit the service of their master when tired, but are bound, not only for all their lives, but for those of their children and descendants. The better we make them, the fitter will they be to perform their duty. . . . It would be a shame to us, whose part it is to take good care of our irrational domestic cattle, if we permitted men to run wild, and left them in a worse condition than when in their fatherland. Our masters are the foster-fathers of Christ's Church, and if we fail to employ the means in our hands, and do not exert every endeavour to bring these men to the knowledge of the redeeming faith—we shut the doors of that Church."

And among the early marriages recorded in Van Riebeck's diary is that of a Bengalese slave girl, Catharina, to Jan Wonters. This girl had been set free and baptised, and she is spoken of in precisely the same terms "de eerbaare jonge dochter" as the Commander's niece.

By the middle of the eighteenth century these humane sentiments had become entirely lost. On September 3rd, 1754, a slave code of the utmost brutality was promulgated from the Castle of Good Hope. By Article 2 of this Code "death without mercy" was fixed as the penalty for "any

* "Record," p. 397.

B

male or female slave raising his hand against his master or mistress;" and by Article 23, every slave found at the entrance of a Church, when the congregation was leaving the building, was directed to be "severely flogged by the ministers of justice." And for many years in the present century, "Dogs and Hottentots not admitted" was the usual notice placed over the church doors in South Africa.

What is essential in the remaining history of the Company's Settlement can be soon told.

In 1700, the first barrier range was crossed at Tulbagh Kloof, and the settlers spread southwards down the fertile valley of the Breede River. In 1705 the Cape Government issued "loan leases," or occupation licenses which were resumable at any period, and in this uncertain tenure of their farms and grazing lands we have the origin of that nomadic manner of life which, under the form of "trekking," has constituted an important factor in South African history (Note 5).

In 1745, the eastern limit of the settlement was advanced to the Gamtoos River, and a Magistracy was established at Swellendam. During the year 1778, the Governor, Van Plettenburg, made a tour of the colony, and in the course of this tour he held a conference with the Kosa chiefs at Prinslo's farm, on the site of Somerset East. In this conference it was mutually agreed that the Fish River should be recognised as the boundary between the Europeans and the Bantu. The sequel is significant. The very next year the Kosas crossed the Fish River, murdered the Hottentots, and over-ran and plundered the eastern farms. We find again and again in South African history that an attempt on the part of the Europeans to make a peaceable settlement with the Kafirs is the prelude to a murderous attack. The reason is simple enough. The Kafir is like a child, the only sanction with which he is acquainted is the sanction of physical

EARLY HISTORY AND OCCUPATION 19

force. In all such cases he argues, "The white man wishes to make peace with me, therefore the white man is afraid of me. This, then, is the time for me to attack." Finally, in 1786, the Fish River was formally declared to be the eastern boundary of the Company's territory, and a Magistracy was established at Graaf Reinet, among the scattered graziers who had settled at the foot of the Sneuwberg Mountains.

All this time the great trading corporation, the Dutch East India Company, to which the settlement owed its existence, was growing weaker and weaker, and by the end of the century it had become hopelessly bankrupt and effete. The attempt to reform its administration made in 1791, when Commissioners-General were appointed by the Stadtholder (afterwards William I.) to discover abuses and effect reforms, proved unsuccessful, and shortly afterwards the States-General assumed the direct control of its possessions. As regards the Cape, the commercial basis upon which the Company's government was built had become increasingly insufficient for the expanding European population.

The condition of the settlers is revealed by the memorial which they presented in 1779. In this memorial they pray that the Fiscal, the highest law-officer of the Government, may be restrained from arbitrarily committing burghers to prison, and from compounding crimes by private fines; and that the practice of deportation to the Indian factories may be prohibited. At this time, the end of the eighteenth century it must be remembered, it appears that no books, except the Bible and editions of Clement Marot's version of the Psalms, were to be found in the settlement outside of Capetown. It was respectfully prayed, therefore, that "authentic copies of the particular placaats and ordinances" in force in the settlement should be furnished from Holland; or that a printing press should be established and a printer appointed. The rigour with which the Company's trading monopoly had been maintained is demonstrated by Article 18; in which the directors are humbly solicited to allow the Cape Colonists "that two ships may be laden annually, for the account of the Cape citizens, with such wares as shall be purchased by their appointed agents —the burgher representatives binding themselves to send back the said ships laden, for their account, with Cape produce," which was to be "consigned to the Honourable Company, to be sold by public auction in payment of the imported goods."

This memorial was referred to the law officer of the Cape Government, the Fiscal Boers. His reply is extremely significant. The request for political freedom is met by the broad denial of the right of the settlers to place themselves on an equality with the "privileged free citizens" of the United Provinces. "It would be a mere waste of words," he says, "to dwell on the remarkable distinction to be drawn between burghers whose ancestors nobly fought for and conquered their freedom from tyranny . . . and such as are named burghers here, who have been permitted as matter of grace to have a residence in a land of which possession has been taken by the Sovereign Power, there to gain a livelihood as tillers of the earth, tailors, and shoemakers." The prayer of the settlers for commercial freedom, for the "rights of trading beyond the colony, in ships freighted by them, to Europe, to the African coast, to India, to barter the produce of other lands for that of this country," is similarly met by a frank statement of the theory of the old colonial system. "Now it is clear, and requires no lengthy argument, that for the purpose of enabling a subordinate colony to flourish as a colony, it is not always expedient to apply these means which, considered in the abstract, might be conducive to its prosperity. The object of paramount importance in legislating for colonies should be the welfare of the parent

EARLY HISTORY AND OCCUPATION

state, of which such colony is but a subordinate part, and to which it owes its existence." *

It is not surprising, therefore, that when Commissary Sluysken, on the 16th September 1795, capitulated to Admiral Elphinstone and General Craig, the settlers at Swellendam and Graaf Reinet were in open revolt against the Company's government. The English occupation of the Cape, which terminated the period of the Dutch East India Company's government, arose out of the French war. It was necessary to prevent a point of such strategical importance—forming a convenient base from which India and the Indian trade could be attacked—from falling into the hands of France. After the treaty of Amiens, by which peace was concluded between France and England, the Cape Settlement was restored to the Dutch; and during the short period (1803-6) that it was administered by the representatives of the States-General every possible reform, commercial and political, was introduced. Subsequently on the renewal of the struggle between France and England, the Cape was again occupied, in 1806, by an English force under Sir David Baird. Since that time the English flag has not ceased to fly over the Castle at Capetown.

By the end of the last century, when the period of the government of the Dutch East India Company came to a close, the south-western corner of the continent of Africa was thinly peopled by a European population some twenty thousand in number. Towns had been founded at Capetown, Stellenbosch, Swellendam and Graaf Reinet. In the capital and its immediate neighbourhood the inhabitants had attained some measure of material prosperity; that is to say, they were housed in substantial and comfortable dwellings, and had made some progress in agriculture and viticulture. Elsewhere the settlers, living for the

* Verantwoording Van Fiscal Boers, as translated by Judge Watermeyer in "Three Lectures on the Cape of Good Hope:" Capetown, 1857.

most part in isolated homesteads, gained a scanty subsistence by the pastoral industries and hunting. There were no roads, there was no trade, no system of education, and the government was at once tyrannical and ineffective.

At the same time the Company had spread a European population over a district as large as the United Kingdom, and, if we confine our notion of a colony to the narrow limits of what would be the Company's definition, we must admit that they had been successful. They had accomplished the special object which they had in view. They had established a convenient post of call where supplies could be obtained for their fleets, and they had made this naval station self-supporting by means of the European settlers whom they introduced. Moreover, the policy which they pursued towards the natives was both humane and prudent. If, however, we take a wider view of the responsibilities of the Company, we must decide that they signally failed. It is not merely that their system of government was bad, and their trade policy uneconomic. Regarded from this point of view, it is not enough to say of the Company's system, as the late Judge Watermeyer has said,* that "in all things political it was purely despotic; in all things commercial it was purely monopolist." If we hold them responsible for the well-being of the community to which they gave birth, the directors of the Dutch East India Company were guilty of a political crime of the gravest character; they allowed a European community to become degraded and de-civilised. And it is this decivilised European community that England lightly essayed to govern at the commencement of the present century.

In comparison with the magnitude and variety of the interests involved in the South Africa of to-day, this account of the actual foundation of the Cape Settlement must necessarily appear somewhat trivial. But the

* "Three Lectures."

EARLY HISTORY AND OCCUPATION 23

traveller will gladly turn aside to visit the little stream which is the source of some great river, grudging neither the time nor the labour which he expends. Neither should we, who have embarked upon the study of the past history and present circumstances of South Africa, regret the time which we devote to a study of the details of this early period. For a knowledge of the period of Dutch occupation is a condition precedent to the adequate comprehension of those great questions of South African administration which will hereafter claim our attention.

Not only do almost, if not all, of these questions arise, but they appear in their simplest and most intelligible form. In the controversy between Van Riebeck and the directors of the Company, with reference to the course to be pursued in punishing the murderer of David Janssens, we have the prototype of those endless "divergences of opinion" between H.M.'s Government and the colonial administrators which have filled the pages of innumerable blue-books. In the reasoning of the Hottentot prisoner, who "spoke tolerable Dutch," we have an epitome of those arguments which were afterwards employed with such grave results by the great philanthropic societies of England. And in the mingled despotism and weakness of the Company's government we see the explanation of that unreasoning aversion to law and order which has unhappily characterised the rural settlers of Dutch origin, and intensified the difficulties of South African administration.

I have spoken of South African history under the figure of a river. The analogy is one which will bear pressing, for there is a curious similarity between the progress of South Africa and the course of a South African river. It is no smooth stream, flowing in a single channel down a gently falling incline. On the contrary, its brief course is diversified by every variety of incident, its waters are diverted into separate and distinct channels, and its current is alternately checked by obstacles, and precipitated onwards by abrupt descents.

And if this be a true description of the nature of South African history and progress, there is no need to add that the study of such a subject will repay the student. With its native question, its nationality difficulty, and its consolidation problem, is it too much to say that in South Africa we have an epitome of those problems upon the solution of which the stability of the Empire depends?

CHAPTER II

THE KAFIR WARS.

IN that beautiful ode,* in which Euripides dwells with loving fulness on the graces of his native Attica, he places in the forefront of his enumeration the fact that her citizens dwell in a "sacred and unravaged" land. With how much greater propriety could an English poet point to that immunity from the ravages of war which has characterised the life of later generations of Englishmen. But there are some who maintain that the discipline of war is necessary for the perfecting of national character. Such persons can find a quick consolation in the reflection that this immunity is by no means the universal experience of the Anglo-Saxon race. Putting the United States on one side—where, in the course of four years, one million lives were lost, and property and labour to the estimated value of two thousand million pounds sterling were squandered—and confining ourselves to the Anglo-Saxon communities within the Empire, there is abundant evidence to show us, who read the history of England as it is written in Canada, in India, in New Zealand, and in South Africa, that the gates are seldom entirely closed upon our British Janus. Of all the Anglo-Saxon communities which have been exposed to the ravages of war—I speak, of course, not of professional soldiers but of non-combatants, civilians, women, and children—none have been exposed more continuously or more fatally to this baneful influence than the English in South Africa.

* In the *Medea*.

But why speak of *English*? We have traced the growth of a European community at the Cape, but it was a community exclusively of Dutch and French origin. How is it that we speak of English?

The permanent English occupation of the Cape commenced in the year 1806. At first our possession rested upon the mere naked right of conquest, but subsequently our position was legitimised by the Convention of London, when, in 1814, the Cape of Good Hope, Ceylon, and a part of Guiana, were formally ceded by Holland to England. For the first twenty years—the reason for this limit will appear afterwards—the Cape Colony was governed in the arbitrary manner usual at that time and under like circumstances. There was, however, no "series of ignorant and absurd governors" at the Cape, to use the rather harsh language of Sidney Smith in his second essay on Botany Bay. The Cape was preserved from such a fate by two circumstances; its strategic importance, as commanding the maritime route to India, and the natural difficulty of administering the government of an alien population. The early governors of the Cape were men of high character and ability. They governed arbitrarily, no doubt—how arbitrarily may be seen from those two lines of Pringle, in which he sums up his experience of life at Capetown—

" Oppression, I have seen thee face to face,
And met thy cruel eye and clouded brow "—

but they were all marked by that sense of responsibility which happily characterises Englishmen of their class. And it was to Lord Charles Somerset, the most arbitrary of them all, that the first introduction of a considerable body of Englishmen was due. Lord Charles Somerset was so pleased with the appearance of the country immediately to the west of the Great Fish River that he recommended the district to the Home Government as

THE KAFIR WARS

suitable for colonisation. His suggestion came at an opportune moment, for just then the labour market of England was terribly over-stocked. By the peace of 1815 a large amount of labour, hitherto locked up in the military operations which England had been conducting against Napoleon and his allies, was set free. Out of 90,000 applications the Government accepted some 4000, and English and Scotch emigrants to that number landed at Algoa Bay between the months of April 1820 and May 1821. The bulk of them were established in the parallelogram of land formed by the Fish and the Bushman rivers, the district of Albany; and from this centre they and their descendants gradually spread themselves over the whole of the eastern provinces of the colony. It was on these English settlers that the brunt of the inevitable conflict between the Europeans and the Bantu naturally fell.

In the year 1826—the date which terminates what I have called the period of early governors—the colonial Commissioners, who had been despatched by the Home Government to the Pacific Settlements and the Cape, presented their reports. As regards the Cape, they suggested, in addition to certain administrative reforms, a number of measures which all tended in the direction of Anglicising the colony. These measures were many of them good in themselves, but they were vitiated by a common fault. They took no account of the fact that the great majority of the population—probably six in seven—were Dutch, not English. It is at least certain that such measures, under like circumstances, would never have been proposed now in any country under British rule. For example: in 1827, English was ordered to be used as the official language, although the proportion of Dutch to English was what I have stated it to be—six in seven. In 1828, the old Dutch system of local government and the Courts of Landdrost and Heemraden were abolished, and an English system, with Resident Magistrates and Civil Commissioners, was established in its place. And in this same year General Bourke's famous ordinance, placing the free coloured population of the colony on an equality in point of law with the Europeans, was issued. We shall not understand the full significance of this measure until we have become familiar with the conditions of Natal; it is enough, however, to remark here that the removal of the Hottentots from the control of those special laws by which their life had hitherto been regulated was regarded by the Dutch colonists as a dangerous and revolutionary measure. But a more far-reaching change was to follow. In 1833 the Abolition Act was passed by the Imperial Parliament. By this Act the institution of slavery was abolished throughout the British dominions. It is not necessary that we should study the arguments by which it was sought to maintain, on political or social grounds, what Lord Brougham has called "the wild and guilty fantasy that man can hold property in man." But it is necessary that we should be acquainted with the actual circumstances under which the emancipation of slaves was carried out at the Cape; otherwise we shall be at a loss to understand how it was that a measure so essentially just and humane should have excited such feelings of indignation and alarm among a European community.

In the first place, we must recollect what the conditions of the colony were at this time. If we put the total European population at 50,000 we shall probably be stating what is not far from the truth. Of this small population all, with the exception of a few officials and merchants in the towns, depended for their subsistence upon agriculture and stock-raising. Both of these industries were carried on by means of slave labour; and, for reasons which we need not now enter into, it was, in some cases, impossible, and in all cases difficult, to replace this slave

THE KAFIR WARS

labour by free coloured labour within the five years provided by the Act, or at all.

Emancipation at the Cape meant, therefore, an entire dislocation of the main—almost the only—industries of the community. In the next place it involved the colonists in an immediate loss of nearly £2,000,000—a large sum to be lost by so small a community. This sum of £2,000,000 is obtained by merely taking the difference between the officially appraised value of the slaves and the amount which actually reached the slave proprietors as compensation (Note 6). In some cases individuals—often those who could bear such a blow least well, orphans, widows, and aged persons—were reduced to absolute penury; while, speaking of the community as a whole, we may say that there was scarcely a home in the colony which was not at this time darkened by the shadow of pecuniary embarrassment.

But even this last measure, grievous and oppressive though it was felt to be, would not have driven the eastern farmers of Dutch origin to so desperate a remedy as that of expatriation—the remedy to which they now had recourse —unless it had been followed by a remarkable instance of Imperial indiscretion.

In 1834 Sir Benjamin Durban was sent out to the Cape as Governor. He was instructed to carry through slave emancipation, to initiate rigorous administrative retrenchments, and to place the relations between the Europeans and the Kafirs on a better footing. It was this last which immediately claimed his attention. On his arrival at Capetown, Sir Benjamin was confronted by two opposite opinions. On the one hand there was a small party (Note 7) of which Dr Philip, the Superintendent of the London Missionary Society's Missions in South Africa, was the head, and of which the then *Commercial Advertiser* was the mouth-piece, which represented the alarms of the eastern colonists as visionary, and the intention of the

Kafir chiefs as pacific. On the other hand there were almost all the colonial officials, civil and military. They regarded the condition of the eastern border as most unsatisfactory, and believed that a Kafir invasion was imminent. Under these circumstances Sir Benjamin Durban took what was obviously the right course. He commissioned Dr Philip to visit the Kafir chiefs and obtain from them assurances of their pacific intentions. Dr Philip did so, and on his return to Capetown he sent in a report to that effect. Meanwhile another person, the Chief Justice, Sir John Wylde, had in the course of his circuit visited Grahamstown for the purpose of holding the assizes. There he had met Macomo, who held the position of paramount chief of the Gaikas. Sir John Wylde's impressions of the intentions of Macomo and of the Kafirs in general was the very opposite of Dr Philip's. He was accompanied by the late Judge Cloete, then Mr Advocate Cloete, and the rest of the story can be given in Cloete's own words.*

"On our return to Capetown, at a numerous convivial meeting, to which Sir Benjamin had invited myself and my family on New Year's Eve, I could not help dilating somewhat at length on the hostile disposition of these tribes, to which his Excellency appeared to listen with particular interest—but nothing else indicated the slightest disturbance in society, except (what only was remembered afterwards by some of us) that Sir Benjamin had occasionally absented himself for a few minutes from the party. Good humour and hilarity prevailed until we had hailed in the New Year, when every one gradually returned to their houses; but on the next morning, on returning to town, I found the astounding intelligence universally spread abroad that the evening before his Excellency had received the account that the Kafirs, to the number of 12,000 or 15,000 men, had invaded the whole frontier from every quarter on Christmas-day, burning and destroying every farm-house,

* "Five Lectures," iii. p. 67.

murdering the inhabitants, and carrying away all their cattle and property.

"Still doubting this information," Cloete appealed to the Governor himself. " He, in his wonted gentle and yet firm manner, not only confirmed the report, but jocularly observed that he had received the sad intelligence while we were assembled there, but that he had done all that could be done, and had not wished to disturb the harmony of the party by divulging such intelligence.

"That night already every order had been given to despatch every disposable soldier, to call out all the burgher forces, and to send off Colonel Smith, the Quarter-Master General of the forces . . . who had started in the middle of the night, and in five days reached Grahamstown, where he found everything in an indescribable state of panic and confusion."

The official returns show us what a Kafir war meant for these unhappy eastern colonists. When the returns of the losses sustained by the farmers on the immediate frontier were made up, it was found that 456 farm-houses had been burnt and entirely destroyed, 356 farm-houses had been pillaged and partially destroyed, 60 waggons, 5715 horses, 111,930 head of horned cattle, and 161,930 sheep had been captured and irrecoverably lost. Within the first week fifty Europeans had been surprised and murdered.

After twelve months' hard fighting, in which the British troops were supported by the burgher forces of the colony, the Kafirs were driven out of the colony. Meanwhile it became Sir Benjamin Durban's duty to devise measures which would prevent the recurrence of such a disaster. With the approval of his colonial advisers, civil and military, Sir Benjamin determined to advance the frontier from the Keiskamma to the Kei, to place a belt of European settlers holding land on military tenure between the Fish and the Keiskamma rivers, and then eastwards, to locate a number of loyal Kafirs between the Keiskamma and the Kei rivers, with a chain of forts in their midst. In this way Sir Benjamin Durban thought that he would erect a barrier sufficiently strong to resist the pressure of the Bantu peoples who were continually crushing southwards. These proposals were duly communicated to the Home Government for approval.

At this time there were two pictures of the Kafir before the English world. In one he was represented as a noble savage who was engaged in a heroic struggle for his fatherland against European aggressors: a being, indeed, of primitive impulses, but one which was capable of almost indefinite development in the direction of morality and civilisation. In the other he appeared as a murderer, who knew no distinction of age or sex; as a destroyer, who placed his brand to the homestead for the mere pleasure of hearing the timbers crackle, and seeing the flames leap up to heaven. The first picture was illuminated by the soft rays of philanthropic enthusiasm: the second was seen in the hard, dry light of facts (Note 8). At this time the first picture only was known to Englishmen; and the temper of England was reflected in the despatch which Charles Grant, afterwards Lord Glenelg, wrote on December 26th, 1835, almost the very anniversary of that cruel and unprovoked invasion. In this despatch the opinion was maintained that it was the colonists and not the Kafirs who were the real aggressors; that the action of the Kafirs was, in fact, only a natural and legitimate result of a long series of oppressions which had been inflicted upon them; and the measures which Sir Benjamin Durban proposed to take—had, in fact, taken—were revoked, and the whole frontier policy was reversed.

The sensation which this despatch created in the colony may be understood from Cloete's comment *:—

"A communication more cruel, unjust, and insulting to

* "Five Lectures," p. 73.

the feelings,—not only of the Commander who, wholly intent upon conciliatory measures with the Kafirs, had been suddenly attacked, and seen the country placed under his authority and protection invaded, but of the inhabitants, who had not only been engaged in a twelve months' warfare of the most harassing and dangerous character, but who were smarting from a system pursued during fourteen years, by the local government never affording them redress for their most serious losses and grievances on this subject,—can hardly have been penned by a declared enemy of the country and its governor. . . ."

Then it was that the eastern farmers of Dutch origin, who had shared with their English neighbours the disasters of the war, and who, unlike them, were bound by no ties of sentiment to the British connection, determined to withdraw themselves from the jurisdiction of the British Government, and seek fresh homes beyond the borders of the colony.

Meanwhile certain movements among the Bantu tribes beyond the frontier had taken place, which show that this determination was not so desperate as it seems at first sight.

In the year 1783 a little brown baby was born on the banks of the Umvolosi River, in the centre of Zululand. That little brown baby grew into a man, who exceeded Nero in cruelty, and Napoleon in ambition. Before he was grown up, Tshaka—for that was his name—quarrelled with his own father, and took refuge in the kraal of a neighbouring chief, Dingiswayo. This Dingiswayo had heard of the great wars in Europe, and how soldiers could be trained so perfectly that a whole regiment would move with the spontaneity of a single man, and he resolved to train his braves on this principle. Tshaka became the favourite general of Dingiswayo's army, and, when the old chief died, the favourite of the army was elected to fill his place. Then Tshaka commenced a career of conquest. At the end of this career he had raised the Zulu tribe from an insignificant position to the headship of the Bantu race, and made himself paramount lord from the Limpopo to the borders of Kaffraria. His method was a very simple one. With the exception of a few of the handsomest girls and the strongest boys, whom he incorporated into his system, he exterminated every tribe he attacked. It is estimated that between the years 1812 and 1828 he devastated thousands of square miles of country, and caused the death of one million human beings. The manner of his death was worthy of such a life. Tshaka's two brothers, Dingan and Umhlangana, having been in terror of their lives for a long time, at length conspired together and slew him. Then Dingan "got rid" of Umhlangana, and became king of the Zulus. Meanwhile, on the western side of the Drakensberg a like war of extermination had been going forward under Moselekatse, a runaway general of Tshaka. And so at this time, the year 1835, the greater part of what is now Natal, the Free State, and the South African Republic, was depopulated and unoccupied country. It was to these regions that the dissatisfied farmers resolved to retire.

The emigrants sold their properties for what they would fetch; they packed their household goods into their great canvas-covered waggons, and set out, with their flocks and their herds, like the patriarchs of old. During the years 1835 to 1838, trains of waggons with their long teams of patient oxen were continually traversing the sandy plains, and slowly winding up the sides of the mountain ranges. They crossed the Orange River, and there, in what is now the Free State, they founded Winburg, the place of victory, so-called in commemoration of their victory over Moselekatse and his Matabele Zulus. They scaled the Drakensberg, and, descending the eastern side of the ranges looked forth upon the terrace country of Natal. Here they founded Weenen, the place of weeping, where Dingan butchered whole companies of their people, and Pietermaritzburg, so-named after two of their leaders. Subsequently they recrossed the Drakensberg, and passing into the Transvaal, founded Lydenburg in the high country in the north-east, and Potchefstroom in the south.

And in the meantime what was the English Government doing?

When first the Colonial Government heard that it was the intention of the dissatisfied farmers to leave the colony, they referred the matter to the Attorney-General, Sir Antony Oliphant. He advised the Government that he knew of the existence of no law, Imperial or colonial, which forbade British subjects to leave a British territory. After this, that is to say for the next eight or ten years, the Colonial Government, acting under instructions from home, contented themselves with merely refusing to recognise the existence of the white communities which were being so irregularly brought into existence. There was, however, an exception to the application of this principle—Natal. The case of Natal was peculiar. In the first place, there was already a small English population at Durban, and in the next, Natal was a maritime province, and, therefore, of more importance than the interior districts. In 1839 Durban was occupied by a military force, and in 1843 it was proclaimed British territory. At the same time, the Government endeavoured to protect the natives of the interior from the aggressions of the emigrant farmers by entering into alliances with various native chiefs, of whom the most important was Moshesh, chief of the Basutos.

In 1846 a fresh Kafir war broke out. In the course of this war a large number of British soldiers lost their lives, and a large amount of British capital was expended; and after this experience the Imperial Government decided that a more energetic policy was necessary in South Africa. Accordingly they appointed Sir Harry Smith Governor of the Cape in 1847, and instructed him to give effect to this change of views.

When Sir Harry Smith arrived at Capetown he issued a proclamation extending the boundaries of the colony northward to the Orange River and eastward to the Keiskamma. The country between the Keiskamma and the Kei was created a native territory under the name of British Kaffraria. That is to say, as regards the eastern border, Sir Harry Smith now put into effect the measures which he, in concurrence with Sir Benjamin Durban, had recommended twelve years before. He then crossed over the Orange River and visited the emigrant farmers there. He recognised the futility of the half measures which had been taken partly in pursuance of the non-interference policy and partly under the influence of an exaggerated belief in the capacity and pacific intention of the native chiefs, and proclaimed the country between the Vaal River on the north and west, the Orange River on the south, and the Drakensberg Mountains on the east, a British territory under the name of the Orange River Sovereignty. He placed the emigrant farmers within the Sovereignty under the independent control of a British official, and delimited the boundaries between them and the natives, the Griquas on the west, and the Basutos on the east.

These were measures which were sound in themselves, and which met with almost universal approval in the colony: but unfortunately they came *too late*. Sir Harry Smith was scarcely back in Capetown before he received intelligence that the emigrant farmers in the Sovereignty— the men who five years before had vainly petitioned the British Government to take them under their jurisdiction— had risen, and politely but firmly requested Major Warden, the British resident, and his handful of officials and

THE KAFIR WARS

police, to withdraw from Bloemfontein. It was not long before Sir Harry Smith was on the other side of the Orange River. He met the insurgents under Pretorius at Boomplaats, on August 29th, 1848, and dispersed them: and he then re-established the Sovereignty government on a firmer basis. This affair had scarcely been settled before another Kafir war broke out. This war, lasting from 1851 to 1853, was really a continuation of the preceding war of 1846-7; for the Kafir chiefs subsequently admitted that they had only made peace in order to allow themselves time to collect the stores of food necessary for a fresh campaign. Sir Harry Smith was considered responsible in some unaccountable way for this fresh outbreak, and he was recalled. Before he left the colony, and while he was conducting operations in person against the Kafirs, he received a communication from Major Warden, stating that Pretorius, who had retired beyond the Vaal after the battle of Boomplaats, had intimated his intention of raising the emigrant farmers in the Sovereignty unless the independence of himself and his followers beyond the Vaal was recognised by the Government. Sir Harry Smith had no soldiers to spare, so he acceded to Pretorius' demands in order to save the Sovereignty, and thus, on the 17th January 1852, by the Sand River convention, the South African Republic, or the Transvaal, came into existence.

Sir Harry Smith was succeeded in March by Sir George Cathcart. The Kafir war had scarcely been brought to an end before news came of fresh disturbances in the Sovereignty. This time it was the natives, the Basutos, who were the cause of the trouble, and not the emigrant farmers. Sir George Cathcart crossed the Orange River with quite a considerable force, 2500 men, and encamped on the bank of the Caledon River. From this position he sent an ultimatum to Moshesh, the Basuto chief. He required 10,000 head of cattle, and 1000

horses as a compensation for the losses inflicted by
Moshesh and his people on the farmers. No doubt
Moshesh would have been quite willing to have acceded
to these demands, but unfortunately he was not an
absolute, but only a constitutional, ruler. He had to
pay attention to the opinions not only of the chiefs,
but even of the commoners of the tribe; and the mass
of the Basutos were unwilling to part with so large an
amount of cattle without a struggle. Moshesh ultimately
sent 3500 head of cattle, with an expression of regret
that he could not provide the full amount. Then Sir
George Cathcart invaded Basutoland with his troops in
three columns. One of these columns was fortunate
enough to capture 4000 head of cattle. Another encountered a strong body of Basutos, and an engagement
ensued at Mount Berea, in which the Basutos rather more
than held their own against the British soldiers. And
now the wisdom of Moshesh appeared. The old chief
was not deceived for a moment by this success, or led
to suppose that his people could ultimately withstand
or conquer the British troops; on the contrary, that
very night he sent for his missionary adviser, Mr Casalis,
and despatched this letter :—

THABA BOSIGO,
Midnight, 20th December 1852.

YOUR EXCELLENCY,—This day you have fought against
my people, and taken much cattle. As the object for
which you have come is to have a compensation for
Boers, I beg you will be satisfied with what you have
taken. I entreat peace from you—you have chastised
—let it be enough; and let me be no longer considered
an enemy to the Queen. I will try all I can to keep
my people in order in the future.—Your humble servant,
MOSHESH.

Sir George Cathcart had seen enough of the Basuto

THE KAFIR WARS

country, and of the fighting qualities of its inhabitants, to make him quite ready to accept this qualified submission, and he then withdrew his forces. In the report which he sent to the Imperial Government he recommended that one of two alternatives should be pursued. Either the Sovereignty should be altogether abandoned, or a Lieutenant-Governor, with a force of at least 2000 men, should be established at Bloemfontein. The Imperial Government chose the former alternative, and despatched a special Commissioner, Sir George Clerk, to arrange for the transference of the government to a Committee of the emigrant farmers, and so, on the 23rd February 1854, by the convention of Bloemfontein, the Free State was created.

We have now reached a point in the history of South Africa where it is convenient to pause a moment, and look round.

First, we must notice that five out of the ten or twelve political divisions marked on the map of South Africa to-day are already in existence. We have the Cape Colony, Natal, and British Kaffraria—all three British possessions; and, in addition, the two independent communities founded by the emigrant farmers, the South African Republic, and the Free State. Moreover, the Imperial Government, taught by the experience of the last twenty years, have now arrived at two conclusions. In the first place they have decided to give the colonists a larger share in the management of their affairs. In these successive Kafir wars a large number of British soldiers—four hundred men went down in the transport *Birkenhead*, under circumstances of heroism which are still remembered—had been sacrificed, and a large amount of British capital had been wasted. Not only so, but the eastern farmers claimed compensation for the losses inflicted upon them by the Kafirs in these wars, and during the intervening depredations, on the ground that the

Imperial Government, through their agent, Lord Glenelg, had accepted the entire responsibility for the reversal of the colonial frontier policy in 1835. This claim was not allowed; at the same time almost the entire cost of the military operations against the Kafirs was defrayed by the Imperial exchequer. The Imperial Government had very practical evidence, therefore, of the evils resulting from the disregard of local opinion and advice; and in 1853 a representative Constitution was granted to the Cape Colony. By this Constitution two elective chambers, an upper-chamber, or Legislative Council, with fifteen members, and a Legislative Assembly with forty-six members, were created. Full parliamentary freedom, responsible government, was not granted until twenty years later, in 1872. The executive officials were still appointed by the Governor, instead of being chosen from among the representatives elected to Parliament, and they were, therefore, responsible for their actions to the Crown, and not to the people of the colony. At the same time the colonists had henceforward a means by which they could bring their wishes and their opinions in a direct and effective manner before the colonial, and ultimately, before the Imperial authorities.

The second conclusion was the determination not to interfere in affairs beyond the borders of the British possessions, and to leave the emigrant farmers and the natives to adjust their differences by themselves. It is quite true that certain limitations were imposed by the conventions upon the Boer governments in respect of the treatment of the natives. At the same time, it is perfectly clear that at this time the Imperial Government, without formally surrendering its paramount position, intended to retire from the task of controlling the European expansion, and the consequent disintegration of the Bantu peoples. Both the Sand River and the Bloemfontein conventions contained clauses in which Her Majesty's Government disclaimed any intention of making any further treaties with native chiefs outside the limits of the British possessions. This decision was based on a feeling which Tennyson has called "the craven fear of being great." It was an attempt to escape from responsibilities which naturally and rightly belonged to England as the paramount power in South Africa. As an attempt to escape responsibilities it was both unsuccessful and disastrous. It was unsuccessful, because the same difficulties arose at a later period, and had then to be met under less favourable conditions. It was disastrous, because by this policy of non-intervention the Imperial Government became a party to a process which Sir George Grey has called "the dismemberment of South Africa." By this process the Europeans, as representing the forces of civilisation, were weakened by separation and division in the conflict with the Bantu peoples, as representing the forces of barbarism; and the moral intervals which had from the first separated the two sections, Dutch and English, were emphasised and perpetuated.

Meanwhile, in spite of war and devastation, in spite of drought and blight, in spite of administrative blunders and political misunderstandings, the colonists were steadily advancing in wealth and civilisation. The Drakenstein range had been pierced by Lord Charles Somerset at French Hoek, and again, by Sir Lowy Cole, at Hottentots Holland. In 1844, Colonial Secretary John Montagu projected, and Colonel Mitchell and Mr Andrew Bain executed, that system of roads which Sir Harry Smith declared "would do honour to a great nation instead of a mere dependency of the Crown;" and on the 31st of March 1859, the first sod of the Capetown and Wellington railway was turned by Sir George Grey. Merino sheep, the producers of fine wool, were introduced from Saxony by Reitz and Breda in 1812, by Lord Charles Somerset and by the Albany settlers in 1820; and thus early the foundation of the staple industry of the colony was laid. By 1865 the ostrich—the wildest of birds—had been tamed but not domesticated; but in 1869 Mr Arthur Douglass of Albany perfected his artificial incubator, and under the stimulus of this invention, the export of ostrich feathers rose in a single year from 17,000 lbs. to 28,000 lbs.

The missionaries, too, were at work. Moffat was established at Kuruman, Livingstone was exploring regions beyond the reach of his enemies the emigrant Boers, and demanded at this early period the free navigation of the Zambesi. And in 1841 the Kafir College of Lovedale, perhaps the most important individual agency for civilisation in South Africa, was founded by Govan.

All this time the earth was waiting to reveal her treasures. The ample stores of coal in the Transvaal and Natal remained unharvested; the golden reefs of the Randt Basin were as yet untouched by the prospector's hammer; the diamonds of Kimberley lay close packed in the blue earth of their volcanic pipes in a despised corner of the Free State. In a word, the Cinderella of the Empire had not yet been visited by her fairy godmother.

CHAPTER III.

SIR BARTLE FRERE AND CONFEDERATION.

AT the end of the period 1806-1854, the Imperial Government had arrived at two conclusions with regard to the future administration of South Africa. In the first place they had decided to restrict their administration to the limits of the Cape Colony, Natal, and British Kaffraria. In the next, they had determined to give to the colonists a larger share in the management of their affairs, and in 1853 a Parliament, with two representative chambers, was established at Capetown. It is with this last decision that we must connect the appointment of such a governor as Sir George Grey;— a governor, that is to say, who was qualified not by military experience, but by a capacity for administration, in part natural and in part acquired during the discharge of the duties of that office in South Australia and New Zealand.

The period of Sir George Grey's administration, lasting from 1854 to 1862—for he was recalled and reinstated— is remarkable in many respects. We will select two. He originated a method of dealing with the Kafirs which was at once more effective and more humane (Note 9), and he formed a remarkable forecast of the future history of South Africa. In condemning the policy of non-intervention, and the consequent dismemberment of South Africa, he foresaw two important movements—that the Bantu would one day be tempted by the separation and apparent weakness of the Europeans to contest the supremacy of race, and that, in the event of a second conflict between the Imperial Government and the Dutch population, the strength of the resistance to be encountered would be measured, not by the conditions of the Dutch within the colony, but by those of their more strenuous and independent kinsmen. Sir George Grey not only foresaw these dangers, but he suggested appropriate remedies. He recognised the danger of leaving the growing Zulu people in utter barbarism, and he therefore recommended that European residents and magistrates should be introduced among them as well as among the Kafirs. He recognised that the attitude of the whole Dutch population in South Africa would be determined by that of the independent States, and he therefore proposed to bring back these States within the sphere of Imperial control by uniting them to the British Colonies in a federal tie (Note 10). Had these suggestions been carried out, England might have been saved the disaster of Isandlhwana and the disgrace of Majuba Hill.

As it was, the Imperial Government maintained their policy of non-intervention with fair consistency for the next fifteen years. During this period, partly owing to the improved methods of dealing with the Kafirs, introduced by Sir George Grey, and partly owing to the weakening of the warlike Amakosa clans—the Gaikas and Galekas—by the extraordinary self-destruction which took place in the year 1857, there was no outbreak on the eastern border (Note 11). During this period, too, the colonists made slow but steady progress, the sort of progress which is typified by the ox-waggon, the national vehicle of South Africa. But though this progress was slow, it was real enough to justify the Imperial Government in contemplating the extension to the Cape Colony of that full parliamentary freedom which they had already granted fifteen years ago to the Pacific Colonies: and in 1869 Sir Henry Barkly was appointed

SIR BARTLE FRERE AND CONFEDERATION 45

Governor and instructed to carry through the measures necessary for the introduction of responsible government. The new constitution was at length proclaimed on the 29th of November 1872. But before this date an event had occurred which very materially altered the attitude of England to South Africa. This event was the discovery of diamonds in 1869, and the subsequent establishment of the diamond industry at Kimberley in 1870. The non-intervention policy was at once abandoned. In 1871, British authority was proclaimed over the diamond fields, together with a large district to the north of the Orange and the Vaal Rivers, and the new territory was named Griqualand West. By this action the Imperial Government were brought into conflict with both of the Boer States. The Government of the South African Republic protested that the proclamation of British authority over so much of Griqualand West as was north of the Vaal River was a contravention of the third Article of the Sand River convention—

" Her Majesty's Assistant Commissioners hereby disclaim all alliances whatever, and with whomsoever, of the coloured tribes to the north of the Vaal River."

The Free State Government declared that the actual diamond fields, the district enclosed between the fork of the Vaal and Orange Rivers, was part of their territory, and had in fact been part of the original "sovereignty" as proclaimed by Sir Harry Smith in 1848.

The dispute with the South African Republic was referred to arbitration. A commission was appointed, over which Mr Keate, the Lieutenant-Governor of Natal, presided. The Keate Award was in favour of the Imperial Government. The Volksraad thereupon repudiated the engagement to abide by the result of that award which had been made on its behalf by President Pretorius, and Pretorius resigned. The matter was then left in abeyance, and the question of the delimitation of the south-west boundary of the South African Republic was not finally settled until the provisions of the convention of London were enforced by the Bechuanaland expedition of 1885. To the Free State Government it was replied that the land in question had been acquired by purchase from a Griqua chief, Waterboer by name; and the Free State protested and withdrew. Subsequently, however, a land court was established in Griqualand West, and the claims of individual owners were subjected to legal scrutiny. It was then discovered that the title of Waterboer to the diamond fields was bad; for all claims to land based upon grants made by Waterboer were rejected by this Court. President Brand then proceeded to London, to lay his case before the Colonial Office. It was a simple case. The Imperial Government had based their right to the diamond fields upon Waterboer's grant. It had been held by a British Court of Justice that Waterboer's title to the land was bad, and therefore, since no vendor can give his purchaser a better title than that which he himself possesses, the title of the Imperial Government was equally bad. Then the Colonial Office produced a new argument. They reverted to the position which England had held in South Africa before the Sand River and the Bloemfontein conventions. They declared that the Imperial Government, as the supreme authority in South Africa, had the right to interfere in the affairs of these otherwise independent communities when the safety or well-being of South Africa as a whole required such interference. At the same time Lord Carnarvon, who was then Colonial Secretary, recognised that the Free State had a grievance, and he arranged a compromise. Ultimately a sum of over £100,000 was paid to the Free State Government by way of compensation.

Now, although this principle, that the responsibility of England as paramount power must be accompanied by

SIR BARTLE FRERE AND CONFEDERATION 47

corresponding rights over the whole of South Africa, is both sound and necessary, and although the special contention of the Colonial Office, that these paramount rights and powers were not waived by the two conventions, can be shown to be just, since both these documents contain requirements and stipulations which could only be rendered effectual by the maintenance of England's relationship of paramount power towards the states in question : at the same time it was unfortunate, to say the least, that this principle should only have been brought forward by the Colonial Office after the title by purchase had fallen through. We are reminded in a very awkward manner by this action of the Colonial Office of that much quoted line in Horace, in which the man of the world is satirically represented as advising his pupil,

"Si possis, recte, si non quocunque modo rem."

"Make money, honestly if you can, if not—somehow or other." And we who believe, to use Lord Rosebery's phrase, that the British Empire is "the greatest secular agency for good known to the world," have a right to expect, and to require, that England shall not be placed in so equivocal a position either by the want of foresight, or by the mere carelessness of her officials.

The establishment of the diamond industry had an immediate effect upon the prospects of the Cape Colony. Within the five years succeeding the date of the discovery the revenue of the colony was more than doubled. And it was on the strength of this increasing revenue that the first premier, Sir John Molteno, was able to commence an extensive programme of railway construction by which the two chief towns, Capetown and Port-Elizabeth, were connected, and the inland districts brought into direct railway communication with the ports. But there were other results from the working of the Kimberley mines which were less happy. The rough work of excavation and of raising the diamondiferous earth was done by natives. These Kafirs came from various parts of South Africa, and engaged themselves for periods of three months, or six months, as the case might be, and then returned to their homes with earnings which represented to them, with their moderate ideas of wealth, very large sums. With an extraordinary disregard of the interests of the other European communities, the Government of Griqualand West permitted the natives to spend part of their wages in the purchase of firearms. Among those who did so were some members of the Hlubi tribe—a tribe which was located on the western borders of Natal. Now the laws of Natal which regulated the possession of firearms by the Kafirs were necessarily very strict. Every native on becoming possessed of a gun was required to register his name with the magistrate of his district. These Hlubis neglected to do this; and Langa, their chief, was summoned to Maritzburg to answer for the misdemeanour of his people by the Governor of Natal, who, under the Natal constitution, was paramount chief of all the Kafirs in the colony. Langa neglected, or refused, to obey the summons; ultimately the law was enforced by the co-operation of the Cape Government, but not before the Europeans in South Africa had experienced a very ugly feeling of alarm.

It was just at this time, when South Africa was beginning to attract population and capital from England, that Lord Beaconsfield's government came into power, and Lord Carnarvon became Secretary for the colonies. The conditions of South Africa were better known now, thanks to the diamond fields, and Lord Carnarvon saw in those conditions two strong reasons for establishing a central government—the necessity of adopting a common policy towards the natives as evidenced by the Hlubi incident, and the desirability of avoiding further conflicts with the Boer States. Moreover, Lord Carnarvon had, in 1867, introduced a bill uniting the British North American colonies

SIR BARTLE FRERE AND CONFEDERATION 49

in a single federal system, the Canadian Dominion, and he naturally sought to apply the same remedy to South Africa. That same year, 1874, he sent out despatches in which he recommended that the Cape government should summon representatives from the various colonies and states to attend a conference on federation; and he despatched the late Mr J. A. Froude to act as his own representative. Unfortunately, through some misunderstanding between the Colonial Office and the Cape ministers, that conference was not summoned, and an opportunity for uniting South Africa was lost. Events subsequently happened which made the necessity for the creation of this central authority all the more obvious. In the year 1876 the government of the South African Republic practically collapsed. Sikukuni, a Kafir chief in the mountain country in the north-east of the Transvaal, revolted, and defeated the burgher forces which were sent against him under the command of the president Mr Burgers. At the same time the Boers had become involved in a dispute respecting their eastern border with Ketshwayo, the formidable king of the Zulus. Under the strain of military service the farmers became impoverished, and the Transvaal treasury was at one time so empty that there was not money enough to pay for the carriage of ammunition from Durban to Pretoria. By an application of the principle already mentioned—the principle that England was responsible as paramount power for the well-being of South Africa as a whole—the Imperial Government decided, under certain circumstances, to establish the Queen's authority in the Transvaal; and a commission was issued empowering Sir Theophilus Shepstone to take the necessary measures, if certain eventualities were realised. The "emergency" contemplated by the commission subsequently appeared to have arisen, and on the 12th of April 1877, Sir Theophilus Shepstone, who had ridden into Pretoria with a small body of police, raised the English flag (Note 12). Meanwhile Lord Carnarvon had carried a second South Africa bill through the Imperial Parliament, and selected a very able Indian administrator, Sir Bartle Frere, to obtain the adoption of its provisions by the local legislatures.

Sir Bartle Frere reached the Cape on March 31st, 1877. He was in no way responsible for the annexation of the Transvaal. The news of this event did not reach him officially until the 30th of April. And before he could address himself to the work of South African union a native insurrection had broken out, in August, on the eastern frontier of the colony. First the Gaikas under Sandille, and then the Galekas under Kreli, revolted. Sir Bartle Frere went himself to the disturbed districts in order that he might personally supervise the measures taken to suppress the revolt. As a result of his energetic action the area of the disturbance was from the first confined, and, in general, the colonists in the eastern provinces were preserved from the horrors and losses of a long-protracted Kafir war of the old type. It was not, however, until the following May that peace was entirely restored. Meantime a more formidable champion of the Bantu peoples had entered the arena to dispute the supremacy of race in South Africa. This was Ketshwayo, the grandson of Tshaka. It has already been mentioned that, at the time of the annexation of the Transvaal, the Zulus were engaged in a dispute with the Boer farmers on the eastern border. After the annexation Ketshwayo transferred his quarrel to the new Transvaal Government; and as early as December 10th, 1877, Sir Henry Bulwer, the Governor of Natal, informed Sir Bartle Frere that, though a "general collision" between the Zulus and the Boers might be avoided, it was impossible to prevent conflicts between individual farmers and parties of Zulus. In that despatch* he also spoke of a "bitter feeling" against the new Transvaal

* C—2000.

SIR BARTLE FRERE AND CONFEDERATION 51

Government as existing on the part of the Zulus, and further suggested that a "third party" should be appointed to arbitrate between Ketshwayo and the Transvaal Government. Sir Bartle Frere decided to undertake the duties of arbitrator himself, and in September 1878, he visited Natal with a view of settling the dispute. After examining the evidence of the frontier commission, he gave his award in favour of the Zulu claim. At the same time he accompanied the announcement of that award with certain requirements which he deemed necessary to secure the peace of South Africa. The most important of these requirements were (1) that Ketshwayo should disband his army; (2) that he should receive a British resident at Ulundi, his capital; (3) that he should surrender certain persons known to have committed an offence on Natal territory; and (4) that he should give certain guarantees for the better government of his people.

Now, as it is obvious that, if Ketshwayo acceded to these demands, he would have reduced himself from a position of independence to that of a vassal of the British Government, the question arises whether Sir Bartle Frere was justified at this time in sending what was practically an ultimatum to the Zulu king. Before we are in a position to answer that question we must inform ourselves on two material points—the nature of the Zulu system, and the conditions of Natal.

By methods analogous to those of ancient Sparta, that is to say, by turning the entire physical resources of his people in one direction, that of war, Ketshwayo was in possession at this time of a "military organisation which enabled [him] to form out of his comparatively small population an army, at the very lowest estimate, of 25,000 perfectly trained and perfectly obedient soldiers, able to march three times as fast as we could, to dispense with commissariat of every kind and transport of every kind, and to fall upon [Natal] or any part of the neighbouring colony in such numbers, and with such determination, that nothing but a fortified post could resist them, making no prisoners, and sparing neither age nor sex."*

The conditions of Natal were these. There were in Natal at this time rather more than 20,000 Europeans. The remainder of the population was composed of over 300,000 Bantu, of whom the majority, we will say two-thirds, were Zulus: that is to say, they were members of Ketshwayo's own tribe, and a large proportion of them had crossed the border in order that they might enjoy the peace and security offered by the Natal Government (Note 13). If, therefore, Ketshwayo invaded Natal with his army—still more, if he fought a successful engagement on colonial soil—there was a grave danger, amounting almost to a moral certainty, that the mass of the Bantu in Natal would, by a mere instinct of self-preservation, join the invaders.

Moreover, it must be remembered that the designs of Ketshwayo were by no means confined to the destruction of Natal. "Wherever there has been disturbance and resistance to authority of Government," Sir Bartle Frere writes on the eve of the war,† "between the Limpopo and the westernmost limits of Kafir population, there we have found unmistakeable evidence" of a "common purpose and general understanding" among the Bantu people to shake off the domination of the Europeans. Of this movement Ketshwayo was the "head centre," and the Zulus the "main strength."

In order to form a clear understanding of this most material point—the relationship of the Zulu power to the civilised communities of South Africa at this crisis—we

* Despatch of Frere to Sir Michael Hicks-Beach (who had succeeded Lord Carnarvon as Secretary for the Colonies), March 1st, 1879. C—2316.
† Despatch, Dec. 10th, 1878. C—2222.

SIR BARTLE FRERE AND CONFEDERATION 53

will take an imaginary case. We will suppose that an aggressive person has taken up a position at a street-corner, with a loaded gun raised to his shoulder; we will suppose, further, that he covers with his piece a passer-by. What, then, is the duty of the policeman? Is he to wait until this aggressive individual has actually discharged his piece and wounded an innocent person, or must he advance at once and disarm him? Again, would the policeman consider it a sufficient answer, if the armed man objected, "But I have not yet fired my gun. You need not be alarmed; I always carry a loaded gun about with me, and often raise it to my shoulder." Plainly not; neither did Sir Bartle Frere consider that he was justified in allowing the Zulu army to further menace the peace of the Europeans throughout South Africa "We may blind ourselves as we will to the truth," he writes,* "gunmakers and gun-runners may make excuses for gun-running. Philanthropists may find reasons for barbarisms, and persuade themselves of good intentions, belied by every word and act of the chief's lifetime. Lawyers may talk of constitutional rights, which would find a more natural and congenial habitation on the deck of a private vessel, and every one in active life may agree to postpone the correction of a vicious system, 'which may last our time,' to some more convenient season, when 'something may turn up' to save us trouble, or throw it on our successors. But the fact remains, that no one can really sleep in peace and security within a day's run of the Zulu border—save by sufferance of the Zulu chief."

When Ketshwayo had refused, or rather neglected, to comply with these demands, Sir Bartle Frere entrusted the enforcement of his requirements to Lord Chelmsford, who was then in command of the British force in Natal.

Lord Chelmsford crossed the lower Tugela early in

* Despatch, Dec. 2nd, 1878. C—2222.

January 1879. One column advanced as far as Etshowe, fortified a position there, and remained in the heart of Zululand until it was ultimately relieved six months later after the battle of Ulundi. The main body under Lord Chelmsford advanced in a north-westerly direction until camp was formed at Isandlhwana. On the 22nd of January Lord Chelmsford again advanced, intending to select a fresh position, leaving in camp a force of 700 British and colonial, and 600 native troops. The Zulus, 15,000 strong, evaded Lord Chelmsford's force, and advanced in crescent shaped formation upon the camp at Isandlhwana. Before the horns of the impi united forty Europeans escaped. Two officers, lieutenants Melvill and Coghill, made a gallant attempt to save the colours of the 24th; but they were pursued and overtaken at the Buffalo River. The rest fought as long as their ammunition lasted — and then they died. After the force at Isandlhwana had been destroyed, 4000 Zulus advanced to Rorke's Drift, to occupy the ford by which the Buffalo River could be crossed and Natal entered. Fortunately a small force, rather more than 100 men of the 24th, under lieutenants Chard and Bromhead, had been left at Rorke's Drift. They occupied a mission house which they strengthened by biscuit tins and bags of mealies. Behind this defence they offered so strenuous a resistance that the Zulus were compelled to retire without seizing the position, and Natal was saved from immediate invasion.

Lord Chelmsford then fell back upon his base in Natal, and waited for reinforcements. Ultimately he advanced again into Zululand, and on the 4th of July he engaged the enemy at Ulundi. The force under his command amounted to 4000 British and colonial troops and 1000 natives: the number of the Zulus in action he estimated at 20,000. On the 6th of July he was able to report * to the Secretary for War, that he felt he had a

* C—2482.

SIR BARTLE FRERE AND CONFEDERATION 55

right to say "that the result of Ulundi would be sufficient to dispel the idea that Ketshwayo could defeat British troops in the open from the minds of the Zulu nation, and of every other tribe in South Africa for ever." On 27th August Lord Wolseley, who had superseded Lord Chelmsford immediately after Ulundi, reported * that, "with the exception of the north-western corner inhabited by Makuluni, the whole of Zululand might now be considered safe for the smallest parties of Europeans." And on 12th December he again reported † to the Secretary for the Colonies that "the force under Colonel Baker Russell's command had stormed and taken Sikukuni's stronghold" on the 28th of November.

Since that time the supremacy of the European race has not been seriously contested in South Africa.

The subjugation of the Bantu—that which had been a condition precedent to the union of the South African Colonies and States—was now accomplished, and Sir Bartle Frere was able to resume the work which he was specially commissioned to carry out.

In the meantime a new factor had been introduced into the already complicated problem of South African politics. After the disaster of Isandlhwana, cable communication had been established with England. The unhappy notoriety which the country acquired in the Zulu war had rendered the English public more familiar with the affairs of South Africa, and the comments and opinions of the leaders of the two great parties were quickly reproduced in the colonial papers by means of the telegraph. In order to trace the effect produced by the play of English party politics upon the measures taken to forward South African federation, it is necessary to go back for a moment to the affairs of the Transvaal.

The annexation, accomplished in April 1877, as already related, was welcome enough to the inhabitants of the

* *Idem.* † C—2505.

towns, who were for the most part of English or German origin, but it was resisted from the first by the farmers —that is to say, by the actual Boer population. Delegates from the Volksraad were at once despatched to the Colonial Office to ask for the restoration of independence. This delegation, and a second delegation which visited England in the following year, were alike unsuccessful; but towards the end of 1879, the year of the Zulu war, a ray of light came from an unexpected quarter. In the autumn of that year Mr Gladstone embarked upon his Midlothian Campaign. In one of the speeches in which he arraigned Lord Beaconsfield's administration, he spoke in terms of frank condemnation of the annexation of the Transvaal. In February of the following year, 1880, an address,* signed by the Africander population in the Cape Colony, was forwarded to Mr Gladstone; and in this address he was asked to use his influence on behalf of the restoration of the independence of the Transvaal. In April of that year the Liberal party came into power, but Mr Gladstone then informed a further delegation that he was unable to advise the Queen to withdraw the British Government from their country. At the same time the Boer leaders, Messrs Kruger and Joubert, had received assurances of sympathy from private members of the Liberal party, and on their return to South Africa they resolved to commence an agitation in the Cape Colony. It was just then—at the opening of the winter session of the Cape Parliament—that the proposals of the Cape Ministry for a Federation Conference were brought before the Cape Parliament. The Boer delegates, acting under the advice of the leaders of the Africander opposition, obtained promises of support from the members who represented Africander constituencies. These members agreed to oppose the Federation proposals of Sir Gordon Sprigg's ministry on the ground

* Enclosed in Despatch, March 8th, 1880. C—2695.

SIR BARTLE FRERE AND CONFEDERATION 57

that the question of Transvaal independence ought to precede the question of South African Union. After a prolonged debate the Ministry ultimately avoided defeat by withdrawing their Conference proposals on June 29th, 1880. As soon as the despatches containing reports of the debates in the Cape Parliament, and information of the virtual defeat of the Colonial Ministry on the Federation question reached England, Lord Kimberley, the new Secretary of State for the Colonies, at once telegraphed to Sir Bartle Frere that the Government had advised the Queen to replace him by another Governor.*

The news of Sir Bartle Frere's recall (Note 14) produced a very general and a very sincere expression of regret. Addresses containing such opinions were forwarded from all parts of the Cape Colony. Judged by the test of "interests involved," no community was better able to pronounce an opinion on the merits or demerits of Sir Bartle Frere's administration than the inhabitants of the Albany district. The verdict of Albany was clear and unmistakeable:—

"Never did colonial governor find himself at the very outset of his duties confronted with so many and such startling difficulties as met you soon after you reached our shores. Never did governor more effectually grasp the situation, and more successfully deal with these difficulties than you did. You carried the Galeka war, . . . to a successful issue. . . .

"We have watched with the most anxious interest your career during that eventful period when the affairs of the neighbouring colony of Natal were administered by you; we perfectly understand that at that crisis the deep-laid plans and cruel purposes of the savage and bloodthirsty King of the Zulus were just reaching their full development, and that his inevitable and long-effected encounter with the British power could no longer be averted; it was, no doubt, unfortunate for your personal convenience

* C—2655.

at the present time; it would appear also to have been temporarily unfortunate for your reputation, but it was extremely fortunate for that colony, and for the honour of the British name, that you were on the spot ready to sacrifice every personal consideration, and to undertake one of the heaviest and most tremendous responsibilities ever undertaken by servant of the Crown. Your excellent plans, your steady determination, your unflagging perseverance, led to the downfall of a barbarous tyrant, the break-up of a most formidable and unwarrantable military power, and the establishment of peaceful relations, which, properly managed, might have ensured the lasting peace and prosperity which you have systematically desired to secure for South Africa." *

Meanwhile the Boer leaders, Messrs Kruger and Joubert, were writing to their sympathisers in England, "The fall of Sir Bartle Frere will be . . useful." † It is a significant fact that the letter in which this sentence occurs was dated June 26th, that is to say, three days before the actual decision of the Cape Parliament (June 29th). It is significant, because it shows to how large an extent the defeat of the colonial ministry, and the failure of Sir Bartle Frere to carry through the South African federation, was due to the fact that it was known in the colony that he—the governor of the colony—was deprived by a swing of the political pendulum of the support of his official superiors, and—what was still more important—of the support of public opinion in England.

I do not think there is a more painful record in the annals of colonial administration than this story of the abandonment and betrayal of Sir Bartle Frere.

We need not trouble ourselves with the reproofs administered from Downing Street, with the complaint that he had exceeded the letter of his instructions in not referring to the Imperial Government before he sent

* C—2740. † C—2655.

what was practically an ultimatum to the Zulu king. Sir George Grey, who had anticipated Frere in the circumstances of his own recall, had also provided a sufficient answer to this and similar complaints, when, twenty years before, he penned the indignant question :—*

"Can a man who, on a distant and exposed frontier, surrounded by difficulties, with invasions of Her Majesty's territories threatening on several points, assumes a responsibility which he guided by many circumstances which he can neither record nor remember as they came hurrying on one after the other, be fairly judged of in respect to the amount of responsibility he assumes by those who, in the quiet of distant offices in London, know nothing of the anxieties or nature of the difficulties he had to encounter?"

But how was England misled? How was it that England was thus unjust to the man, who was, after all, only faithfully and skilfully discharging the duties of his office? Sir Bartle Frere was in no way responsible for any military error. The disaster of Isandlhwana, by which he was discredited, was in reality the clearest evidence of his foresight, and the most complete justification of his action; for a barbarous power, which could annihilate a British regiment in the open, was obviously no safe neighbour for Natal; and what security could there be for the 400,000 Europeans in South Africa so long as the absolute master of that power entertained the design, or even believed in the possibility of uniting the 3,000,000 Bantu in a war of race?

There is an explanation which lies ready to hand. We can turn to that storehouse of political experience, the literature of ancient Greece, and read in the pages of the historian of Athens the comprehensive verdict, "a Democracy is incapable of Empire."

But is this sufficient? Is it sufficient for us who believe that a democracy *is* capable of empire, of an empire with

* "Correspondence," etc., printed April 17th, 1860, p. 26.

wider boundaries and higher aims than any empire yet recorded in history? I think not. I think we shall seek for a temporary disorder before we admit the existence of an incurable malady in the body politic.

At the time that this blow fell England had lately stood face to face with her great world-rival Russia; and in the moment of that ordeal she had realised, as she had never realised before, the dignity and the responsibility of her Imperial position. What wonder if, at such a time, when the multitudinous interests of an empire in four continents were crowding upon her, England forgot the suspended union of South Africa, forgot the deadly peril of Natal, forgot the iniquitous system by which a whole people had been converted into a man-slaying machine, forgot that Ketshwayo was the grandson of Tshaka, and knew only that a British regiment had been sacrificed to a barbarous enemy.

Was it strange, too, if England in her vexation and alarm did not discriminate too nicely in visiting her displeasure?

" Yes, we arraign her, but she,
The weary Titan, with deaf
Ears, and labour-dimmed eyes,
Regarding neither to right
Nor left, goes passively by,
Staggering on to her goal ;
Bearing on shoulders immense,
Atlantēan, the load,
Well nigh not to be borne,
Of the too vast orb of her fate."

And the remedy? It lies in the creation of a central authority which shall embody the consolidated resources of the empire. Such an authority must include representatives from every province of the empire, that so it may be informed with equal exactness of the necessities of each component part, and control without dispute the Imperial exchequer formed by their united contributions. Entrusted to such an authority, we may hope that an Imperial policy will at length be unaffected by the side issues of party politics, and unrestricted by the exigences of national finance.

CHAPTER IV.

THE BOERS.

EARLY in the year 1881 Englishmen were startled by the receipt of strange intelligence. The garrisons in the Transvaal had been surrounded and isolated by insurgents. On the 20th of December a detachment of the 94th, more than 250 strong, marching from Lydenburg to Pretoria, were attacked in a narrow defile, Bronkhorst Spruit; the commanding officer and fifty-four men were killed, seven officers and ninety-one men were wounded, and the rest were taken prisoners. At the end of January General Colley, who was in command of the troops in Natal, advanced to the relief of the garrisons in the Transvaal. He found that his way was barred. Lang's Nek, at the entrance of the pass over the Drakensberg leading from Natal to the Transvaal, had been occupied by the insurgents. The attack made by the force under General Colley, 1100 strong, on the 28th of January, was repulsed with heavy loss. Colonel Deane and all the staff and mounted officers were shot down, and 190 rank and file were reported as dead, wounded, or missing. Ten days later, on the 8th of February, as General Colley was patrolling the road to Newcastle with a force of 300 men, in order to maintain his line of communication between that place and the camp at Mount Prospect, he was attacked at Ingogo Heights. In this engagement four officers were killed, and three were wounded, and 150 men were reported killed or wounded. But the crowning disaster was still to come. On the night of the 26th of

February, General Colley left the camp at Mount Prospect with 600 men, intending to turn the insurgents' position at Lang's Nek by occupying Majuba Hill, an eminence which commanded the Boer lines. He detached part of this force to maintain communication with the camp, and posted the remainder, some 400 men, on the level top. The next morning, when the Boer leaders saw that the level plateau of Majuba was fringed with redcoats, they at once realised the significance of the movement. One hundred and fifty volunteers offered to make an attempt, which seemed hopeless enough, to scale the hill and dislodge the English. At four o'clock it was known at Mount Prospect that the Boers had carried the hill soon after mid-day. It was subsequently ascertained that General Colley was shot in fighting line with two officers close by him, that ninety-two men had been killed and 200 wounded and captured.

In these and some minor engagements as many as 800 English officers and men had been killed or wounded. On the other hand, the Boers had lost eighteen men killed and thirty-three wounded.

And who, then, were these Boers, and what were their circumstances?

The replies elicited by these enquiries heightened the extraordinary character of the intelligence, and increased the bewilderment of the public. For it appeared that the enemy which had inflicted these successive and severe defeats upon the British arms were the burgher force of a community of farmers—a community numbering only 50,000 inhabitants, that is to say, with a population smaller than that of an English town of the third rank. Their present circumstances, the actual grounds of their quarrel with the Imperial Government, were imperfectly understood. What their previous relationship to England had been, how they came to be in possession of a country scarcely less in area than the United Kingdom, and shrewdly guessed to be the most valuable in South Africa,

THE BOERS

above all, what was the special experience which had made them such daring patriots, such intrepid foes, and such consummate marksmen—on all these points the public were profoundly ignorant, and, before they had time to inform themselves, the armistice of the 7th of March was succeeded by the cessation of hostilities on the 23rd, and the Transvaal war had become a thing of the past.

This interesting and neglected chapter of South African history now claims our attention.

The events which led to the great emigration of 1835-1838, when 10,000 Dutch farmers left the Cape Colony and passed into the interior, have already been related, and a mention of the bare heads under which those events can be grouped will be sufficient to recall the circumstances. There were the injudicious measures which accompanied the Anglicising of the Colony; there was the indiscreet interference of the missionaries and the odium cast by the philanthropic societies in England upon the Dutch population at the Cape; there were the direct and indirect losses occasioned by the emancipation of slaves; and, lastly, there was the reversal by the Imperial Government of Sir Benjamin Durban's measures for the protection of the eastern settlers from future Kafir inroads. To these must be added two subsidiary causes: the depopulation of large areas in the interior by the murderous wars of Tshaka and Moselekatse, and the northward flow of the Europeans. The first of these has been already described, but the second needs some brief explanation. The northward expansion of the whites (contrasting with the southward flow of the Bantu) is as noticeable a feature in South African colonisation as the eastward expansion is in North America. It is due to two simple and easily understood causes: the unproductiveness of the soil and the unprogressiveness of the Boer, or South African farmer. The joint result of these two causes may be stated to be this:— each son in a Boer family requires just as much land for his support as his father has held before him. This northward expansion commenced at the beginning of the century. Some European half-castes, uniting with the Mantatees, produced the Griquas, and this race subsequently occupied lands near the confluence of the Vaal and Orange Rivers. The colonists maintained intercourse with the Griquas, and early in the century the eastern graziers, discovering that, owing to the more constant rainfall, the pastures were more fertile in these districts than in the colony, began to make a practice of driving their cattle across the Orange River at certain seasons of the year. They had, however, no intention of leaving the colony; on the contrary, they returned and paid their *opgaaf*, or annual assessed taxes, as regularly as before. At the time of the emigration, therefore, the eastern farmers had in this way become acquainted with part of the country between the Orange and Vaal Rivers.

The first party of emigrants, one hundred in number, left the colony in the year 1835. They made their way to the extreme north-east of the Transvaal. There they divided into two parties. One of these parties was attacked and almost entirely destroyed by the natives. The survivors of the other party, after enduring extremes of famine and fever, reached Delagoa Bay, and eventually sailed to Natal. In August of the next year (1836) a party of two hundred emigrants, under Hendrik Potgieter, crossed the Orange River and reached Thaba N'chu on the north bank of the River Caledon. Here they were received willingly enough by a Barolong chief, Maroko; and from this point they advanced northwards and formed encampments on the south bank of the Vaal. Hendrik Potgieter and a small party of men then crossed the Vaal, and explored the country further north. On their return they found that their encampments had been attacked by the Matebeles under Moselekatse, and that twenty-five European men and women had been murdered. Potgieter at once went into "laager"* on a suitable hill, Vecht Kop, and there awaited a fresh onslaught. Behind the waggons the men shot straight and quick, and their mothers and wives loaded the guns. The Matabele were repulsed, but they carried off all the emigrants' sheep and cattle. The party was now in great peril, for they had no oxen to yoke into their waggons, and therefore could not retreat. Ultimately they managed to communicate with Maroko; and this chief, and Mr Archbell, a missionary, sent friendly natives with oxen to their assistance; and in this manner they were able to retire to Thaba N'chu.

Meanwhile a larger company, headed by Gert Marritz, starting from Graaf Reinet, and other companies from Uitenage and Albany, had crossed the Orange River. The emigrants were now strong enough to attack Moselekatse. A commando of 200 men, under the leadership of Marritz, crossed the Vaal River, and recovered some waggons and 7000 head of cattle. At the same time the position of the emigrants was so perilous that many of them began to entertain the idea of returning to the colony. It was just at this crisis that they were joined by Pieter Retief. Retief was a colonist of Huguenot extraction. He had held a command under the Colonial Government, but he had suffered severely from the Kafir invasion of 1834-5, and he had been censured for some measures which he took for the restraint of Hottentot vagrants. So he resolved to throw in his lot with the emigrants, and sold his property. On Retief's arrival a

* "These 'laagers,' or camps, were formed by their waggons being brought up into a square, the poles and waggon gear of one waggon being firmly secured under the perch of the next waggon; and when time admitted branches of the thorny mimosas were also wattled in under each waggon, so that no entrance could be effected into the enclosure without forcibly tearing up all these impediments."—CLOETE, iii. p. 77.

government was organised. The emigrants assembled at Winburg. A constitution was drawn up on June 6th, 1837, and Retief was elected Commandant-General. At the same time some of the emigrants expressed the opinion that Natal would be a more suitable country for settlement than the Orange River district, and Retief himself favoured the opinion. He determined, however, before deciding to lead the emigrants across the Drakensberg, to himself visit Dingan, the Zulu king, and ascertain whether Dingan would cede Natal. While he was absent on this mission a second commando, consisting of 135 mounted men and some friendly natives, was organised by Potgieter and Jacobus Uys. After nine days' desperate fighting the Matabele were so severely punished that Moselekatse retired to the north of the Transvaal, and ultimately crossed the Limpopo. There he attacked the Mashonas, and after depopulating the southern portion of their country, settled with his people in the district now called Matabeleland.

Retief found that Dingan was willing to allow the emigrant farmers to settle in Natal; and, early in the next year (1838), he led a large company across the Drakensberg. They formed encampments on the Blue Krans River; and then Retief, with a party of seventy Europeans and thirty natives, proceeded to Dingan's capital, Umkungunhlovu, to arrange for the formal cession of the country. On the 4th of February a deed of cession, which had been drawn up in English by a missionary named Owen, residing there, was read to Dingan. He expressed himself as satisfied with its terms, and affixed his mark to it. On the following morning the emigrants were informed that Dingan wished them to drink beer in the royal hut before they set out on their homeward journey. Retief and his companions, having no suspicion of treachery, left their guns at the entrance of the hut. When they had entered Dingan suddenly bade his guards seize them. The whole party were at once led to the place of execution, and barbarously murdered. This order was followed by another. Ten regiments were bidden to advance without delay against the encampments, and destroy them. The nearest party of emigrants were murdered—men, women and children —with the exception of one young man who was herding cattle at a distance from the waggons. This single survivor was able to warn the more distant parties, and these latter were able to go into laager before the Zulus came upon them. The Zulus were unable to force the laagers, but they destroyed, or rather massacred, 600 Europeans and natives before they retired.

Meanwhile Uys had reached the Drakensberg with a second party, and was preparing to descend into Natal. Both he and Potgieter collected fighting men, and hastened to assist the emigrants at the Blue Krans River. Subsequently a force of 1500 natives, headed by 17 Englishmen from Durban, and a commando of 350 farmers, crossed the Tugela, and attacked Dingan. Both of these forces were defeated, and Natal was again overrun by the Zulus. The English settlers * at Durban were forced to take refuge on board the *Comet*, a man-of-war which was fortunately anchored in the bay; the emigrants defended themselves successfully behind their waggons. After the Zulus had again retired, the emigrants remained in a position of great danger until the month of November, when they were joined by Andries Pretorius, and a force of 450 men collected in the Orange River districts. Pretorius was, like Retief, a man of higher social grade, and he at once assumed a commanding position among the emigrants. He had resolved, moreover, to avenge

* Natal was colonised under a concession from Tshaka by Englishmen as early as 1825. In 1835 the settlers petitioned that their settlement at Durban might be called "Victoria," and taken under the protection of the Imperial Government.

his people. He crossed the Tugela with the force he had collected, and advanced carefully, laagering at every stage, until he arrived at the neighbourhood of Dingan's capital. Then Dingan let loose all his regiments upon the farmers' camp. On the evening of the 16th December, ever afterwards celebrated by the Boers as Dingan's day, 3000 Zulus lay dead outside the waggons, but within only four men had died of their wounds. Then Dingan was seized with terror. He set fire to his town, and retreated to the north. From among the smoking ruins of Umkungunhlovu Pretorius carried back Retief's skull, and the actual deed of cession with Dingan's mark upon it.*

When Pretorius returned with these melancholy relics to his people in Natal, he found that Durban, the port, had been occupied by a military force under Major Charters. The emigrants in the interior, however, were not interfered with by the soldiers, and in the spring of 1839 Pietermaritzburg, the present capital of Natal, was laid out by them. In September they were joined by an important ally. Dingan had quarrelled with Panda, his half-brother, and this Panda had withdrawn with a large following, and now offered his services to the emigrants. In January of the next year, 1840, Panda advanced into Zululand, supported by a force of emigrants under Pretorius. In the battle which followed Dingan was ultimately but decisively defeated. He fled to the neighbourhood of Delagoa Bay, and was there murdered. On the 14th of February Pretorius issued a proclamation in which he, as "Commandant-General of the Right Worshipful Volksraad of the South African Society of Port Natal," in the first place declared Panda King of the Zulus in succession to Dingan; and, secondly, claimed possession of the whole of Natal by right of conquest. Just at this

* "This deed was delivered over to me by the Volksraad in 1843, and is in the archives of the Colonial Office."—CLOETE, p. 94.

time the British force, a detachment of the 92nd regiment, was withdrawn by Sir George Napier, who was then Governor of the Cape Colony, in pursuance of instructions received from the Home Government.

Although Sir George Napier declined to make any formal acknowledgment of the existence of the settlement, the emigrants had now practically achieved their independence. Towards the end of the year 1840, however, Pretorius committed an act not only of extreme barbarity, but of extreme folly. He attacked a chief, N'capai by name, who lived 200 miles from Natal, on the border of the Cape Colony. Pretorius killed N'capai's people, captured his cattle, and carried off seventeen young children into slavery. Sir George Napier then sent a force of 250 infantry to the Umgazi River, to watch the movements of the emigrants, and to prevent any further expeditions against the natives. At the same time he applied to the Home Government for instructions. Ultimately the Imperial Government decided to occupy Natal; and in pursuance of a despatch, written by the then Lord Stanley on the 13th December 1842, Mr Cloete arrived as British Commissioner at Durban on the 1st of May 1843, and a permanent administration was established. In the years 1846 and 1847, the bulk of the emigrants withdrew from Natal, some to the Orange River district and some to the Transvaal. They had a very simple reason for withdrawing. A land court had been established, and they were dissatisfied with the amount of land assigned to the Europeans, both collectively and individually. They objected to the apportionment of any part of Natal to the Bantu, for they regarded the whole country as belonging to them by right of conquest, and at the same time the possession of a large area of land was, as I have already pointed out, necessary for the very existence of the Boer.

The subsequent history of the emigrants in the Orange

River district and beyond the Vaal has already been related as part of the main stream of South African history. It will, however, be convenient at this point to consider in a connected form the main acts and measures which indicate the varying relationship maintained by the Imperial Government to the Boers.

The first military occupation of Durban was made under a proclamation of Sir George Napier, dated November 14th 1838. The object of that occupation was there stated to be :—"To put an end to the unwarranted occupation of the territories belonging to the natives, by certain emigrants, from the Cape Colony, being subjects of Her Majesty."

The same principle appears in the reply which Sir George Napier made to the communication of the Volksraad of "the South African Society of Port Natal," forwarded in January 1841, and containing a request for an acknowledgment of independence and a commercial treaty. Sir George Napier then said :—"That Her Majesty could not acknowledge the independence of her own subjects, but that the trade of the emigrant farmers would be placed on the same footing as that of any other British settlement, upon their receiving a military force to exclude the interference with, or the possession of, the country by any other European power."

The emigrants on receipt of this communication issued a fresh declaration of their independence as "Dutch South Africans." Sir George Napier then announced, by proclamation of 2nd December 1841, his intention "of resuming the military occupation of Natal."

Lord Stanley's despatch (already mentioned) contained definite instructions as to the nature of the administration which was to be established over the emigrants.

The Commissioner was directed to call the inhabitants together, and give them an opportunity of stating the nature of the institutions they required; but legislative

THE BOERS

power was not to be conceded as yet. "I think it probable," Lord Stanley says, "looking to the nature of the population, that they will desire those institutions to be founded on the Dutch, rather than on the English model, and, however little some of those institutions may be suited to a more advanced state of civilisation, it is the desire of Her Majesty's government, that in this respect the contentment of the emigrants, rather than the abstract merits of the institutions, should guide our decision."

There were, however, certain limitations to this freedom of selection. 1, No distinction or disqualification, founded on "colour, origin, language, or creed," was to be recognised. 2, No "aggression upon natives beyond the colony" was to be sanctioned under any plea whatever. 3, Slavery in any shape or form was declared to be "absolutely unlawful."

It is impossible not to feel that the principle of this despatch is both just and generous : and any opinion we may form of the subsequent dealings of the British Government with the Boers must be largely modified by the remembrance of the equitable character of these original proposals, and of the one reason—the greed of land—which prevented the emigrants from remaining under the administration so established.

In 1848 British authority was effectively established over the emigrants in the Orange River districts by Sir Harry Smith : it was withdrawn when the Free State came into existence under the Convention of Bloemfontein in 1854. Two years previously the independence of the emigrants beyond the Vaal was recognised by the Sand River Convention (1852).

It was undoubtedly the intention of the Imperial Government to rid itself of any further responsibility by these conventions. That object was not attained. On the contrary, when circumstances made it necessary for England to resume the part of paramount power in South

Africa, it was found that she had placed herself in a position of great disadvantage. For these conventions not only recognised the independence of the emigrant farmers, but they bound the Imperial Government not to make any fresh alliances with the native chiefs north of the Vaal River. Moreover, while the Imperial Government agreed to allow the emigrants to obtain arms and ammunition freely in the British possessions, they pledged themselves to prevent the natives from procuring fire-arms.*

When the discovery of diamonds had shown that South Africa was a more valuable possession than had ever been supposed, England began again to exercise the paramount rights which had remained dormant for nearly fifteen years. In 1868 the Imperial Government interfered between the Free State and the Basutos. At that time the Free State Government had at last, after four years' fighting, succeeded in reducing Moshesh to submission. They proposed to punish him by confiscating a large part of his territory. The ground on which the Imperial Government interfered was the belief that the dispersion of the Basutos, which would result from this action of the Free State, would endanger the peace of South Africa. In 1871 British authority was proclaimed over Griqualand West, a territory including country north of the Vaal and the diamond fields—a part of the Orange Free State. The justification for this act was the belief that the district which contained so valuable a possession as the Kimberley diamond mines ought to be administered by the paramount power. And in 1877 the Queen's authority was established in the Transvaal, on the ground that the weakness and bankruptcy of the local government constituted, in view of the growing disturbances amongst the natives, and the organisation of the Zulus under Ketshwayo, a menace to the supremacy of the Europeans in South Africa (Note 15).

    * Despatch of Sir George Grey, 1858, § 10.

We have now returned to the point in what has been called the main stream of South African history from which we diverged to trace the history of the Transvaal Boers.

When it became evident to the Boer leaders that, in spite of Mr Gladstone's condemnation of the annexation, and in spite, too, of the very practical proof of Africander solidarity which had been afforded by blocking the federation proposals of the Cape ministry, the Imperial Government did not intend to withdraw from the Transvaal, they resolved to resort to the arbitrament of arms. The affairs of the community were entrusted to a Triumvirate—Messrs Kruger, Joubert, and Pretorius; and on the 16th December —Dingan's day—the flag of the South African Republic was floated in the breeze on the desolate uplands of the Witwatersrandt.

The successes which attended the insurgents have already been related.

But now, when, to use an expressive phrase of General Wood, "the Boer leaders had lit a fire which had got beyond their control," happily all those parties in whose control that fire lay hastened to extinguish it.

The Imperial Government poured overwhelming reinforcements into South Africa. At the time of the cessation of hostilities, the 22nd of March, General Wood had 10,000 men massed on the slopes of the Drakensberg, eager to avenge, if need be, the defeats suffered by the British arms. General Roberts and his staff had arrived at Capetown, and 10,000 additional troops were on their way to South Africa. President Brand, of the Free State, used the whole of his influence on the side of peace, and he was successful in preventing the Free State, as a state, from taking part in the quarrel (Note 16). Mr Hofmeyr, the leader of the Africander party in the Cape Colony, exhorted the Boer leaders to moderation (Note 17). General Wood (who had succeeded to the command of the troops on the death of General Colley), without sacrificing a single point in the game of war,* showed both tact and patience in the very difficult negotiations which he conducted, and won the confidence of the insurgent leaders. And so the armistice of the 7th of March was followed by the cessation of hostilities on the 22nd. The sum of the terms actually offered by General Wood, and accepted by the Boer leaders, were these :—

1. A complete amnesty was guaranteed to all the insurgents, including the leaders, except persons who had committed acts contrary to the rules of civilised warfare.

2. A commission was to be appointed for the purpose of restoring the independent Transvaal Government, and the names of the persons composing this commission were to be named forthwith. They were Sir Hercules Robinson, the new Governor of the Cape, Chief Justice de Villiers, and General Wood himself. It was also stipulated that President Brand should be present at the meetings of the commission.

3. Complete self-government under the British suzerainty was to be granted, at the latest, within six months from the cessation of hostilities, and under the terms arranged by the commission (Note 18).

It has been sought to represent the retrocession of the Transvaal as an act justifiable on grounds other than those of political expediency. But that is a contention which cannot be maintained. The retrocession came twelve months too late. If it was intended that it should rank as an act of grace, the independence of the Boers should have been granted in May 1880. If a man asks an alms of us, and we refuse him ; if he then threatens us with violence, and we empty our pockets, can we claim to have been actuated by motives of philanthropy ? But that is not all. It was wrong, no doubt, to subject a community of 50,000

* Despatch 93, C—2837.

THE BOERS

farmers to an alien government. But was it right to desert the 10,000 loyalists in the towns? It was right, no doubt, to recognise the wishes of the Africander population in the Cape Colony, being the Queen's subjects, but was it right to expose the English colonists, also the Queen's subjects, to the degradation and contempt which they endured at the hands of their Dutch neighbours during the years 1881 to 1885?

No, the retrocession of the Transvaal must be justified on the ground of political expediency. But let us understand clearly the nature of this expediency. The Boers had the whole of Dutch South Africa at their backs: they emphasised the fact of Africander solidarity by shooting down 800 English officers and men. It was more expedient to surrender the Transvaal than to run the risk of having to subdue the whole Dutch population in South Africa by force of arms—that is to say, it was expedient under the then existing political conditions of South Africa. But how can we justify the course of action which created those conditions? In other words, was the crisis which arose at the end of 1880 one which could have been neither foreseen nor prevented by the exercise of reasonable foresight and address on the part of the Imperial Government?

Let us look at the information which was placed before them as to the condition of the Transvaal during the twelve months which immediately preceded the revolt.

On the 29th of October 1879, Lord Wolseley, who was then administering the Transvaal, reported to the Secretary for the colonies, "That he was informed on all sides that it was the intention of the Boers to fight for independence," but he also stated that, in his opinion, the insecurity of the important section of loyalists would be "an insuperable obstacle to retrogression."

On the 2nd of March 1880, he wrote in justification of certain energetic measures which he had taken to uphold the Queen's authority *—measures which had been censured by the Imperial Government—that the object of the meeting of the Boer leaders in December 1879 was to see how far they "would be suffered to advance in open repudiation of the Queen's authority"; that the tolerance of such proceedings was regarded by the mass of the Boer population as "sufficient evidence of the inability of the administration to defend its authority," and was "the seal of success upon rebellion." "It appeared to me," he continues, "to be quite clear that the longer this false idea of the timid collapse of British sovereignty was suffered to germinate, the more dangerous would become the audacity of the leaders and instigators of the agitation, and the more confirmed and intractable would be the feelings of the people."† And in his despatch of July the 6th, 1880, Sir Bartle Frere placed first among the causes to which was due the refusal of the Colonial Parliament to pledge itself to the Conference proposals, the distrust and uncertainty which was felt regarding the course of H.M. Government in the Transvaal, Zululand and Natal.‡

I have spoken of the disgrace of Majuba, and I used the word advisedly; but the disgrace of Majuba does not lie in the defeat of the British arms. I believe that if the special conditions and circumstances of the engagements of the Transvaal Revolt are studied, it will be found that our soldiers fought with no less than their accustomed gallantry (Note 19). The disgrace of Majuba lies in the fact that it was the sign and seal of the disasters which attend a vacillating policy, an evasion of responsibilities, and the desertion and abandonment of a faithful servant.

There are passages in the lives of nations, as in the

* The arrests of Pretorius and Bok.
† C—2584.
‡ C—2655.

THE BOERS

lives of individuals, where the office of history is confined within the narrowest limits. In such passages there is no room for picturesque description or complacent detail, still less for the eloquence which is naturally stimulated by the contemplation of wise counsels or brave deeds. It remains solely to trace the connection of cause and effect; and in proportion as the analysis is accurate and exact, is the possibility of achieving a useful purpose. Such a passage is the story of the relationship of England to the Boers: and I have endeavoured to relate the facts with some completeness, for an account of mistakes and errors, and of the disasters resulting from them, is only useful when it is so clear that it becomes a means by which like errors can be avoided in the future.

Well, the Boer has been left in undisturbed possession of his inheritance in South Africa for fourteen years, and during that time he has passed from poverty to opulence —through the exertions of the aliens to whom he denies the franchise.

Let us do justice to the Boer. Let us acknowledge the reality of the original grievances which drove him beyond the limits of the British jurisdiction; let us admit the magnitude of the services which he rendered to South African civilisation by destroying the murderous power of Dingan, and driving the Matabele hordes beyond the Limpopo; let us forget the occasions on which he lapsed into the inferior morality of the previous century in his treatment of the natives; let us freely admire the determination and the intrepidity which he displayed in defence of his independence.

We may do all this and still feel that something is wanting to justify him in the occupation of the fairest districts of settled South Africa. He has won his promised land from the heathen. It is exceedingly improbable that he will ever be disturbed again in the possession of this inheritance by any external force. But he has still to justify his possession of these ample pastures, these rich and fertile valleys, and these stores of gold and of coal.

If he can enlarge his mind, if he can reform existing abuses, if he can expand an archaic system of government and render it sufficiently elastic to meet the requirements of an enlarged population and important and increasing industries—well and good. If not, let the Boer beware: for he will place himself in conflict with the intelligence and progress of South Africa.

Then the Boer system will be condemned by a higher authority than the Colonial Office or the opinion of England; and from the high court of nature—a court from which no appeal lies—the inexorable decree will go forth—" Cut it down; why cumbereth it the ground?"

CHAPTER V.

NATAL AND THE KAFIR PROBLEM.

THE gain which has been achieved by humanity during the present century has invited criticism by its very magnitude. Matthew Arnold and Ruskin have told us, each in his own characteristic manner, that a material gain may be a spiritual loss. Mr William Morris, as the social reformer—not "the idle singer of an empty day"—has attacked the dearest doctrine of economic science, and declared that "division of labour" is *wage*-saving not *labour*-saving. Henry George has warned us that the progress of the few may bring poverty to the many, and that while the rich are getting richer, the poor are getting poorer.

To these weighty indictments against the age of progress, the late Mr Pearson has added his gloomy forecast. This new criticism is no longer confined to a single society, or to some one aspect of contemporary life. Its contentions are supported by observations covering the whole range of political and social movement throughout the world; and the doom which is here pronounced is not that of a single community but of civilisation in general.

In spite, however, of the persistency with which the prophets of the age have warned societies and individuals against any unreasoning hopes of the future, certain ideals have hitherto survived. Among them the most captivating, and perhaps the most practical, is a belief on the part of the various members of the Anglo-Saxon family that their race is destined to spread civilisation throughout the world. It is on this ideal of a beneficent and imperial mission that Mr Pearson's criticism falls most heavily. For, if it be true that the coloured races, protected and assisted by European civilisation, will rapidly increase in population, and ultimately circumscribe and paralyse the white races, we Englishmen, the conquerors and administrators of India, beyond all others are "the blind instruments of fate for multiplying the races that are now our subjects, and will one day be our rivals." *

Natal is a case in point.

But before we proceed to discuss this aspect — the aspect which appears the most characteristic and stimulating of the life of Natal—we must first consider those broad necessary facts which will enable us to form a general notion of the colony as a whole.

The most important events in the early history of Natal have already been mentioned. To these events—told incidentally as forming part of general South African history—only one or two fresh facts need be added. The basis of the English population was laid during the years 1848-51, when immigrants, to the number of nearly 4000, arrived in the colony, attracted thither by the representations of a Mr Byrne, an English gentleman who had visited the country in 1843, the year in which a British administration was first permanently established. For three years, 1845-48, Natal was governed as a dependency of the Cape Colony. It was then erected into a separate colony, governed by a Lieutenant-Governor and an executive council. In 1855, after the visit of Sir George Grey, a legislative council was established. In 1866 representative members were admitted to this council. In 1873 the Hlubi trouble, to which reference has already been made,† arose, and in consequence of the facts dis-

---

* "National Life and Character," p. 83.
† Chap. iii. p. 48.

closed by this incident, Lord Wolseley was sent out as special commissioner, to enquire into the relations existing between the Natal government and the natives. As a result of the enquiries then made, certain reforms were introduced into the system of native administration by Sir Henry Bulwer, who became Governor of Natal, on the departure of Lord Wolseley, in August 1875. The progress of the colony was disastrously affected by the Zulu and Transvaal wars; but, since that time—since 1881—Natal has rapidly advanced in prosperity; and in 1893 responsible government was established.

Under the present constitution there is a Legislative Council, of eleven members, nominated by the Governor-in-Council and holding their seats for ten years, and a Legislative Assembly of thirty-seven members, elected by the various constituencies for four years. Under the very special circumstances of Natal the Imperial government have thought fit to make a reservation in conferring parliamentary government upon the colonists. The Governor is empowered to designate not more than six offices "political" offices, and to reserve these for "crown" appointment. Provision is also made for the application of a due proportion of the colonial revenue to the payment of the salary of the Governor, and of the salaries of these political officers, and to native education.

The Natal franchise is liberal. A European is entitled to vote for members of the Assembly if he possesses real property of the value of £50, or occupies such property at an annual rental of not less than £10; or if he is in receipt of an annual income of £96 or upwards. In both cases he must also have resided in the colony for three years. The natives, too, are admitted to political privileges; but in their case a time of probation is required. A native is entitled to vote if, in addition to possessing one or other of these qualifications, he has lived for seven years exempt from the action of the special native laws; that is to say, if he has become, to all intents and purposes, a civilised being.

The area of Natal is rather more than twenty thousand square miles (20,460), or a good deal less than half that of England without Wales and Scotland. The country falls into three natural divisions. There is a coast belt, extending for eight or nine miles inland, where the temperature is raised by the warm Mozambique channel which flows past the coast, and where sugar, tea, arrowroot, and other tropical products are raised. Then, passing inland and westwards, there are the midlands, where the country rises from 900 feet above sea level to 3000 feet. Here horned cattle are depastured, and maize —but not corn—is grown. And, lastly, there are the uplands, rising from 3000 feet in elevation to 5000 feet, where they spring into the Drakensberg. This is where the sheep farms are; and, in the north, there is a great coal-field, estimated at 2000 square miles in extent, where coal is raised in considerable and increasing quantities.

The population of Natal we may take to be in round numbers 600,000 (588,576). Of this total 45,000 persons are Europeans, 40,000 are coolies or Indian immigrants, and 500,000 are Kafirs. The European population is in the main concentrated in the two towns, Durban, the port, and Maritzburg, forty-five miles inland, the seat of Government.

The volume of annual trade passing through Durban is four and a half millions.* Of this amount rather more than three millions (£3,212,259) represents imports, and

---

* The figures in the text are for 1892, and are taken from the "Statistical Abstract" for the Colonies, &c. (C—7144), published in 1893. Later returns show a diminution of about a million in the volume of trade, due mainly to the diversion of the transit trade from Durban, owing to the establishment of better railway communication from other ports to the O. F. State and the Transvaal. As, however, the Natal railway has been extended to Johannesburg and Pretoria in September 1895, I leave the '92 returns as most representative.

a million and a half (£1,535,903) exports. But probably only two-thirds of the imports, and less than a half of the exports, belong to Natal. In order to understand the significance of these figures, we will compare the trade of Natal with that of New Zealand. I say New Zealand, because the total of the population of New Zealand is nearly the same as that of Natal, while the numerical relationship between the Europeans and the natives is almost exactly reversed, for in New Zealand we have a small (45,000) and dwindling population of Maories in the midst of Europeans. The volume of the New Zealand trade reaches over sixteen millions, of which nine and a half millions (£9,534,851) are exports, and seven millions (£6,943,056) imports. The native, therefore, both consumes and produces very much less than the European.

In the Natal exports the chief items are the wool export, £583,385, of which part only is produced in Natal, and the sugar export, £119,461, which is exclusively Natal produce. And to these figures we must add the fact that, in 1892, 141,000 tons of coal were raised in the colony. Of this amount three-fourths (117,000 tons) came from the collieries of a single company, the Dundee Coal Company, which only commenced work in 1890.

Now as to the employment of the Europeans. Of the 13,000 adult males, more than one-half are artisans and mechanics. The remainder are chiefly distributed among the farmers who raise the wool, the planters who grow the sugar, the officials and professional men who, in addition to conducting the general affairs of the colony, control the native population, and the agents and middlemen who forward the goods received at the port, Durban. For Durban serves not only Natal, but the south-eastern corner of the Transvaal, the eastern corner of the Free State, and the native territories lying north and south of the colony. This inland or "overberg" trade requires the services of these agents, and provides employment for a commercial class quite out of proportion to the actual trade of Natal. The existence of this forwarding trade has benefited the colony in two ways. It has made the creation of a complete and relatively extensive railway system necessary and possible ; and it has caused the colonists to spend both energy and capital in improving the port. The harbour of Durban consists of a land-locked stretch of water enclosed between the Bluff promontory and the town. Across the entrance, the Bluff Channel, there runs a bar of sand which prevents vessels of deep draught from reaching the secure waters of the harbour. Between the years 1854 and 1881 the average depth of water over the bar was 6 feet 5 inches. By various harbour works 7 feet 7 inches have been gained, and the maximum draught registered in 1892 was 19 feet 9 inches—a depth which will admit all but the largest class of ocean-going steamers.

I need only speak at length of one of the Natal industries—the sugar industry ; for the South African wool export will be discussed in a subsequent chapter, and the collieries do not, of course, present any characteristic features. In this industry some eight hundred pounds sterling (£830,500) is invested. There are 26,000 acres under crop, and of this area half is reaped annually. There are thirty-six factories, and in the year 1891-1892 the output of sugar amounted to 15,000 tons. The plantations are worked by some 6000 coolies, and a small number of Kafirs. This fact—the fact that the planters have to go to India for their labour when they have a large mass of unemployed Kafirs at their doors—is the most significant feature of the sugar industry. It appears that the Natal Kafirs cannot be induced to submit to the restraints of regular employment. The whole question of Indian immigration was carefully considered by a commission which sat from 1885 to 1887 ; and it was then found that it was impossible to dispense with Indian immigration

NATAL AND THE KAFIR PROBLEM 85

without ruining the industry. This was felt to be too heavy a sacrifice, so the planters continue to bring over coolies from India under contracts for three years' service. The immigrants appear to be exposed to no hardships; on the contrary, many of them settle in Natal after their contracts have expired, and a good deal of the retail trade of the colony has passed into their hands. The commencement of coal mining has benefited the sugar industry, for the cheap supply of fuel allows the planters generally to avail themselves of the diffusion process for the extraction of the juice of the sugar-cane. By this process the juice is first dissolved out of the cane by hot water, and then the liquid so obtained is solidified by evaporation. Both of these treatments require a large expenditure of fuel, and therefore the fact that coal can now be obtained at 21s. 6d. the ton at Durban, has obviously an important bearing upon the prospects of the industry.

Now we are free to approach the subject of the government and administration of the Kafirs.

The physical basis upon which the Natal Government rests consists of (1) a garrison of the Imperial troops, in number from 1000 to 1500 men; (2) the Natal Mounted Police, a small permanent colonial force with a commandant, eight officers, and 280 men; and (3) the volunteers. This latter force amounts to a total of all arms—mounted rifles, artillery, infantry, and a coast corps—nearly two thousand (1835) strong.

Every native who is responsible for a hut is required to pay an annual hut-tax of 14s., and by means of this charge —a charge which is very cheerfully borne—the Kafirs are themselves made to pay for the expenses of administration.

The Letters Patent issued in 1848, by which Natal was created a separate territory, directed that there should be "neither interference with, nor abrogation of, any law, custom, or usage" prevailing among the natives, except so far as these might be "repugnant to the general principles of humanity recognised throughout the whole world." We may compare this proviso with the corresponding proviso in the Constitution Act of an ordinary British colony. By such Imperial Acts a Colonial Legislature is empowered to make laws, and these laws are declared to be valid, except so far as they are "repugnant to the law of England." In the following year, 1849, the Lieutenant-Governor of Natal was created by ordinance "Supreme Chief" of all the natives within the colony, and empowered to administer native law through such persons as he thought fit to appoint for that purpose.

In Natal, therefore, the tribal organisation has been preserved instead of being broken up, as we saw was done in the Cape Colony under the policy initiated by Sir George Grey; and the authority of the chiefs has been utilised for the purposes of government. At the present time the administration of justice is effected by means of three kinds of courts—those presided over by European magistrates, chiefs' courts, and mixed tribunals. In these latter cases between Europeans and natives are heard, and European magistrates and chiefs sit side by side. In all these courts Kafir law and custom, as modified by the Colonial Statutes, are recognised. The Natal Laws also include a number of statutes intended merely to preserve order among the natives. Such laws are of two kinds—those which regulate the relationship between the Europeans and natives, *e.g.* such laws as those which forbid the sale of intoxicating liquors, or of firearms, by a European to a native, under very severe penalties, and a class of laws which deal with what may be called special police regulations applicable to the natives only. These latter cover such matters as "passes," or the written permission which a native is required to procure from a magistrate before he changes his residence; the curfew, or the nine o'clock bell, after which the Kafirs retire to their huts in Maritzburg and Durban; and the registration of firearms.

The system resembles that of India rather than that of

NATAL AND THE KAFIR PROBLEM 87

the Cape Colony. The natives have been left practically to themselves :—not altogether, because there are now a small number (73) of native schools at work; but this effort is too slight to produce any effect as yet upon the solid mass of Kafirdom against which it is directed. Considered only as a means of *governing* the natives, the Natal administration has been successful, for, with the exception of the Hlubi trouble, there has been no serious outbreak among the Kafirs since Natal was constituted a separate government. But now, in the view of the experience of the last ten years, in view, that is to say, of the very rapid growth of the Kafir population in the colony, the question is being raised whether it is enough merely to govern without civilising. This question constitutes what I have termed the " problem " of Natal.

We will take the figures as Mr Pearson gives them. In 1863 the European element constituted one-seventh of the population of the colony, in 1891 it constituted only one-twelfth; and again, in 1879, the year in which the Zulu war broke out, there were 319,934 Kafirs in Natal, in 1891 there were 455,983 (Note 20).

Making due allowance for the undoubted fact that this increase is very largely due to immigration, the figures are still sufficiently significant. And what applies to Natal applies also to South Africa generally.

Let us take the fact of the Bantu increase as Mr Theal states it:

" That the Bantu population in South Africa from the Limpopo to the sea has trebled itself by natural increase alone within fifty years, is asserting what must be far below the real rate of growth." *

The chief causes of this rapid increase are disclosed by a very interesting enquiry initiated by the Native Department of the Cape Government in 1855. A circular containing a series of questions was distributed among the

* Appendix to " The Republics " (" History of South Africa ").

magistrates, missionaries, and traders. The collective evidence of these authorities attributes the increase to the "controlling power of the civilised Governments" which has removed certain ancient checks on population, such as tribal wars and feuds, and executions on charge of witchcraft, and lessened the action of others, such as "ignorance of medicine" and "uncertainty of food supplies." At the same time, most of these authorities are of opinion that the present rate of increase will not be maintained in the future. They indicate that already certain new checks are coming into operation. The most important of these new checks are :—

(*a*) The rapid limitation of the food supply which can be produced by the primitive methods of cultivation practised by the Kafirs, and

(*b*) The adoption of European dress and manners. This last introduces a higher standard of comfort, a recognised check on indiscriminate reproduction ; and also appears to slightly deteriorate the physique of the South African native.

Still, there is no doubt that the Bantu are increasing very rapidly in South Africa; and the broad fact remains, that in South Africa the Europeans must be prepared to share the country with the coloured races, instead of exclusively occupying it as they have done in North America and Australia.

And if this is so, the question of native education becomes especially important.

What, then, is being done in South Africa to educate the native, to make him a civilised being, to fit him, in short, for this partnership with the European? As I have already said, in Natal there has been no serious effort made in this direction. No effort has been made in the Native Territories, nor in the Republics. Experience shows that, in order to produce any permanent results, two conditions are necessary. There must be an efficient machinery for educating the young, and there must be a sufficient European background to prevent the civilised native from falling back into barbarism. The only part of South Africa where these conditions are at all realised as yet are some districts of the Cape Colony. It is to the Cape Colony, therefore, that we must go, if we would learn what has been already achieved in this direction, and what results may be expected in the future.

In the Cape Colony an extensive and efficient machinery for native education has been at work for many years past. From a report of the Superintendent-General of Education (Sir Langham Dale), published in 1883, we learn that, in the preceding year there were 396 mission schools with an attendance of 44,307; 226 aborigines' day schools with an attendance of 13,817, and 21 boarding and trade schools with 2519 pupils. It should also be added that about one-third of the Annual Education Grant (amounting in 1889 to £85,000) is appropriated to the purposes of native education.

Of all these native schools and institutions, Lovedale is the most remarkable; and a record of the work done at Lovedale will give some insight into both the methods pursued and the results attained by the native educator.

In the same report it is stated that there were 300 pupils at Lovedale, and that the yearly turnover was £15,000. There is a college department in which native clergy and teachers are trained; there are workshops where young men are taught bookbinding, printing, and smiths' and carpenters' work, and where young women are taught sewing and laundress work; and there is an elementary school for boys and girls. As evidence of the reality of the trade instruction given at Lovedale, the fact is recorded that the work of thirty-five apprentices for one year realised the sum of £2200.

Writing on the general question of native education —a question which has been warmly debated at the Cape

—the Superintendent-General of Education says, in a supplementary report issued in the following year, that the supporters of native education "appeal to such facts as the large interchange among natives of letters passing through the post-office; of the utilisation of educated natives as carriers of letters, telegrams, and parcels; of the hundreds who fill responsible posts as clerks, interpreters, school-masters, sewing-mistresses, and of the still larger number engaged in industrial pursuits, as carpenters, blacksmiths, tinsmiths, wagon-makers, shoemakers, printers, sailmakers, saddlers, etc., earning good wages, and helping to spread civilisation among their own people." Among the opponents of native education he finds "conflicting opinions." "On the one hand," he says, "the schools are abused as worthless, and educated natives decried; on the other hand, I find it affirmed that the aborigines are getting a better education than the white people, and that the native apprentices from the trade schools become successful rivals in industrial employments."

To clench the argument I have made some extracts from the South African Circular issued by the Emigrants' Information Office in October 1894. After saying that the bulk of the labour employed, both in agriculture and in mining, is supplied by the natives, the Circular continues, under the heading " Mechanics "—

"It should be remembered that large numbers of Malays and other coloured men, in all parts of Cape Colony, now compete with whites as skilled mechanics at lower wages.

"Nearly all the reports received (from various commercial centres) state either that none but natives are employed, or, that . . . if Europeans are employed . . . the supply is sufficient.

"In the Transkei Europeans receive 10s. to 15s. a day, but they are rarely employed . . ."

This is very practical and conclusive evidence of the value of native education at the Cape.

NATAL AND THE KAFIR PROBLEM 91

We will now enlarge the area of our observations once again, and pass from a consideration of the growth of the Bantu population to the wider question of the ultimate numerical relationship between the higher and lower races raised by the late Mr Pearson, who was for many years Minister of Education in Victoria, in his work entitled "National Life and Character: a Forecast."

Mr Pearson's forecast depends upon two main propositions.

1. The lower races will in the future increase at so disproportionate a rate (as compared with the white populations) as ultimately to predominate over the higher races.

2. The stationary condition of society to which the higher races are to be thus reduced will involve a general deterioration of national life and character.

The arguments by which Mr Pearson seeks to establish the first of these two propositions are contained in the chapter on "The Unchangeable Limits of the Higher Races." He points out that, with the exception of small acquisitions, such as that of the Mediterranean seaboard of Africa by France, and of Western Turkestan by Russia, the white races are not likely to add any considerable territories to those which they already occupy. From the evidence collected on this head Mr Pearson concludes that "by far the most fertile parts of the earth, and [those] which either are or are bound to be the most populous," cannot possibly be the homes of any of the higher races. Meanwhile the dense yellow populations of China, India, Japan, and the Malay Archipelago, the black populations of Central and Southern Africa, the negroes of the United States, and the Indians of Central and South America, are bound to multiply with an ever-increasing rapidity. And thus, in Mr Pearson's words—

"The day will come, and perhaps is not far distant, when the European observer will look round to see the globe girdled with a continuous zone of the black and yellow races, no longer too weak for aggression or under tutelage, but independent, or practically so, in Government, monopolising the trade of their own regions, and circumscribing the industry of the European; when Chinamen and the nations of Hindustan, the States of Central and South America, by that time predominantly Indian, and it may be the African nations of the Congo and the Zambesi, under a dominant caste of foreign rulers, are represented by fleets in the European seas, invited to international conferences, and welcomed as allies in the quarrels of the civilised world. The citizens of these countries will then be taken up into the social relations of the white races, will throng the English turf, or the salons of Paris, and will be admitted to intermarriage . . . We shall wake up to find ourselves elbowed and hustled, and perhaps even thrust aside by peoples whom we looked down upon as servile, and thought of as bound always to minister to our needs." *

In order to get a definite notion of the nature of the change which is here predicted, it is necessary to form some idea (approximately correct) of the relative numbers of the higher and lower races, and of the manner in which they are respectively distributed over the surface of the globe. Mr Pearson himself subsequently states the ratio between the white and coloured populations to be as one to two. Assuming that this is so, let us suppose Europe, North America, and Australia to belong exclusively to the 400,000,000 Europeans in and out of Europe, and Asia, Africa, and South America similarly to the 800,000,000 Chinese, Hindus, Africans, and Indians, which form the bulk of the population of these continents. In this way we get 400,000,000 of whites occupying 15,000,000 square miles, as opposed to 800,000,000 of coloured people occupying 35,000,000 square miles of the earth's surface. This calculation omits to take account

* P. 84.

of 2,000,000 square miles, and 200,000,000 people; but as both areas and populations would be fairly evenly divided among the higher and lower races, the omission does not affect the argument.

As the population of South America is too small to have any immediate significance, it is in China, in India, and in Central Africa that we may expect the first signs of the disproportionate increase which is to reverse the present relationship of the higher and lower races.

Our knowledge of the population of China is eminently unsatisfactory. But in the absence of definite information, there are two considerations which are valuable as tending to mitigate the alarm caused by the migratory tendencies lately developed by the most populous nation in the world. In the first place, by far the greater portion of its 400,000,000 * inhabitants are confined to China proper, that is to say, to an area one-third only of the four and a half million square miles of the empire, and equal to India. Assuming, therefore, that the opportunities of expansion permitted to the Chinese by the remaining three million square miles of sparsely peopled territory are not more than equivalent to the sanitary and other advantages of British administration enjoyed by the people of India, we may conclude that the rate of increase in China is not likely to exceed that in India. Accordingly, if we find that the increase of population in India does not at present indicate any such expansion as Mr Pearson's forecast requires, we may, in the absence of any positive evidence to the contrary, conclude as much with regard to China. In the second place, China has already been brought face to face with Russia.† Con-

* Generally stated now as 350,000,000.
† "It is Russia who threatens her frontiers in Chinese Turkestan and on the Pamirs; Russia who is always nibbling, in scientific disguise, at Tibet; Russia who has designs in Manchuria; Russia whose shadow overhangs Korea; Russia who is building a great trans-continental railway that will enable her to pour troops into

tinued development, therefore, will bring the Chinese increasingly into collision with a state which is, perhaps, the most powerful military state in the world, and one whose population has increased *by natural increment* during the last hundred years at the rate of more than 200 per cent.*

With India the case is, happily, different. Here we have census returns which reveal the movement of population with increasing fidelity. The census for 1891 shows that the entire population under both British and feudatory rule now reaches a total of over 284,000,000, having increased during the decade 1881-91 at 12·36 per cent. The population of British India, however, now numbering 220,000,000, has increased (deducting the increment due to the acquisition of fresh territories) at the lesser rate of $9\frac{1}{2}$ per cent. The apparently more rapid increase in the native, as compared with the British territories, is referred by the Census Commissioner to the receipt of more faithful returns, arising partly from a better disposition in the natives, and partly to the fact that many of these feudatory states are now more directly under British control than they have been previously.† We may therefore fairly conclude that $9\frac{1}{2}$ per cent. represents the rate at which the Indian peoples have increased by natural increment during the last decade. If we compare this $9\frac{1}{2}$ per cent. with the 13·98 per cent.‡ of natural increase in England, and the 14·40 per cent. of natural, and 24·86 per cent. of actual increase in the United States §—to say nothing

China at any point along 3500 miles of continuous border."—"China in relation to the Powers," *Times*, February 10th, 1893. The fact that Russia is the natural rival of China (and of the yellow races) is emphasised by the results of the war between China and Japan.

* Giffen, in *Statistical Society's Journal*, June 1885, p. 103.
† Preliminary Report by Mr J. A. Baines, Census Commissioner to the Government of India.
‡ Preliminary Report, etc., of the Census (England and Wales), 1891.
§ Statesman's "Year-Book," p. 1069.

NATAL AND THE KAFIR PROBLEM 95

of even higher rates reached in Australia—we can scarcely avoid the conclusion that India, at any rate, affords but slight confirmation of Mr Pearson's contention.

Apart from the evidence I have already mentioned as indicating that a new set of checks are in operation which will prevent the Bantu race in South Africa from increasing in the future at the present abnormal rate, we can form some estimate of the probable rate of increase of the Central African generally from the progress of the race in the United States. Even here the census returns are not altogether reliable. In 1870 in particular the numbers of the blacks were so much understated as to produce an apparent rate of increase for the decade 1870-80 so high as justly to cause serious apprehension. But an examination of the decennial returns for the century 1790-1890 indicates that, so far from the black race increasing in an ascending ratio relatively to the white, the proportion of negroes to Europeans is appreciably less now than it was a hundred years ago.

TABLE SHOWING COMPARATIVE GROWTH OF THE WHITE AND COLOURED POPULATION IN THE UNITED STATES.*

Years.	Population.		Number of coloured to 100,000 white.	Per cent. of Increase.	
	White.	Coloured.		White.	Coloured.
1790	1,271,488	689,884	54,258	...	...
1800	1,702,980	918,336	53,925	33·94	33·11
1810	2,208,785	1,272,119	57,594	29·70	38·52
1820	2,831,560	1,653,240	58,386	28·20	29·96
1830	3,660,758	2,187,545	59,757	29·28	32·32
1840	4,632.530	2,701,901	58,325	26·55	23·51
1850	6,222,418	3,442,238	55,320	34·32	27·40
1860	8,203,852	4,216,241	51,393	31·84	22·49
1870	9,812,732	4,555,990	46,429	19·61	8·06
1880	13,530,408	6,142,360	45,397	37·89	34·82
1890	16,868,205	6,996,166	41,475	24·67	13·90

* The United States "Census Bulletin," No. 48, March 27th, 1891.

In connection with this table it is necessary to point out that (1), the States included in the enumeration contain fifteen-sixteenths of the total coloured population; and, (2), the number of immigrants from Europe or from the northern States of the Union is so small as not to appreciably affect the rate of increase of the whites. This calculation is the more significant from the fact that it comes from a country where the negro race is already in the enjoyment of those advantages of European administration which Mr Pearson thinks would, if extended to the race in Central Africa, produce a disastrous and disproportionate increase. *

In his concluding pages Mr Pearson invites his readers to think of civilised society under the figure of an old man, "with his intellect keen, with his experience bitter, with his appetites unsatiated, with the memory of past enjoyment stinging him."

Society is "doomed to live on into the ages, with all that the best ordered polity can secure it, with all inherited treasures of beauty, with a faith in science that is perpetually mocked by weaker and weaker results, and with no spiritual sense to understand what surrounds it, with the mind's vision growing dim, with the apprehension of art dwarfed to taking comfort in bric-a-brac, with no hope or suggestion of sight beyond the grave..."†

It is a more hopeful and a more just thought to present the Anglo-Saxon race to the mind under the figure of a youth.

During the last hundred years not only has the population of Europe risen from 145,000,000 in 1788 to

* The general conclusion, based upon returns for a hundred years (given above), does not differ materially from Mr Pearson's conclusion as stated in Appendix ii., p. 348 :—"Assuming the facts of the last census to be unimpeachable, it seems to result that whites and blacks increase in nearly the same ratio." But this is obviously insufficient for the purposes of his contention.

† P. 337.

350,000,000 in 1888, but during the same period the European population out of Europe has grown at a far more rapid rate, increasing from 5,000,000 to 70,000,000. To this remarkable increase the Anglo-Saxon people have been by far the largest contributors; and Dr Giffen estimates* that, "in another century, at the past rate of progress, there will be nearly 1,000,000,000 of this race alone in the world." If, therefore, the growth of population in Europe should be checked, either by the operation of war, or by mere stagnation such as we see in France, it is to the Anglo-Saxon settlements in America, Australia and South Africa that we must look to maintain the predominance of the white races in the world.

It is then that the citizens of America, Australia and South Africa will justify their occupation of these continents. The European traveller will no longer scrutinise their title deeds, or contrast the broad unfinished streets and the wildernesses of corrugated-iron sheds and shanties in their growing towns with the splendours of the historic capitals of Europe, or compare their arid and unfertilised plains with the soft luxuriance and settled beauty of an old world landscape. Even the harsh tone of colonial life will have been forgotten. Or rather, it will then be seen that for these and other deficiencies there is a large and generous compensation. For it is the sense of youth permeating the life of these new communities that causes that unreasonable—as it seems—complacency with conditions of existence so palpably defective, and that irritation at the application of any old world test, which seems to characterise Americans and Australians.

And yet this complacency is not so unreasonable after all. For what man of mature years would not exchange his great possessions, or high position, for the thirty, or twenty, or even ten years of vigorous action with its glittering possibilities that a young man, untrained and

* *Journal of the Statistical Society*, June 1885, p. 101.

untried, inferior to the other in all else but this boon of youth, alone possesses ? So it is with our greater England : it is instinct with the energy of anticipated existence, and the torch of life which is delivered into its hands burns ever brighter and stronger with the flames of Science Industry, Peace and Justice.

CHAPTER VI.

THE BECHUANALAND SETTLEMENT.

THE original possessors of the soil of South Africa were not the dark-skinned people, the Bantu, whom we have been led by unhappy associations to regard as the "natives," but a yellow-skinned race, differing in little but their woolly hair from the Chinese and the Malays. At the time of Van Riebeck's expedition—in 1652—they had already deeply degraded in the scale of civilisation. To-day their descendants, the 50,000 or 60,000 Hottentots, Bushmen, Namaquas and Korannas, have no political or social importance.

With the dark-skinned race, the Bantu, who occupied the southern extremity of Africa contemporaneously with the Europeans, the case is very different. They outnumber the Europeans in the proportion of six to one; and they have plainly signified their intention of sharing the country with them.

Hitherto we have been mainly concerned with the warlike tribes of this family, the Kafirs, the Zulus, and the Matabele Zulus; we have now to consider the relations of the Europeans with one of the peaceable tribes, the Bechuanas.

The distribution of the military and industrial Bantu is significant. The military Bantu are found in possession of the most fertile regions. They are found between the Drakensberg mountains and the Indian Ocean, and in the fertile districts to the north-west—the Zoutpansberg—and to the south of the range—Kaffraria. The industrial Bantu are found clinging to the mountains as in Basutoland, or scattered over the high plateau which forms the greater part of the Free State and the Transvaal, or on the confines of the Kalahari desert, or on those of the deserts and karoos south of the Orange River. The desert was their ultimate retreat when they were compelled to retire before their more warlike kinsmen.

The military and industrial Bantu differ in their tribal organisation, in their dwellings, and in their pursuits. They are both armed with the same weapon, the assegai * or spear; but the assegai of the military Bantu is short-handled and broad-bladed. It is not thrown away, but used for fighting at close quarters. The manner in which the assegai is used, and the general method of the attack of the warlike tribes, are well described by Pringle in his poem "Mokanna's Gathering":

> "Grasp each man short his stabbing spear,
> And when to battle's edge we come,
> Rush on their ranks in full career,
> And to their hearts strike home."

More than one disaster inflicted upon the British troops has borne witness to the terrible effect of this "rush." The assegai of the industrial Bantu is long in the shaft and light in the blade; it is used as a javelin, and is intended mainly for the purposes of the chase. Among the military Bantu the chief is a despot against whose word there is no appeal: among the industrial Bantu the power of the chief is limited; first, by the council of lesser chiefs—his brothers, as he calls them—and, secondly, by the *pitso*, or general assemblage of the freemen of the tribe. The town of the military Bantu is designed solely with a view to defence. The chief's hut and the cattle pens are placed in the centre, and around these the remaining huts are built in concentric

* From *hasta* through the Portuguese.

THE BECHUANALAND SETTLEMENT 101

circles. The town of the industrial Bantu is open; that is to say, it is intended to serve the requirements of a peaceable people. Again they differ in their respective pursuits. The sole business of the military tribes was warfare; they planted just so much corn, and raised just so many cattle as would provide for their immediate wants. Outside the town of the industrial Bantu we find plots of garden ground cultivated, and they are acquainted with the art of smelting ore and working in iron.

The chief seats of the industrial tribes are Bechuanaland and Basutoland. Of these the former, Bechuanaland, is interesting to Englishmen as being the scene of the labours of some of our most famous missionaries, Robert Moffat, David Livingstone, and Mr John Mackenzie. It is politically important, because this region, inhabited by peaceable tribes was, and is, the trade route from the Cape Colony to Central Africa. For a long time it was the only door into the interior of Africa, and this door would have been permanently closed by the Boers except for the interposition of the broad shoulders of a single Englishman, Livingstone. After his house had been plundered by a Boer commando towards the end of 1852—the year of the Sand River Convention—Livingstone turned from his missionary labours to the work of exploration. In his own words—" The Boers resolved to shut up the interior, and I determined to open the country."* To the missionaries, therefore, we owe— quite apart from their general services in the cause of Christianity and civilisation—the establishment of British authority in Bechuanaland, and, indirectly, the acquisition of the whole of the vast central region now administered by the British South Africa Company.

Had time permitted it would have been interesting to have considered Basutoland in detail. In some respects the Basutos are the most interesting of the

* "Missionary Travels," 1857.

Bantu peoples in South Africa. We find the tribal organisation most completely developed among them, and they inhabit an exceedingly picturesque country, the Switzerland of South Africa it has been called. Moreover, it is impossible not to sympathise with Moshesh, the old chief, who could express the requirements of political expediency in a phrase so beautiful as that in which he petitioned for the protection of the Imperial Government. This was in 1868, when he and his people were threatened with extinction, or at any rate dispersion, at the hands of the Free State. Moshesh then prayed :— " Let me and my people rest and live under the large folds of the flag of England before I am no more." This request was granted; but in 1871 Basutoland was annexed to the Cape Colony. In 1880 the Colonial Government endeavoured to enforce the disarmament measures, which they had been led to adopt in consequence of the general disturbances among the Bantu at the period of the Zulu war, in Basutoland. After an expensive and unsuccessful campaign, they determined, in 1883, to abandon the country. The Imperial Government regarded this proposal as disastrous to the prestige of the Europeans in South Africa, and they again " took over " Basutoland in 1884.

To return to Bechuanaland.

Tradition tells us that in the distant past one Morolong led the Baralongs from the far North, and that the tribe settled on the Molopo River under Mabua, fourth in descent from Morolong. Here the Baralongs were attacked and dispersed by the Matabele Zulus, under Moselekatse. On their dispersal one section was led by Moroko southwards to Thaba N'chu. Two other sections, respectively led by Taoane, the father of Montsioa, and Machabi, also found their way into the country between the Orange River and the Vaal. In 1836 the emigrant farmers entered this same district, and shortly afterwards the Boers, under Hendrik Potgieter, entered into an alliance with the Baralongs for the purpose of attacking Moselekatse. After the "old lion of the North" had been defeated and driven beyond the Limpopo, Taoane returned with his following to the south bank of the Moroko. By virtue of this conquest Hendrik Potgieter issued a proclamation in which he laid claim to the whole of the country which had been overrun by the Zulu chief. Under this proclamation the Boers (and the Transvaal Government) claimed to exercise sovereign powers over all the Bechuana tribes; and in 1868, President Pretorius issued a proclamation by which the Transvaal authority was declared to extend as far as Lake N'gami. The British Government, however, at once protested against this proclamation, and it was withdrawn. Although some of the Bechuana chiefs recognised the sovereignty of the Boers, both Taoane and Montsioa, who succeeded his father in 1849, appear to have repeatedly refused submission. They maintained that the Baralongs reoccupied their country as of right, and not by permission of the Boers. On March 27th, 1870, Montsioa wrote to the Landdrost of Potchefstroom to complain that taxes had been demanded of his people by an official of the Transvaal Government. "If there is not soon made an end of this lawless matter," he wrote, "I shall be obliged to hand it over to Her Britannic Majesty's High Commissioner, Sir P. E. Wodehouse, with the earnest request to arbitrate between me and my most noble allies."*

In 1871 Griqualand West was occupied by the Imperial Government, and in the same year an attempt was made to settle this question of the South-Western frontier of the Transvaal, by arbitration. The Keate Award was, however, repudiated by the Volksraad, and the question remained in abeyance. In 1877 the Transvaal was annexed, and the border was delimited. In 1878 Bechuana-

* "Bechuanaland," by a member of the Cape Legislature, p. 2.

land was in a state of great disturbance, and the Griqualand West police occupied the country for some time. After they had been withdrawn Imperial agents were placed with two of the chiefs, Mathlabane and Mankoroane. In 1881 the independent Transvaal Government was re-established under the terms of the Convention of Pretoria. In November of that year the High Commissioner, Sir Hercules Robinson, telegraphed * to the Civil Commissioner at Kimberley, informing him that "in consequence of the final definition of the Transvaal boundary, the Government did not intend to continue to maintain representatives outside the Colonial frontier." These agents were then withdrawn. In the next two years, 1881-3, Bechuanaland became more and more disturbed. Montsioa, the Baralong chief, was at war with his brother Moshette, and Mankoroane, the Batlapin chief, was engaged in a struggle with David Massou, the head of the Korannas. Of these four chiefs, Montsioa and Mankoroane claimed the protection of the Imperial Government, while Moshette and Massou acknowledged the sovereignty of the Transvaal. All four chiefs were assisted by European volunteers, or "freebooters," who were to be rewarded for their services by grants of land; that is to say—by the land taken from the rival chief, by the spoils of war in fact.

In November 1883, the Transvaal delegates, Messrs Kruger, Du Toit and Smit, arrived in England. The object of their visit was to obtain certain modifications of the Convention of Pretoria. In this object they were successful, and on February 27th, 1884, the Convention of London was signed. As this Convention governs the existing relationship between Great Britain and the South African Republic—the name which was now formally recognised as the designation of the Transvaal State— and as there appears to be a good deal of misunder-

* C—3098.

THE BECHUANALAND SETTLEMENT

standing on the subject, I give the telegram in which Lord Derby, the then Secretary for the Colonies, announced the result of these negotiations. This telegram was addressed to Sir Leicester Smyth, the acting Governor at the Cape; for Sir Hercules Robinson had also come to England in order that the Colonial Office might have the benefit of his advice at this time.

"Convention signed to-day, new south-western boundary as proposed to the east of trade road. British Protectorate over the country outside Transvaal established with Delegates' consent. They promise appointment of border commissioners inside the Transvaal, co-operating with ours outside. Mackenzie British Resident. Debt reduced to quarter million. Same complete internal independence in Transvaal as in Orange Free State. Conduct and control of diplomatic intercourse with foreign governments conceded; *Queen's final approval to treaties reserved.* Delegates appear well satisfied, and cordial feeling between two governments. You may make above known." *

Meanwhile the Imperial Government had taken a new departure. They had determined that the Governor of the Cape Colony, in his capacity of High Commissioner, should assume the responsibilities towards the natives which would have been assumed by the Federal authority which Lord Carnarvon had endeavoured to establish. On February 9th, 1884, a fortnight before the new Convention was signed, a new Commission had been issued to Sir Hercules Robinson. By this Commission he, as High Commissioner, was placed in much the same relationship to the natives outside the Republics and the territories of foreign powers, as that in which the Governor of Natal had been placed to the natives in that colony by the ordinance of 1849, which created him supreme chief.

* C—3936. See Appendix, where the text of the Convention is given in full.

The special articles in the new Commission were as follows:—

IV. And we do hereby require and empower you as such our High Commissioner . . . to take all such measures and do all such things in relation to the native tribes in South Africa with which it is expedient that we should have relations, and which are not included within the territory of either of the said Republics or of any foreign power, as are lawful and appear to you to be advisable for maintaining our possessions in peace and safety, and for promoting the peace, order, and good government of the tribes aforesaid, and for preserving friendly relations with them.

V. And we do hereby authorise and empower you, by instruments under your hand and seal, to appoint so many fit persons as you shall think necessary . . . to be your Deputy Commissioners, or to be resident Commissioners or assistant Commissioners . . . [Such Commissioners to have the powers, etc., within their districts of the High Commissioner.]

VI. And . . . we further authorise, etc., you to appoint such border agents and other officers as you shall think necessary, if provision shall have been made for their payment . . .

This was a very significant departure, for, in undertaking the administration of the territories occupied by the natives, the Imperial Government had assumed the further and very necessary duty of regulating and controlling the northward expansion of the Europeans.

In pursuance of this new policy Colonel (now Sir) Marshall Clarke took over Basutoland in March (1884), and in May Mr Mackenzie arrived in Bechuanaland for the purpose of giving effect to the newly proclaimed protectorate.

When Mr Mackenzie arrived in Bechuanaland he found that the volunteers in the service of Moshette and Massou

THE BECHUANALAND SETTLEMENT 107

had established two independent communities, the "republics" of Land Goshen and Stellaland. The burghers of Stellaland submitted, but the burghers of Land Goshen refused to acknowledge the authority of the Deputy Commissioner. During the next few months the country remained in a state of anarchy, which culminated in the outrages perpetrated by the freebooters of Rooi Grond at the end of July and in the month of August. Rooi Grond, it should be explained, was the capital of Land Goshen. It had been cleverly placed on the line of the new southwestern boundary of the Transvaal, so that the town stood partly in the Transvaal and partly in the protectorate. On the 30th of July Mr Mackenzie was withdrawn by Sir Hercules Robinson. It was stated, at the time the appointment had been made, that the mere fact of Mr Mackenzie being a missionary, and therefore known to sympathise with the natives, was sufficient to render his success impossible. As a matter of fact, it appears that Mr Mackenzie's actions as Deputy Commissioner were both equitable and prudent; and it seems probable that, if he had been properly supported, that is to say, if he had received the 200 police for which he asked, he would have established his authority in spite of the very great opposition with which he met. In deference to the opinion of his colonial ministers, which Sir Hercules Robinson was bound to consider, Mr Mackenzie was however withdrawn, and Mr Cecil J. Rhodes, a colonial ex-minister, was appointed to succeed him. Mr Rhodes was accompanied by Captain Bower, who filled the newly created office of Imperial Secretary. These two gentlemen fared no better, but rather worse, than Mr Mackenzie.

The freebooters of Rooi Groud were contemptuously indifferent to the arrival of these new officials. They did not even think it worth while to desist from the attack upon Montsioa's town, in which they were then engaged, and scarcely allowed them an opportunity of delivering their message.

At this point in the history of South Africa the authority of the Imperial Government was "at its lowest ebb." Mr Mackenzie writes in "Austral Africa"—*

"No Imperial officer before or since was ever in such a position—dogging the steps of freebooters in the Transvaal with proferred repudiation of our own accredited and official actions within an English protectorate, and dogging their footsteps in vain. Cape Colonist, Free State farmer, roving European—each and all became aware that day that there was no Imperial or Colonial authority in Bechuanaland. Delarey and Van Niekerk were masters, but they gladly acknowledged that they too had a master —the Transvaal Government, then represented on the border by General Joubert; and they accordingly proceeded to lay the affairs of the protectorate before General Joubert at Goshen, while the Secretary of the High Commissioner waited the turn of events, and the wishes of others, at Mr Delarey's farm."

On September 10th, President Kruger issued a proclamation by which "in the interests of humanity" he "proclaimed and ordained" the contending chiefs, Moshette and Montsioa, to be under the protection of the South African Republic. The proclamation was stated to be made "provisionally" and subject to Article iv. † of the Convention of London.

Now the Transvaal had gone too far. The broad contempt of the Imperial Government, and the cynical disregard of the interests of the mother colony, which the Boers had manifested in this action, produced a revulsion of public opinion in the Cape Colony. It was seen that what had been represented as a question of nationality was also a question of principle; that the question at issue was not merely whether the Dutch or

* Vol. I. p. 433.
† Under Article iv. the S. A. Republic remains within the sphere of British influence as regards its foreign relations.

THE BECHUANALAND SETTLEMENT 109

the English should take the lead in South Africa, but also whether the inevitable northward expansion of the Europeans should be an honourable triumph over the forces of nature and of barbarism, or whether this advance should be polluted by crime and injustice. And when this was realised there arose in the minds of all law abiding colonists an earnest desire for the intervention of England (Note 21).

When this state of affairs was made known to the Imperial Government they very naturally hesitated. They declared—the declaration was made publicly by Mr Evelyn Ashley, the Under-Secretary for the colonies—that, before England could again interfere by force of arms in the affairs of South Africa, she must be assured of the support of public opinion in the Cape Colony.

The reply to this challenge came in the form of a great public meeting which was held in the Corn Exchange at Capetown on September 24th. This meeting was both large and representative. It was declared by the *Volksblad* to be "the most important public meeting held in the colony," since the meeting held in 1849 to protest against the formation of a penal settlement at the Cape. Among the resolutions passed the first recorded the opinion :—

"That the intervention of Her Majesty's Government in Bechuanaland for the maintenance of the trade route to the interior, and the preservation of native tribes to whom promises of Imperial protection had been given, was an act dictated by the urgent claims of humanity no less than by the necessities of a wise and far-seeing policy."

And the second :

"That any failure on the part of Her Majesty's Government to maintain its just rights under the Convention of London, entered into with the Transvaal, and to fulfil its obligations towards the native tribes in the protectorate of Bechuanaland would be fatal to British supremacy in South Africa."

After this assurance of moral support the Imperial Government proceeded to take action. On the 9th of October the High Commissioner formally called upon the Government of the South African Republic to withdraw their proclamation; and this was at once done. Meanwhile an expedition was equipped and despatched sufficient to establish the Queen's authority in Bechuanaland, if necessary, by force of arms: and the command of the expedition was given to Sir Charles Warren.

While the Bechuanaland expedition was being despatched, the Colonial Government made an attempt to settle the Bechuanaland question without the intervention of the Imperial Government. Their object in making this attempt was stated to be "an earnest desire to avert bloodshed and avoid the creation of race bitterness and national jealousies." They were also of opinion that the appearance of an Imperial force in South Africa at this crisis would cause a "risk being run of feelings being aroused which might lead to a calamitous race war, and of unsettling society in every relation." Acting under this belief, two members of the Colonial Ministry (the Premier, Sir Thomas Upington, and the Treasurer-General, Sir Gordon Sprigg) proceeded to Rooi Grond; and on the 22nd of November certain conditions submitted by these ministers were accepted by the representatives of Land Goshen. The agreement provided for the annexation of "the territory known as Land Goshen" to the Cape Colony; and it was transmitted *in extenso* by telegraph to the Imperial Government. After a fortnight of suspense it was known at the Cape that the Imperial Government had refused to ratify the settlement. In the opinion of Sir Hercules Robinson the terms proposed were "equivalent to recognition as a *de facto* Government of freebooters who had made war on the British protectorate, and to acknowledgment of the *bona fide* character of the claims of the brigands to land in Montsioa's country."*

* C—4275.

THE BECHUANALAND SETTLEMENT

General Warren arrived at Capetown on December 4th, and on the following day the decision of the Imperial Government was communicated to the Colonial Ministry. Within less than a year, on the 10th of November 1885, he was reading an account of the Bechuanaland expedition at the Colonial Institute. This expedition stands out in the history of South Africa as perhaps the one completely successful armed intervention of the Imperial Government, and therefore a somewhat lengthy extract from this account * will not be out of place.

The duties with which Sir Charles Warren was charged by the terms of his commission were:—

"To remove the fillibusters from Bechuanaland, to pacificate the country, to reinstate the natives in their land, and to take such measures as were necessary to prevent further depredations, and, finally, to hold the country until its further destination [was] known."

"There was every intention," Sir Charles Warren says, "to fight on the part of the fillibusters, and on the part of those who sympathised with them, but when they found that we were prepared at all points, they did not know how to commence. They received no provocation, and they simply retired before us and disappeared. This was due in a great measure to the rapidity with which the troops were organised, disciplined and drilled and marched up the country. In four months from the date of leaving England we had occupied Land Goshen, and driven the fillibusters out. Within a month of our leaving England, viz., on December 13th, the head of the column was encamped on the Orange River, and recruiting was going on rapidly; three regiments of colonists of 500 men each, and a battery of artillery and corps of guides were enrolled: two of them, namely, the 2nd mounted Rifles and the Pioneers, were brought together from all parts

* "Our Portion in South Africa," by General Sir Charles Warren, "Proceedings of Royal Colonial Institute," Vol. xvii.

of the colony, and the 3rd mounted Rifles was recruited from the Diamond Fields. Methuen's Horse, which did not arrive in the colony till December 26th, and which was composed entirely of English volunteers, was taken straight up by rail to the Orange River, and there organised and drilled, and by January 22nd (1885), that is to say, within six weeks from our arrival in the Cape Colony, the whole of the troops had marched up ninety miles through Griqualand West, and were assembled at Barkly Camp on the Vaal River, numbering nearly 5000 men ; 2000 horses had been bought and shod, saddles fitted, and men mounted and drilled. Within six weeks of that date the head of the column had occupied Rooi Grond, and the whole line of communication down to Barkly, a distance of 230 miles."

Certain military details which Sir Charles Warren gives are interesting. In the first place we notice that troops were employed which had been raised in the colony. These included men who could not only shoot straight, but who had been trained to shoot in the very difficult atmosphere of South Africa. Next, the officers and men were "dressed alike." It will be remembered, in connection with the engagements in the Transvaal revolt, that there was a very heavy relative mortality among the officers ; the fact being that the Boer marksmen shot down the officers first. This fact—the fact of the men and officers being dressed alike— was "described by the Transvaal papers as being 'very unfair.'" Also war-balloons were employed for purposes of scouting. These were a "matter of mystery and alarm, and considered unfair and contrary to their ideas of the usages of war." Again Sir Charles Warren was a "local man," and he was able to make use of his knowledge of the country. The Boers declared that it would be impossible for the British force to reach Rooi Grond without entering Transvaal territory to obtain water. Sir Charles Warren "dug wells, and by the use of tanks prevented the water from flowing back," and thus kept the supply sweet and wholesome.

"On the other hand," he adds, "a blunder, or a desire on the part of any of the officers or men to make themselves conspicuous, and sacrifice the interests of the expedition, must have precipitated an action."

On his return from Bechuanaland Sir Charles Warren was received everywhere with the "warmest enthusiasm." Not only were the receptions at the large towns in the colony described as being of an "unprecedented description," but a "most gratifying" reception was accorded to him by the President and people of the Free State. "There was," he says, "one general sentiment throughout the colony of gratitude to the mother-country for having given peace with honour, having averted civil war, and having restored to Englishmen the prestige and position which they had enjoyed in former days."

After the forces were withdrawn Southern Bechuanaland was created a Crown Colony, and its government was entrusted to an "administrator." Shortly afterwards the original protectorate was extended, and the sphere of British influence advanced to the Zambesi. Subsequently, in 1895, the Crown Colony of Bechuanaland was incorporated into the Cape Colony.

Since this time—that is to say, since the date of the Bechuanaland expedition — England has continued to perform the duties of a central authority in respect to the native tribes outside the Republics; and to-day all these native territories, with the exception of Swaziland, are administered by Imperial or Colonial officers. The burden of these responsibilities, when once it was frankly accepted, has proved less heavy than was anticipated. It is found possible to maintain order and administer justice in a native territory by means of European officials and magistrates supported only by a small body of permanent police; and the expenses of this simple administration are practically defrayed by the proceeds of the hut-tax levied upon the natives, together with those of the trading-licenses paid by European traders.

We can form some idea of the character of the men who are engaged upon out-post duty in this part of the empire from the vivid description of the Bechuanaland Border Police given by Lord Randolph Churchill. He visited South Africa in 1891, and the portion of the force he describes * were then stationed at Fort Tuli, on the northern boundary of the Transvaal.

" Here, some thousands of miles away from England, in a country inhabited by a numerous tribe of savages of noted ferocity, not a hundred miles from the kraal of the great Lobengula, was a tiny group of men holding their own, maintaining their authority partly by their own reputation for efficiency, partly because they represented the might and prestige of the empire; never dreaming, even for a moment, that a shadow even of danger could approach them, never doubting their ability to dissipate any danger should it arise. This is the group of military force which holds for England a portion of South Africa, from Kimberley to Fort Salisbury, comprising a territory as large as Germany and France, replete with elements of a hostile and dangerous nature."

In this and the preceding chapters we have traced the European occupation of South Africa through a period of little less than two centuries and a half. We have seen how the station established by the Dutch East India Company at Table Bay in 1652 became a settlement; and how these settlers gradually advanced into the interior, meeting with little opposition from the yellow races which constituted the sole inhabitants of these regions, and how, by the end of the last century, the south-western corner of Africa was thinly peopled with some 20,000 Dutch-speaking Europeans. Meanwhile, a dark-skinned race—

* " Men, Mines, and Animals," p. 125.

the Bantu—had simultaneously advanced from the north and occupied the fertile regions between the Drakensberg and the Indian Ocean.

At the beginning of the present century the Cape settlements were ceded by Holland to Great Britain, and shortly after this change of administration the stream of European colonisation setting northwards and eastwards met the southward flow of the Bantu. For fifty years the expansion of the Europeans, reinforced by English immigration, became little more than a record of the conflicts between the British troops and the warlike tribes of this family. When the century was half-way through, England, wearied by the burden of the Kafir wars, recognised the independence of the emigrant farmers, and became a party to the dismemberment of the Europeans in South Africa. Twenty-five years later, when the discovery of diamonds had revealed an unexpected source of wealth, English interest in South Africa revived, and an attempt was made to reunite the colonies and states by the creation of a federal government, and so recover the European solidarity which had been lost. The attempt came too late. The evils which a central government could have checked were already full grown. The well-intentioned efforts of the Imperial Government encountered a double resistance— a general rising of the Bantu, and an active and concerted hostility on the part of the Dutch population in and out of the Cape Colony. These forces might have been overcome, and an Imperial policy, at once just and progressive, have eventually triumphed over all opposition, had not the counsels of England been divided. In the Bechuanaland settlement we have reached the turning point in the history of England's administration of South Africa. From that time forward the responsibilities of a central power have been frankly accepted by England, and, in spite of temporary disturbances, there is reason to believe that his declared intention to do justice to the colonists of both nationalities will ultimately reconcile the conflicting claims of Dutch and English, and the conflicting interests of farmer and capitalist.

The remaining chapters are mainly concerned with an account of the gradual development of the material resources of South Africa. We shall find that deficiencies of soil and climate have been counterbalanced by a remarkable profusion of mineral wealth. That under the impulse of gold discovery, commerce has expanded, population increased, railways have been constructed, and European civilisation has been carried up to the Zambesi; but that this material prosperity has brought in its train a new series of problems—not hopeless, but requiring infinite tact, judgment, and determination for their solution.

CHAPTER VII.

AGRICULTURAL AND PASTORAL RESOURCES.

WHEN the Emperor Napoleon I. wished to put a taunt upon England, he called the English a nation of shop-keepers. But Napoleon was scarcely original. Many years before a great English writer had noticed the same thing, that Englishmen were a trading race. The inference, however, which Adam Smith drew, was the very opposite of that which was, presumably, the inference of Napoleon; for Adam Smith adds that the desire of obtaining markets for their produce had led the English to found the Atlantic Colonies and commence the conquest of India. And when Max O'Rell wishes to give a descriptive title to his last book, which contains his impressions of the British Colonies, he calls it "John Bull and Co."

Well, let us accept this continental estimate of our national life and character. For the moment let us forget such names as Shakespeare and Milton, Bacon and Newton, Reynolds and Gainsborough. Without any obtrusive patriotism we can find some satisfaction even in this restricted view of our position in the commonwealth of nations. For the external trade of England—and by England is meant the United Kingdom—is far greater than that of its brilliant and wealthy continental neighbour, far greater, too, than that of its own great daughter state—

"The beacon-bright Republic, far-off sighted."

And that, too, in spite of the marvellous fertility of France and the giant proportions of the United States.

The external or sea-borne trade of England for the year 1889 amounts (in round numbers) to a total value of seven hundred and forty million pounds (*see Appendix, Table II.*)

I take this year, the year 1889, as the basis of my remarks, because it is a fairly normal year. In 1889 the trade of England had recovered from the depression which lasted from 1884-1888; and it was not yet disturbed by the political and financial troubles in South America, nor by the M'Kinley Tariff. Since 1889 the total value of our trade has fallen by some fifty or sixty million pounds; but, in the first place, this shrinkage is confined to the money value (for the *bulk* has increased), and, in the next, there is every reason to expect that the money value of 1889 will be reached again and even exceeded.

Of this total of seven hundred and forty million pounds, four hundred and twenty-five million pounds represent imports, and three hundred and fifteen million pounds, exports. Of our imports, seven-eighths are food and raw materials, and of our exports—omitting imports re-exported—seven-eighths also are manufactured articles. We can see at once, therefore, what the industrial position of England is. England is a great workshop, the greatest workshop in the world: she imports food for her people, and raw materials which are made up into manufactured articles, and these manufactures she sells to the world.

The food purchase of England amounts to a total of one hundred and seventy-eight million pounds, being 41·7 per cent. of the total imports. Of this purchase the largest item, 53·6 million pounds, nearly a third of the whole, is paid for animal food; and almost the same proportion, 52·2 million pounds, is paid for corn, grain

AGRICULTURAL & PASTORAL RESOURCES

and flour. Then we pay 23·2 million pounds for sugar, 38·3 million pounds for other vegetable products, 8·1 million pounds for spirituous liquors, and 2·6 million pounds for fish.

The purchase of raw materials amounts to a total of 181·4 million pounds. The largest item is that of raw cotton, which is one-fourth of the whole, amounting to 45·8 million pounds. Next to that comes "sheep's wool," one-sixth of the whole, for which 29·7 million pounds is paid. Then follow "metals and ores," 21·7 million pounds; wood, 20·4 million pounds; textiles other than sheep's wool, 15·6 million pounds; and other raw materials which make up the balance, 48·2 million pounds.

Now, let us pause for a moment to consider where England makes her purchases. Speaking generally, we may say that the bulk of her food and raw materials comes from the new Anglo-Saxon countries, the United States and the British Colonies, from Russia and from British India. An analysis of three important imports, grain, cotton and wool, will make this plain. Of the total grain purchase (52·2 million pounds), more than one-third (18·2 million pounds) comes from the United States, and more than one-fourth (14 million pounds) from Russia. The rest comes in decreasing proportions from India, Canada, Australia and elsewhere. More than two-thirds (33·6 million pounds) of the cotton purchase (45·8 million pounds) comes from the United States, and a much less amount, five million pounds worth, from India. And actually five-sixths (25·4 million pounds) of the entire wool purchase (29·7 million pounds) comes from Australasia. To this last import South Africa contributes some three million pounds, one-tenth of the whole.*

* The figures in the text are based upon an "Analysis of the Maritime Trade of the United Kingdom," by Sir Rawson W. Rawson, 1892. The results are exhibited in tabular form in the Statistical Appendix.

While, however, England purchases a part only of her food and raw materials from the British Colonies, nine-tenths, that is to say, practically the whole of the exports of the colonies, omitting the inter-colonial trade, comes to England. The English import, therefore, from any given colony furnishes us with a rough measure of its development. Consequently we can gain, at the outset, a general notion of the agricultural and pastoral development of South Africa, from merely learning that South Africa is a country which contributes *nothing* to the food supplies of England, and only one-tenth of the wool supply.

Canada, Australia, and New Zealand all contribute in proportion to their population as much (or more) to the food supply of England as the United States. New Zealand, a country with an area only one-tenth of South Africa and a European population—600,000—of about equal numbers, in addition to a large grain and meat export, sends nearly twice as much sheep's wool to England as South Africa.

Now we will look a little more closely at the South African exports.* In round numbers they amount to a total of eighteen million pounds. They have reached this total mainly through the rapid increase in the output of gold in the Transvaal, which in 1895, amounted in value to £8,725,000. This, together with £4,000,000 worth of diamonds from Kimberley, and the copper export gives a mineral export of about £13,000,000. The pastoral exports consist of more than £2,000,000 worth of sheep's wool, £500,000 worth of ostrich feathers, the same amount of hides, and more than £500,000 worth of Angora hair.

Taking the production of grain (*See Appendix, Table V.*), horned cattle, and sheep's wool (*See Appendix, Table VI.*), the three primary industries of a new country, as a test, we

* *I.e.* exports passing through Durban and ports of the Cape Colony.

AGRICULTURAL & PASTORAL RESOURCES 121

are forced to the conclusion that the condition of South Africa is very unsatisfactory. And so an account of the agricultural and pastoral development of South Africa seems to resolve itself into an endeavour to answer the question : "To what is this deficiency due?"

In this enquiry it is necessary to remember what are the main physical characteristics of South Africa ; and at the same time we can take the opportunity of ascertaining the position of the chief grain and wool areas.

The first fact that commands our attention is the very high average elevation of the continent of Africa. This continent, the tropical continent *par excellence*, has an average elevation twice as great as that of Australia, more than one-third greater than that of Europe, and nearly one-third greater than that of America, North and South. It is only equalled in this respect by Asia, which contains the greatest mountain masses and the highest mountain summits in the world. In view of the importance of elevation as a factor in climate, this is a fact which must largely modify any estimate we form of the political and commercial value of the central and south-central areas.

The general climatic conditions of South Africa are determined by the position of the mountain ranges. It will be remembered * that they are situated comparatively near the coast, and to a great extent conform to the contour of the coast-line. Physically, South Africa falls into four divisions. The south coast valleys, the east coast semi-tropical slopes, the central plateaux, and the western deserts ; the south and east winds which carry rain-clouds to the interior plateaux and deserts must be not only violent but continuous, since they have to bear the clouds over mountain barriers which reach a height sometimes of 10,000 and 12,000 feet. It is not surprising, therefore, that the interior districts, forming two-thirds of settled South Africa, should have no

* Chap. I. p. 3.

regular or periodic rainfall. Moreover, owing to the rapid fall of the land from the mountains to the coast, the rivers on the south and east, which traverse these broken and terrace-like districts, are practically useless for purposes of navigation and irrigation.

The chief grain areas are these. In the Cape Colony there is a western district extending from Piquetberg to Caledon. It consists of the plains lying between the mountains and the sea at the south-western corner of the continent; and the centre of this district is Malmesbury. In the east of the colony there are two areas of which Graaf-Reinet and Middelburg are the centres; but the most important area is that which lies between the Stormberg Mountains and the Orange River, containing the centres of Hershel and Barkly East. Grain is not grown in the Karoo, nor in the eastern coast districts; for the Karoo is too dry and the atmosphere in the coast districts is too moist. In the Orange Free State there is a district called the "Conquered Territory," which is suitable for grain growing, because it has a periodic rainfall. It extends for 100 miles from Bethlehem to Wepener, and lies on the south-eastern border. In the Transvaal, grain can be grown on the Bankenveldt or Terrace country; that is to say, in the central districts which lie between the "high country" in the south and east, and the "low" tropical belt in the west and north. It includes the districts lying between the River Marico on the west and Leydenburg on the east, and includes the very fertile country on and near the Magaliesberg range. In Natal the only grain which is grown is the Indian corn or mealies, consumed by the Kafirs.

The wool areas are more extensive than the grain areas. In the Cape Colony there is, first of all, a district in the Western Province lying on the south coast from Caledon to Mossel Bay; and, in the eastern provinces and the Transkei, the whole country between the Stormberg

AGRICULTURAL & PASTORAL RESOURCES 123

Mountains and the Indian Ocean. In both of these areas the sheep are pastured upon grass. Then there are the central districts, including the Karoo and the country northward of the great mountain ranges ; here the sheep are pastured on the succulent Karoo plants—plants with leaves, stems, and roots thickened to contain stores of moisture, and therefore able to survive long periods of drought. Passing outside the Cape Colony, we may say that practically the whole of the Free State is suitable for sheep-raising. In the Transvaal the high country is most suitable, and sheep are pastured in Natal on the highest plateau to the north and east of the colony.

In order to complete this rapid survey of the agricultural and pastoral resources of South Africa it is necessary to add a brief account of three special industries of the Cape Colony—mohair, ostrich-farming, and the cultivation of the vine.

By "special" is meant that these are industries which can only be carried on in countries, or districts of countries, which are naturally suitable for them.

The Angora goat, which furnishes mohair, is a native of the central plateaux of Asia Minor, and is also found in the highlands of Persia and Kashmir. The value of the hair of this animal was recognised in very ancient times. It was used for the hangings of the Tabernacle of the Israelites ; and the robes of the kings of Persia consisted of cloth of the same material. Attempts were made to introduce these fine-haired Eastern goats into the Cape by the Dutch East India Company as early as 1725. But this original attempt to bring the goats from Kashmir *via* Ceylon failed. Subsequent attempts made early in the present century were only partially successful; and it was not until forty years ago (1856) that the industry was really established. The honour of founding the industry belongs to Mr Adolph Mosenthal who himself visited Asia Minor to procure the animals. In his quest he was greatly assisted by the late Lord Stratford de Redclyffe, the famous English ambassador at the court of the Sultan. Another name which deserves to be honourably mentioned in connection with this industry is that of Sir Titus Salt, the great Yorkshire manufacturer. The bulk of the goats' wool from the Cape is still made up at the Saltaire works.

The average annual clip per head amounts in weight to five or six pounds, and is worth 20s.

But the Angora goat is not only valuable, it is also a very beautiful animal. Somewhat smaller in size than the domestic goat, it has a small and pretty head, surmounted in both sexes by long, flat, corrugated horns extending from 18 to 24 inches, its fleece falls in natural ringlets almost to the ground, and is white and lustrous. The herds of Angoras roam at will over the veldt, unrestrained by any boundary, but they are docile and easily managed.

The value of the annual export, taking a five years' average, amounts to £400,000; and this Cape export forms one-third of the mohair purchase of England.

The ostrich industry presents an obvious contrast to the Angora industry, for the ostrich is a native—a very old inhabitant indeed—of South Africa. But the industry was not established without effort. There are three stages. At first the wild birds were hunted and killed, and the feathers were so obtained. Next, ostrich chicks (*i.e.* young birds up to seven months of age) were caught and farmed. But these birds, when they were full grown, were found to be very fierce and unmanageable, and the number of birds kept was very small. In 1865, however, as many as eighty ostriches were returned as forming part of the live stock of the colony. The establishment of ostrich farming as a separate industry dates from the year 1869, when Mr Arthur Douglas perfected his artificial incubator. By means of this invention successive generations of birds have been hatched, brought up by hand, and, in this way, being accustomed to man from their birth, the birds have become

AGRICULTURAL & PASTORAL RESOURCES

increasingly domesticated. Now a drove of ostriches proceeding on a Cape road is a sight which is no more alarming, and scarcely more unusual, than a drove of cattle.

Ostriches are kept on farms throughout the colony; but they are not farmed outside the Cape Colony. Within the colony the industry is tending to become specialised. The chief districts are Oudtshoorn on the south coast, and Albany in the eastern province. The price of ostrich feathers varies very much, as the demand is controlled by the changes of fashion, but the average yearly value of the export is £500,000.

Viticulture is, from one point of view, the most interesting of the Cape industries. It is the oldest established, and it is carried on in the districts which have been longest colonised—the mountain slopes and valleys in the south western corner of the colony. The surroundings of the wine farms are very picturesque. The old Dutch homesteads are quaintly built, with coal-black thatched roofs and white-washed walls; and the vineyards, owing to the remarkable fruitfulness of the vines, are richly coloured in the season of the grape harvest. The vine plants are grown without stick or trellis or other supports, and have very much the appearance of currant bushes. The soil of these districts of the Cape is specially suitable for viticulture, yet, from an economic point of view, this industry is the least satisfactory of all, for the amount of wine exported from the Cape is very small. In 1892 it amounted to £18,000.

We are now in a position to answer the question which preceded this review of the agricultural and pastoral resources of South Africa.

The insufficient development of South Africa in respect of these primary industries—grain growing and the raising of horned cattle and sheep—is due to two main causes, one physical and one moral. The physical cause is the insufficiency and uncertainty of the rainfall in the interior;

and the moral cause is the unprogressiveness of the Boer or South African farmer.

Observations * covering a period of thirty-five years show that in the British Isles the annual average rainfall varies (omitting certain abnormal stations) from 22 inches at Greenwich to 38 inches at the Orkney Isles; and in France from 24 inches at Paris to 52 inches in the Department of the Lower Pyrenees. In the Cape Colony observations (again omitting abnormal stations) show a variation from 2 inches at Port Nolloth to the 37 inches which fell in the very wet year, 1876, at King William's Town. Taking averages, we find that the average rainfall in the western districts is 9 inches, in the midland 17 inches, and in the eastern 27 inches.

Combining these facts, we may safely conclude that an average year in the Cape Colony would be considerably drier than the driest year in the United Kingdom or in France. And we may say further, that the weather in South Africa generally is marked by long periods of drought, terminated by torrential rains.

This uncertain and insufficient rainfall, together with the unsatisfactory nature of the South African rivers, and the fact that there is as yet no adequate machinery for water storage and irrigation, is a very real hindrance to agricultural and pastoral pursuits.

The moral cause is the unprogressiveness of the Boer or South African farmer.

Travellers are only too unanimous on this point.

Captain Percival, who visited the Cape of Good Hope in 1796, the second year of the temporary British occupation, writes : †

"The Dutch farmers never assist the soil by flooding, being satisfied with the moisture it derives from the water

* Symon's Tables.
† "An Account of the Cape of Good Hope," by Captain Robert Percival, 1804, p. 227.

AGRICULTURAL & PASTORAL RESOURCES 127

in its neighbourhood. Their only labour is sowing the seed; leaving the rest to chance and the excellent climate. Their ploughs, harrows, and utensils of husbandry are clumsy, ill-formed, and clogged; but they cannot be prevailed on to make any alteration in the system of their agriculture."

And a little further on he says : *
"No part of the world has had its natural advantages so abused as the Cape of Good Hope. The very minds and dispositions of the settlers interfere with every plan of improvement and public utility."

Lord Randolph Churchill, who visited South Africa in 1891, writes, † with special reference to the Transvaal Boer :

"The Boer farmer personifies useless idleness. Occupying a farm of from six thousand to ten thousand acres, he contents himself with raising a herd of a few hundred head of cattle, which are left almost entirely to the care of the natives whom he employs. It may be asserted, generally with truth, that he never plants a tree, never digs a well, never makes a road, never grows a blade of corn. Rough and ready cultivation of the soil for mealies by the natives he to some extent permits, but agriculture and the agriculturists he holds alike in great contempt."

Then we have one whom we may call an impartial witness—the genial Frenchman who disguises his admiration for England under an assumption of literary malice. In "John Bull and Co." Max O'Rell says : ‡

"The Boers are farmers and sportsmen, nothing more. Their ancestors were farmers, and they do not conceive that they themselves could be anything else. Ignorant,

---

* *Idem.* p. 231.
† "Men, Mines, and Animals," p. 94.
‡ P. 305.

bigoted, behind the times, these Dutch Bretons, transplanted in Africa, cultivate the soil like the contemporaries of the patriarchs, and refuse even to look at agricultural machinery."

On the other hand, what can be done even with the difficult soil of the Karoo has been shown by Mr Logan's enterprise. Speaking of Mr Logan's estate of 100,000 acres at Matjesfontein, Lord Randolph Churchill writes:[*]

"Mr J. D. Logan, . . . 100,000 acres . . . has settled himself down on what appears at first sight to be the most unpromising spot for a farmer which the mind can imagine. Here, in the arid plain of the Karoo, producing nothing but low scrub and scanty herbage, he has built himself a large and comfortable house, a spacious homestead with good cottages for his men, and elevates with much success flocks of many thousands of sheep and herds of many hundreds of cattle. The Karoo is far more hospitable and nourishing for live stock than the uninstructed tourist would imagine. The climate is perfect, the air invigorating like that of Scotland, and the only source of anxiety to the farmer is found in the somewhat insufficient rainfall. Sport is to be obtained in plenty . . . . I imagine that many a young English farmer with a good training, an active disposition, and a small capital, might find in the Karoo both a home and a fortune. No rent, scarcely any taxes, and perfect freedom are constituents of happiness which to the ordinary English farmer would appear almost an unrealisable dream."

And he testifies to the capabilities of the Transvaal soil in general: [†]

"All over the Transvaal, and especially round Johannesburg, the well-watered and yet easily drained valleys possess a soil of astonishing fertility, which, with ordinary skill and care, could produce abundant crops of almost every grain, every vegetable, and every fruit. Whether for house-

[*] *Id.* pp. 35, 36.   [†] *Id.* p. 80.

AGRICULTURAL & PASTORAL RESOURCES

building, for use in mines, or for common firewood, the plantation of trees proposes to a landowner munificent remuneration. Such is the geniality of the climate, such the fertility of the soil, that many kinds of useful and valuable trees are estimated by competent authority to make a growth of no less then ten feet in the course of a year."

Lastly there is the evidence of the wine industry. Baron Karl von Babo, the son of the Austrian expert in viticulture, was commissioned by the Cape Government in 1885 to visit and report upon the wine farms. According to his report, the vineyards of the Cape are six times as productive as those of Europe, and eight times as productive as those of Australia. And yet we find that in the year 1892, while the single colony of Victoria, in Australia, exported wine to the value of £63,235, the Cape exported less than one-third of that value (£17,964) (*See Appendix, Table VII.*).

In the face of this evidence we can scarcely avoid the conclusion that the climate and soil of South Africa are not so much at fault as the men who have become, to so large an extent, the possessors of the soil. And if this is so, if, after all, man and not nature is chiefly at fault in South Africa, it becomes interesting, and indeed necessary, to ask, What are the Cape Government doing? What are the men, that is to say, who are from time to time entrusted with the management of the affairs of the colonists, doing?

During the last ten or twelve years we must, I think, admit that the Cape Government have done all that could be reasonably expected of them. They appear to be sensible of the reproach under which their colony labours, the reproach of having the dearest loaf in the world. They are conscious of the necessity which exists for developing the agricultural and pastoral resources of the colony, and during this period a number of useful measures have been introduced with this object in view.

For example, it is well-known that vegetation, forests in particular, promote rainfall. In 1883 the forest department was rendered effective, and the necessary measures were taken to preserve the existing forests, and to raise fresh plantations in suitable districts. The colony is now divided into four forest conservancies, and each of them is placed under the control of a "conservator of forests" and his assistants. Other colonies have followed this example, and now Natal has its "forest officer," and Bechuanaland its "forest ranger"; while the Chartered Company have from the first had a forest department to watch over the woodlands of Mashonaland.

In this same year (1883), also, a select committee was appointed by the Cape Parliament to enquire into the condition of the agriculture and industries of the colony. According to the evidence before this committee,* it appeared that the farmers chiefly complained of the uncertain supply of the native labour which they employed. The committee themselves spoke of "the crying want of irrigation works in various parts of the colony." Acting on the recommendations of this committee, the Government soon afterwards created a "department of agriculture," and established agricultural schools at suitable centres. And so to-day, not only can the young agriculturist obtain scientific agricultural instruction, but the farmers themselves can procure advice from qualified officials on practical matters, such as the treatment of diseases among stock, and the best methods of fertilising the various soils.

Moreover, of late years the Cape Government, in common with other governments in the British colonies, have passed a number of laws regulating the sale and cultivation of their unoccupied areas. All the colonies possess a valuable, though not always a realisable, asset in their unoccupied or "crown" lands. In the Cape one-third of the area of the colony is as yet unappropriated

* Cape Parliamentary Papers, A. 3—83.

AGRICULTURAL & PASTORAL RESOURCES

to private owners. The proceeds of the sale and leasing of these lands form a considerable item in the revenue of a colony. But, apart from these direct profits, the mere occupation and cultivation of fresh areas is advantageous to a new country; and recently the Australasian Governments, at all events, have had a further object in view. They have endeavoured to distribute part of their urban population by settlements in rural districts; for there has been the same tendency in the Pacific colonies to crowd into large towns as we have observed in England.

The system of sale is very much the same in all the British colonies. A distinction is made between "large" and "small" areas. The former are sold by auction, and the latter are practically assigned to applicants by the Land Boards. From time to time the Government announces that such and such blocks of crown lands are to be sold, and the lots are knocked down to the highest bidder. But even in the case of these large areas—areas which might tempt the capitalist or the investor—the purchase is facilitated, for it is not necessary to pay the whole of the purchase money at once. In the Cape Colony a deposit must be paid at the time of purchase, one-tenth of the purchase money within six months, and one-fifth within twelve months. The balance may remain unpaid, and on this balance (properly secured) the purchaser pays a moderate rate of interest, 4 per cent., to the Government. In the year 1892 two million acres of crown lands were sold in the Cape Colony. They realised a total sum of £128,025, that is to say, they sold at an average price per acre of only (about) 1s. 3d.

The small areas are from 8 to 500 acres in extent, and consist of land suitable for occupation by small farmers and agricultural settlers. An applicant sends in an application to the Civil Commissioner of the district in which the land is situated. He must state among other things that he is twenty-one years of age, and does not possess as much as, or more than, 500 acres of land in the colony. His application is referred to the Land Board of the district; and, if it is approved, the applicant receives a license to occupy the holding for five years, on payment of an annual license fee fixed at one-twentieth part of the value of the land, as estimated by the Board. At the end of this period, if he has fulfilled the conditions of the license, the licensee receives a quit-rent title instead of his license, and continues to pay the amount of his license fee as quit-rent. From the issue of the license the licensee is recognised as having an interest in the holding, which he can both sell or assign (under certain conditions), but the Government reserves to itself all rights to gold, silver, or precious stones. Since, in the case of these small areas, the occupation and cultivation of the land is part of the consideration which the purchaser gives, he must fulfil two conditions. He must commence to reside on his holding within six months, and he must bring one-twentieth part of the land into cultivation within two years. Taking the average price of land to be that shown by the sales in 1892, the annual license fee which would be paid on a holding of 500 acres (the largest permitted by the law) would amount to £1, 11s. 6d.

There is need of such settlers, and of the exercise of human skill and ingenuity in the task of fertilising the soil. Remarkable as is the mineral development of the last few years, it is the Veldt, and not Kimberley or Johannesburg, which characterises South Africa. Once beyond the barrier ranges and the undulating plains spread on every side desolate and illimitable. The surface of the earth is broken only by rounded and flat-topped masses, hills with the contour of mountains, weird distortions which serve only to confuse the vision. There is neither tree nor shrub, homestead nor boundary, to arrest the eye. At most a line of mimosa bushes marks

AGRICULTURAL & PASTORAL RESOURCES

the barren track of the periodic water course, and the brown earth at our feet is studded here and there by stunted bushes.

Such is the Veldt, and such is the characteristic landscape of two-thirds of settled South Africa.

Yet even so the human spectator experiences no sense of depression; for over his head the great sun is shining in his might. In the high plateaux of South Africa and the uplands of Australia, where the air is free from all humidity, the increased power of the sun is welcomed, and not dreaded. It is difficult to describe this influence of the sun. Let me try to do so by an illustration. In a recent novel,* the heroine, a young Australian girl, is represented as chilled and depressed beyond all endurance by a wet day in the English summer.

"Gazing out at the wretched day . . . she longed for one little glimpse of the sunlit bush. The barest sandhill on her father's run would have satisfied her, so long as its contour came with a sharp edge against the glorious dark-blue sky; the worst bit of mallee scrub in all Riverina—with the fierce sun gilding the leaves—would have presented a more cheery prospect than this one on the banks of the renowned . . . Thames."

Stimulated by this beneficent influence, the Anglo-Saxon in South Africa will irrigate, cultivate, and fertilise the Veldt, till the whole face of nature has been changed. Does such a prospect seem too remote? If so, let me put this further question — "Do we understand how greatly a country and a climate may be affected by the agency of man?" When I hear men speaking of this and that new country as being unsuitable for European occupation, I wonder whether the speakers have ever considered what England, this garden of the world, was like in the sixth century, the century in which Englishmen first settled here, and in which was born the one nation of the Teutonic

* "A Bride from the Bush," by Mr Hornung.

family absolutely untainted by the moral and physical degeneracy which marked the declining years of the Græco-Roman civilisation.

At that time the famous area which now contains Westminster Abbey, the Houses of Parliament, the offices of Downing Street and Whitehall—a group of buildings which more than any other concentrates in itself the past history and the present life of our nation—was a desolate ridge barely emerging from the surrounding marshes which separated it, by an interval of two miles, from the town of London. The English settlements upon the east and south coasts were isolated from each other, and cut off from the interior of the island, by fen and forest, marsh and ing. Between the Sussex coast and the valley of the Thames lay Andredsweald, a stretch of forest, broken by uninhabited wastes, extending from Kent to Berkshire. From York to Cambridge there ran a succession of ings, marshes, and fens, which effectually barred the progress of the east coast settlers. The greatest manufacturing district of England was covered by the forest of Elmet, which stretched from Nottingham to Cumberland; Wales was protected by the forests of Dean, of Wyre, and of Arden; West Wales, as the counties of Cornwall and Devonshire were then called, by the forest of Selwood. So great were the natural difficulties, and so inhospitable was the climate, that, had there been no convenient estuaries, and above all, no deep and placid rivers to bear the English keels into the heart of the island, the colonisation of Britain by the English might never have been accomplished.

Those who discourage the acquisition of fresh areas in Africa—South and Central—and disparage the value of the territories already colonised, are wanting in this faculty. The dry bones of history and political economy must be clothed by the imagination to assume form and substance. Such persons arrange their facts as the

AGRICULTURAL & PASTORAL RESOURCES 135

Japanese artists arrange their lines; they have no sense of perspective to guide them. They discredit a new country because it cannot satisfy the tests which they would apply to an old country: they condemn the change of to-morrow because it is impossible under the conditions of to-day.

It was no easy task, that task which was undertaken by the English in the sixth century—to clear the forests, to drain the marshes, and reclaim the wastes of Britain; and who shall say that this same colonising race, with its quickened intelligence, its inherited aptitudes, its accumulated stores of knowledge, its ocean-going steamships, its railways, and its telegraphs, shall not teach even the desert of South Africa to "rejoice and blossom as the rose"?

NOTE.—For the effect of the Rinderpest, see Note 31.

CHAPTER VIII.

THE DIAMOND MINES.

IT is certainly somewhat remarkable that the circumstances which attended the discovery of diamonds in South Africa appear to be only imperfectly remembered to-day. There are various accounts; but these accounts differ from each other in some material particular, and that, too, although the events to which they refer happened less than thirty years ago.

This much, however, would appear to be established. In the year 1867, a hunter or trader, named O'Reilly, was enamoured of a white stone which was shown him among a collection of river pebbles at a farmhouse in the Hopetown district of the Cape Colony. This white stone proved to be a diamond, and was sold eventually to the Governor, Sir Philip Wodehouse, for £500. Two years later, in 1869, the farmer himself, Van Niekerk, purchased a similar stone from a Griqua Hottentot for cattle and goods of the estimated value of £400.

This second stone was bought by Messrs Lilienfeld of Hopetown for 10,000 pounds or guineas. It was appropriately christened "the Star of South Africa," and subsequently came into the possession of the Countess of Dudley, who paid £25,000 for it.

This was exciting news, and before long a number of persons were searching for similar treasures over the district at the confluence of the Vaal, the Modder, and and the Orange Rivers. As the white pebbles had been river stones, the diggers first of all directed their attention to the banks of the Vaal, working their way northwards, and finding numerous diamonds. By the beginning of the year 1870 there were 10,000 men on the banks of the Vaal. Towards the end of that year diamonds were discovered on two farms, Dutoitspan and Bulfontein, about 20 miles south of the bend of the river where these "wet" diggings were situated. The diggers now rushed southwards, and established themselves as best they could in the middle of the barren and desolate plain. Next year two new mines were reported, "Old" De Beers and the "Colesberg Kopje," or Kimberley. All these four mines would be enclosed by a circle with a diameter of only $3\frac{1}{2}$ miles, and they produce nine-tenths of the total output of diamonds from South Africa.

Kimberley, as the "dry" diggings came to be collectively called, was anything but a pleasant place of residence. There was no regular communication even by road with the surrounding districts, and no certain supply of food; the miners were sheltered by the most unsubstantial of dwellings; water was scarce, and the dust of an eight months' drought blinded their eyes and choked their throats.

The diamondiferous area is covered by the square formed on the map of South Africa by the intersection of the 28th and 30th parallels of south latitude and the 24th and 26th degrees of east longitude. This square would include the two mines in the Free State, Koffyfontein and Jagersfontein, subsequently discovered and situated to the south of Kimberley, and the river diggings to the north. Almost the whole of this district is enclosed by the wide fork of the Orange and Vaal Rivers, and it has an elevation of more than 4000 feet above sea level.

The diamond mines of Kimberley* are the craters and

* The account in the text is based upon the reports of the De Beers Consolidated Mines, Limited, and in particular on the "Technical Report" of Mr Gardner F. Wiiliams, the general manager, issued in the second Annual Report (1890).

pipes of extinct volcanoes filled with mud, or "blue ground," of igneous or eruptive origin. These oval columns of blue ground occur in the formation known as the Karoo Beds—a formation which extends over the whole of the interior of what we call "South" Africa, and

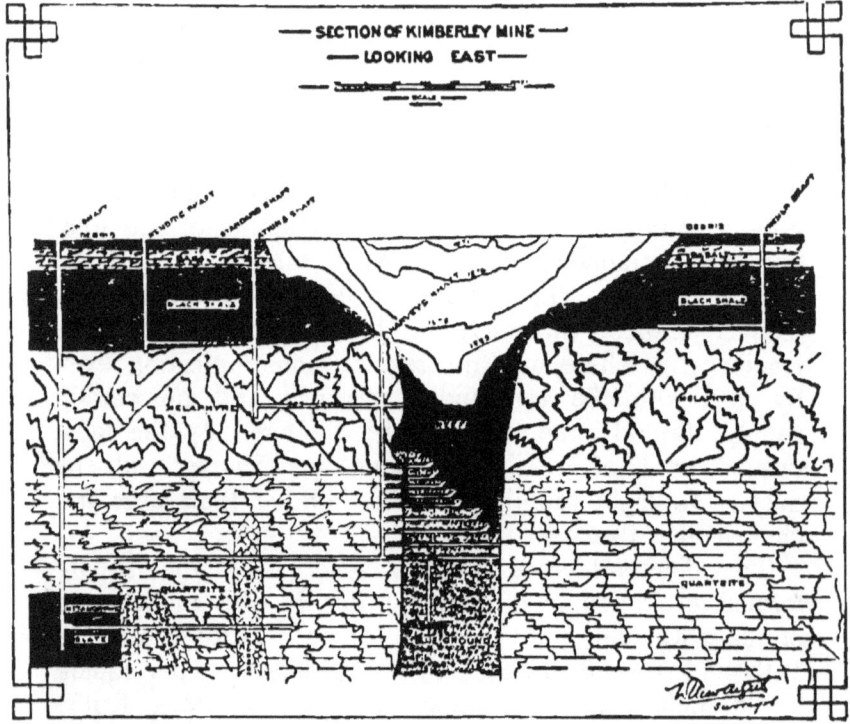

By Permission of De Beers Consolidated Mines, Ltd.

below the surface layers they are encased in horizontal strata consisting of, first, carbonaceous shales, then an amygdaloidal trap called "melaphyre," and, lastly, quartzite.

The thrust which filled the pipes has come from below. That appears from two circumstances. In the first place, the edges of the softer strata, the carbonaceous shales, were found to be turned upwards, and, in the second, fragments of the lower encasing rocks are found in the higher levels of the column in the shape of boulders embedded in the blue ground.

The origin of the diamonds themselves is not yet explained. At first it was suggested that the diamonds, being pure carbon, had been formed by the passage of volcanic steam through the carbonaceous shales; but when the work of excavation proceeded, and the levels of the column below the shales were still found to contain diamonds, this theory had to be abandoned.* That the diamonds were not made in the pipes in which the blue earth is now enclosed is proved by the fact that broken crystals are frequently found : for these crystals, of course, could only have been broken during the movements which accompanied the process of filling the pipes. There is one further fact which is noticeable. It seems that the blue ground has not spread beyond the lips of the craters. This circumstance is accounted for by the supposition that, at the time the columns reached the surface, the country was under water. It was covered, it is supposed, by the waters of a great fresh-water lake in the Karoo area. The waters of this lake subsequently flowed into the sea, over, and through, the barrier ranges, discharged by some great convulsion of nature.

The diamonds were won at first by surface diggings, and afterwards by subterranean workings.

During the first period the mines rapidly assumed the appearance of open quarries. In the Kimberley mine, the richest of the four mines, the blue ground was at first removed by means of roadways which had been left between the claims when the diamondiferous area was first marked out. But in the middle of the second year, 1872, these roadways fell in, and a system

* If, however, as appears to be the case, fresh strata of carbonaceous shales are found below the quartzite, the theory would again become possible.

of bucket haulage had to be adopted. Wire cables were carried from the various workings to the edge of the crater, and the blue ground was carried in buckets running on these cables. In order, however, to keep the numerous cables clear of one another, and provide each proprietor with a sufficient space for hoisting and tipping the buckets at the edge, wooden stagings, with tiers of platforms, were erected round the margin; and by this contrivance the extent of the landing space was multiplied by three.

Meanwhile, as the work of excavation proceeded, the difficulty and cost of raising the blue ground increased. The central, and lowest, claims were flooded by accumulations of drainage water, and the encasing rocks became disintegrated by exposure to atmospheric influences, and fell in. In 1874 the Kimberley Mining Board was established to combat these evils. It represented the combined interests and the combined resources of the miners, but it proved unequal to the task of keeping the workings clear. In 1882 more than half a million of money was spent in removing "reef," as the fallen rock was called; and still the open workings were only partially cleared. Early in the following year the Board desisted from the hopeless conflict. Its books showed a deficit of a quarter of a million, and the banks refused to discount its "reef" bills. And so in the Kimberley mine operations were brought to a standstill.

It was clear that the blue ground must be removed now by subterranean workings; but it was by no means easy to see how these subterranean workings were to be commenced. To pierce the hard rock outside the limits of the crater, and reach the blue ground by transverse drivings, was considered at first both too costly and too lengthy. Moreover, it was not yet ascertained that the supply of blue ground was practically inexhaustible. What was required was some method of reaching the

THE DIAMOND MINES 141

diamondiferous ground which would not entail the performance of an amount of dead work which would eat up the profits. Also the method must be speedy, for the industry required immediate relief. These requirements were met by a scheme put forward by Mr Edward Jones, an engineer. He proposed to reach the submerged blue ground by sinking shafts through the reef itself. The shafts were sunk on the "coffer-dam" principle; that is to say, successive frameworks of wood were let down into successive excavations, and in this way the shifting mass of débris was penetrated without dangerous or inconvenient dislocations of the surrounding soil, and the blue ground was once more reached.

At the same time, however, some of the open workings were again cleared by means of fresh removals of reef. These fresh removals of reef produced fresh, and even more disastrous, subsidences, which both carried away the new shafts and machinery and again submerged the open workings.

In all four mines successive falls of reef occurred, and the open workings were gradually abandoned. By the year 1885 it was admitted that open workings could not be carried on below a certain depth, which varied from 350 to 400 feet; and it was then that the present system of subterranean working was gradually introduced.

Under the new system shafts were sunk outside the margin of the craters, and the blue ground was struck by transverse tunnels. The subterranean workings were in operation first at the De Beers mine; and the introduction of the system caused the annual out-put of diamonds won from that mine by the De Beers Mining Company to rise from half a million to a million carats. At the same time the cost of production was largely decreased by the improved methods which had been simultaneously introduced. Moreover, as the orifice of the pipe was reached, it was seen that the column of blue ground extended perpendicularly downwards, and that the supply of diamond-bearing material was practically inexhaustible. Although the new workings were not yet in operation at the Kimberley mine, it was known that the same formation existed there too.

The diamond industry was now threatened by an entirely different, and quite unexpected, danger, the loss of profits by competition, the diminution of the value of the diamond by excessive production. In 1882 the value of the carat was 27s. 3d., in 1887 it had already fallen to 18s. 5½d.

This disaster was prevented by an amalgamation of the competing companies.

The amalgamation of mining interests was the last of a series of changes of ownerships which had accompanied the changes in the methods of winning the diamonds which we have traced. Originally the diamondiferous area of each mine was marked out in claims. In the Kimberley mine these claims were 31 feet by 31 feet. No person was allowed to hold more than one claim under the early regulations, but the more valuable claims were sub-divided, and so this mine at one time contained 1600 separate mining properties. In 1874 the limit of claims tenable by a single owner was raised to ten; and shortly afterwards it was altogether abolished. As the difficulty and the consequent cost of raising the blue ground increased, a process set in which may be called the elimination of the individual digger. In 1880-1 the majority of the properties held by individuals were converted into Limited Liability Companies; and, in 1883, the Inspector of mines reported, with respect to the Kimberley mine, that it "could never be worked to best advantage until all the payable holdings had been amalgamated." In 1885 the four mines were in the possession of forty-two companies and fifty-six private firms. One mine, the De Beers, however, was divided among only seven companies and three private owners.

Among these companies the most important was the De Beers Mining Company, and this Company became the nucleus for the amalgamation.

The De Beers Mining Company was founded in 1880, with a capital of £200,000. It gradually absorbed the whole of the De Beers mine, and then obtained, by purchase of shares and amalgamation of properties, controlling interests in the remaining three mines. On the 31st March 1883, the De Beers Mining Company became the De Beers Consolidated Mines, Limited; and two years later the directors of the new Company were able to report to their shareholders that the object with which the conversion had been effected, "had at last been accomplished, and the four diamond-producing mines of De Beers, Kimberley, Dutoitspan and Bulfontein were now practically under the control of the Company."

In this way a contest between the proprietors of the Kimberley and De Beers mines, which must have ruinously affected the industry, was averted. The author of this brilliant financial achievement was Mr Cecil Rhodes. Speaking of his part in the amalgamation of the Kimberley mines, Lord Randolph Churchill says: * "It was this great work accomplished in the teeth of unheard-of difficulties, and almost insurmountable opposition, representing the conciliation and unification of almost innumerable jarring and conflicting interests, which revealed to South Africa that it possessed a public man of the first order."

The "De Beers Consolidated Mines," therefore, practically represents the diamond industry of Kimberley, and their methods are the methods of that industry. They were adopted in 1889, and they embody the result of nearly twenty years' experience of diamond mining. Although the Company control all four mines they are at present working only two, Kimberley and De Beers. These two mines afford a sufficient and economic supply of

* "Men, Mines, and Animals," p. 38.

diamond-bearing ground, for it is the policy of the Company to place only that amount of diamonds on the market which it can carry at the present price per carat, about 25s.

The first operation * is to raise the blue ground to the surface. For this purpose tunnels are driven north and south, east and west, through the area of excavation. The rectangular spaces formed by the intersection of the tunnels are successively cleared of blue ground, working from the rock margin inwards. As the process of excavation proceeds the reef or débris gradually falls in and fills up the space created by the removal of the blue ground. The working levels are laid out 40, and the main levels from 90 to 120 feet apart. The "hoisting" is done only from the main levels. The blue ground is "dumped" down through shoots to the main levels, then loaded into trucks and finally "tipped" at the foot of the shaft into the "skip." The skip holds four loads, or rather more than three tons, and Mr Gardner Williams, the general manager of the Company, reports in June of 1893, that an average of 5·3 tons per minute had been hoisted by a single shaft during an eight hours' "shift."

At the head of the shaft the blue ground is tipped into surface boxes, and then drawn off into trucks which carry it, by a system of "endless wire rope haulage," to the "floors" for pulverisation. These "floors" are simply rectangular spaces, 600 yards by 200 yards, marked off on ground which has been cleared of bush, and rendered hard and level by rolling. The length of the main line is three miles, and there are two branches, respectively one mile and three-quarters of a mile in length.

This second operation, pulverisation, is effected by exposing the blue ground to the action of the air and rain, and to assist disintegration the ground is "worked" or broken up, first by men with pickaxes and afterwards by

* This account of the methods pursued is based upon Mr Gardner F. Williams' "Technical Report."

THE DIAMOND MINES

harrows drawn originally by spans of mules, but subsequently by steam power. The length of the exposure required varies from three to six months according to the nature of the blue ground.

The pulverised blue ground is then "washed." The machines are erected in "nests" at various points, and are generally placed on heaps of tailings. The blue ground is carried by mechanical methods to the top of the machines,

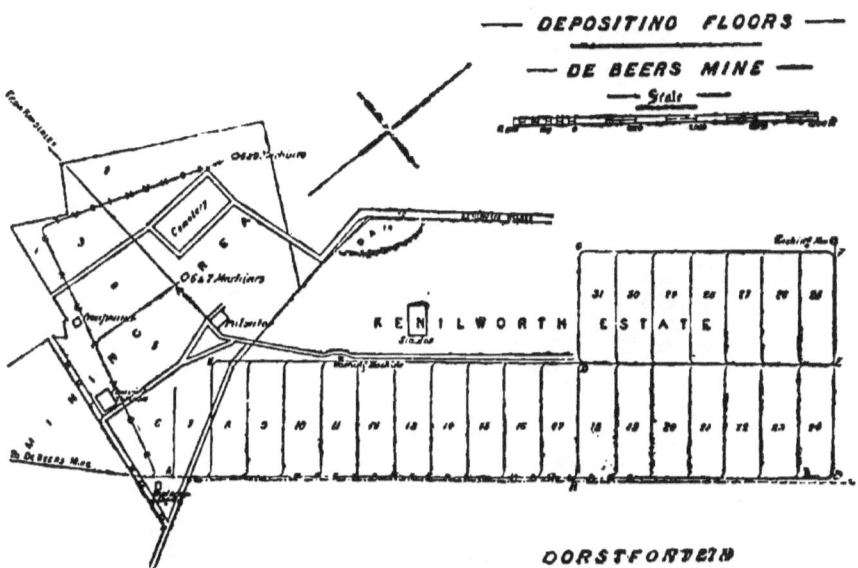

By Permission.

and dumped into a shoot which is furnished with perforated pipes. These pipes supply water and at the same time regulate the downward passage of the mass into the puddling cylinder. The latter is a revolving cylinder, two and a half feet in diameter, with perforations of one and a quarter inch round, and one inch square. Both clear and muddy water is poured into the cylinder with the blue ground. The "coarse" ground passes out at the end of the cylinder and is carried back to the floors

K

for further pulverisation. The "fine" ground passes through the perforations and is shot into the washing pan.

The washing pan is fourteen feet in diameter, and is furnished with ten revolving arms provided with "teeth" so set as to work the solid mass by a spiral course to the edge of the pan, while the lighter stuff is discharged from the centre into a second pan, called a "safety" pan. Each "safety" pan serves two "washing" pans. The solid

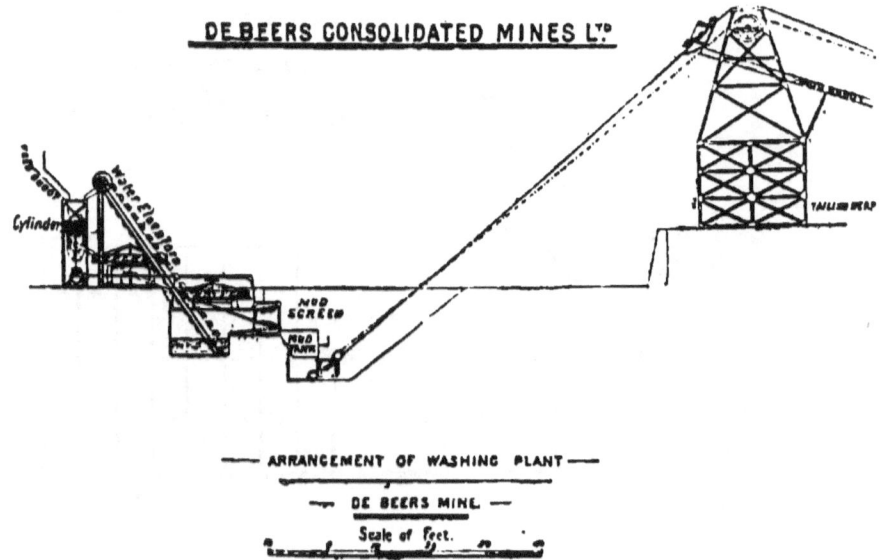

By Permission.

mass, or "deposit" is drawn off by means of a "slot" from the edge of the pan every twelve hours. It is this "deposit" which contains the diamonds.

Meanwhile the water is not wasted. It is carried from the puddling cylinder to a mud screen, and, after being purified, is again hoisted by bucket elevators out of the tank into which it flows from this screen, to the top of the machine. The rate at which the machines work may be gathered from the fact that from forty to forty-five loads

THE DIAMOND MINES

pass through a single pan in one hour. Nor is the efficiency of the machinery inferior to its speed, for by this process the blue ground is reduced to one-hundredth part of its bulk. That is to say, that 100 loads of blue ground are "washed" down into one load of deposit.

This deposit is then "graded," or separated into stones (or gravel) of equal size, and further concentrated by Hartz jigs or "pulsators." The separation is performed by a cylinder, about 15 feet long by $1\frac{1}{2}$ in diameter, made

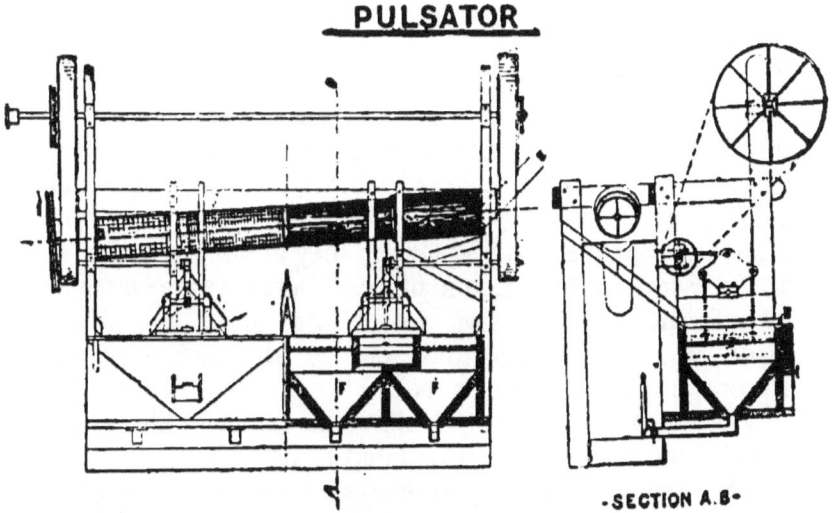

By Permission.

by metal plates with round perforations of four different sizes, namely, from $\frac{1}{8}$th to $\frac{3}{8}$ths of an inch in diameter. The coarse deposit passes out at the end, and is then sorted by hand. The fine deposit passes through the perforations, and flows down on to jigs furnished with screens covered with a layer of bullets, and having square perforations corresponding to the round perforations in the cylinder. The four sizes of stones are collected in V-shaped boxes under the screens. The lighter stuff, however, remains on the surface of the downward flowing mass, passes over the top of the screens, and is carried off to the tailing heap. Out of twelve loads of deposit fed into the cylinder, one would pass out at the end, four would pass through the screens of the pulsators into the boxes, and seven would be carried away as waste.

The deposit thus separated into masses of equal sized stones is then laid out on tables and sorted. The sorting is done first (while the stuff is wet) by European workmen, and afterwards by native convicts supplied by the Cape Government.

The diamonds vary in size from a pin's head to that of the largest diamond as yet found at Kimberley. This measured $1\frac{7}{8}$ inches through the major, and $1\frac{1}{2}$ inches through the minor axis, and weighed in the rough $428\frac{1}{2}$ carats, and, when cut, $228\frac{1}{2}$ carats.* They show all colours, green, blue, pink, brown, yellow, and are both clear and opaque. After sorting they are sent, under an armed escort, to the diamond office. There they are classified by reference to their size, colour and purity, and finally made up into parcels, and sold to the agents of the European diamond-merchants.

The following figures will show the extent of the operations of the De Beers Consolidated Mines :—

The extent of the open works of the four mines is 111.73 acres. The De Beers mine shows an area at the hard rock level of 10·12 acres of which 5·97 are worked; and the Kimberley mine, at the same level, of 4·55 acres, of which 2·69 are being worked. Both mines and works are lighted by ten circuits of electric lamps, with a total illuminating power equal to that of 63,696 candles. The amount of labour employed, according to the Report

* On June 30th, 1893, a diamond was found at the Jagersfontein Mine, in the Orange Free State, which weighs $969\frac{1}{2}$ carats gross, is of fine quality, and blue-white colour, and measures through its longest axis 3 inches. This is probably the largest and the most valuable diamond in the world.

issued in June 1890, was 1261 Europeans, who are comfortably housed at the village of Kenilworth, and 5250 natives, who are imprisoned in the two "compounds." Among the underground workers the wages of the Europeans range from £7 to £4 per week; and those of the natives from 4s. to 5s. per day. The Europeans and native workmen on "the floors" receive respectively from £6 to £3, 12s., and from 21s. to 17s. 6d. per week.

By means of this plant and this supply of labour, in the financial year 1892-93 (in round numbers) three million loads of blue ground were raised at a cost of a million and a half sterling, and the diamonds found realised three millions and a quarter, showing a profit of a million and a half; and out of this profit, after all necessary deductions and reserves, the Company paid two half-yearly dividends of 12½ per cent. on their capital of four millions.

These, then, are the processes by which the diamonds of Kimberley are won. Let me add a description of the town itself. It is the vivid picture contained in Lord Randolph Churchill's "Men, Mines, and Animals." *

"Nothing in the external appearance of Kimberley suggests either its fame or its wealth. A straggling, haphazard collection of small, low dwellings, constructed almost entirely of corrugated iron or of wood, laid out with hardly any attempt at regularity, and without the slightest trace of municipal magnificence, is the home of the diamond industry. It seems that when the diamonds were first discovered some twenty years ago, many thousands of persons settled down suddenly on the spot like a cluster of swarming bees, and established themselves anyhow as best they could in the most rough and primitive fashion, never dreaming but that the yield of diamonds would be of limited extent and short duration, that their fortunes would be rapidly acquired, and that they would pass as rapidly away

* P. 36.

from the place, having exhausted all its wealth-producing resources. The reverse has proved the case. The diamondiferous resources of Kimberley are now known to be practically inexhaustible, but the amalgamation of the mines has restricted employment and checked immigration, and the town still preserves, and probably will always preserve, its transitory and rough-and-ready appearance."

There is one point still to be noted. The special character of this industry has produced some rather curious legislation. In order to protect the diamond industry—an industry in which the product is at once so valuable and so portable—the Cape Parliament has passed a series of enactments which have created a statutory crime known as "Illicit Diamond Buying," and this crime is punished with remarkable severity. The ordinary presumption of the law in favour of the innocence of the accused is abolished, and a man is liable to a maximum penalty of fifteen years' penal servitude for merely neglecting to report to the proper quarter, and at once, a diamond which he may have chanced to have found (Note 22).

In the case of the native employés extraordinary precautions are taken. During the term of their service, for three months and more, they are treated as prisoners. Every day they are stripped and searched on leaving the mines, and for a week before the conclusion of their contract they are isolated and subjected to a *régime* which makes a theft of diamonds a physical impossibility.

The story of the diamond mines wins our interest not so much because of the element of the marvellous which surrounds the commencement of the industry—the weird situation, the strange origin, the chance discovery—but because of the difficulties which beset its development. Twice the industry was threatened with destruction—in 1883 by successive falls of the encasing rocks, and in 1889 by the commencement of a ruinous competition.

THE DIAMOND MINES

The lesson of Kimberley is the value of effort. There was no high motive to elicit this effort. At first sight scarcely a useful purpose was subserved, for the value of a gem is of all values the most artificial, its beauty is of all beautiful objects least securely founded upon utility. But the digger and the capitalist sought not diamonds but wealth: a few were successful, far more were unsuccessful; but South Africa has reaped the benefit of their efforts.

"The pulpit and the press," says Emerson,* "have many commonplaces denouncing the thirst for wealth; but if men should take these moralists at their word, and leave off aiming to be rich, the moralists would rush to rekindle at all hazards this love of power in the people, lest civilisation should be undone."

The history of the diamond mines affords us a striking illustration of this pregnant remark.

The yield of twenty-five years' search in the Kimberley mines has been exchanged for seventy millions of money. This exchange has been a factor of supreme importance in the history of South Africa. The interest of the mother-country was awakened, the railway system of the Cape Colony was developed, and, above all, an energetic and wealthy community was created in the heart of South Africa.

What ultimate developments, political and commercial, will follow the era of gold discovery we cannot tell, but of this at least we may be certain, that the present quickened life of South Africa is the direct outcome of the experience, the energy, and the resources which were concentrated there by the search for diamonds,—that Johannesburg and Fort Salisbury are alike the offspring of Kimberley.

* "The Conduct of Life": Essay on Wealth.

CHAPTER IX.

GOLD-MINING.

IT is the prospect of the rapid acquisition of wealth which makes men leave their home and expose themselves to unknown difficulties and unknown dangers in new countries. The most efficient magnet is gold. In the middle of the century we have seen it at work populating North America and Australia : during the closing years of the century we see this same powerful influence in full operation in South Africa.

The mineral wealth of South Africa is both varied and widely distributed.

Iron is found in the Cape Colony, in the Orange Free State and in Natal, and there are ample deposits of this useful metal in the Transvaal and in the territories of the Chartered Company. At present this metal is not worked.

Copper-mining is the oldest of the mineral industries of (modern) South Africa. The deposits lie in the north-western corner of the Cape Colony. Copper-mining was commenced in 1852 ; and by 1864 the export had risen to £100,000 in value. Since that date the annual output has reached a value varying between £250,000 and £800,000. Out of the annual output of 30,000 tons, nine-tenths (27,000 tons) are raised by the Cape Copper Mining Company. Ookiep, where these mines lie, is connected by a line of railway, ninety miles in length, with Port Nolloth.

Silver is found in the Cape Colony, but not in payable

GOLD-MINING 153

quantities. In the Transvaal there is a district which would be enclosed by a circle with a diameter of 50 miles, immediately east of Pretoria, where there are abundant deposits of silver. A considerable amount of capital has been invested in these Transvaal silver mines, and several companies are at work. So far, however, the industry is promising, but not yet established: its development has been hindered by the superior attractions of the gold fields.

Coal is found in the Cape Colony, in the Orange Free State, in Natal, and in the Transvaal. In the Cape Colony the coal mines on the Stormberg Mountains are being worked. Three of these, Cyphergat, Fairview, and Molteno, furnish an annual output of 35,000 tons,* and provide supplies of coal for the Eastern and Northern Railway systems. The Free State output is about 20,000 tons. The Natal coal deposits are found in the highest and most northern of the three natural formations or terraces into which the area of that Colony is divided. The annual output amounts to 140,000 tons; and of this total more than three-fourths (117,000 tons) was raised by the Dundee Coal Company at the place so named. The coal industry is a valuable ancillary to the sugar industry.† The coal fields in the Transvaal lie in close juxtaposition to the gold fields. Coal deposits are found over a wide area extending from the Vaal River on the south to Middelburg on the north, and from Boksburg (on the edge of the Randt Basin) on the west to the Drakensberg Mountains on the east. Two collieries, the Brakspan and Springs, which have an output of 200,000 tons and 100,000 tons respectively, lie on the eastern edge of the Randt basin, and furnish the gold fields with the necessary supplies of coal at an average price of 20s. 6d. the ton. This convenient and abundant

* The coal figures are taken from the returns for 1892.
† See Chapter V. p. 85.

supply of fuel has largely assisted the rapid development of gold-mining on the Randt.

The subjoined comparison will indicate the significance of these figures—

	Estimated area of coal fields in square miles.	Annual output in tons.
South Africa,	56,000	600,000
New South Wales,	25,000	3,500,000
United Kingdom,	4,000	180,000,000

The coal industry in South Africa, therefore, is in its infancy, but it is capable of indefinite development.

Gold is found in the Cape Colony, but not in sufficient quantities to repay the miner or digger. Both in the Knysna and at Prince Albert in the Karoo, gold winning has been commenced and abandoned. It is also found in Zululand, in Swaziland, in the Transvaal, and in the territories of the Chartered Company. To-day, gold-mining is being actively prosecuted in the Transvaal and in Matabeleland and Mashonaland.

The era of gold development has advanced rapidly. Only ten years ago gold-mining in South Africa was a tradition of the past or a dream of the future. Men looked regretfully at the old Dutch maps in which Mashonaland and Matabeleland were indicated as "The Land of Ophir": or shook their heads when they were asked to buy shares in the Transvaal gold ventures. Up to this time there had been many discoveries and many disappointments.

As early as the year 1854, two years after the independence of the emigrant farmers beyond the Vaal had been recognised by the Imperial Government, discoveries of gold were reported in the Transvaal. But the Boer Government prohibited prospecting. They were afraid— and rightly so—that the introduction of a mining population would endanger their newly acquired independence.

GOLD-MINING

The early explorers were compelled, therefore, to turn their attention to the districts northward of the Limpopo. The history of the discovery of gold offers a contrast to the history of the discovery of diamonds. The searchers for diamonds stumbled at the very outset upon the richest deposits, the four marvellous mines at Kimberley; but fortune seems to have taken a whimsical delight in misleading the prospectors. Hartley, the "pioneer of the gold fields," himself possessed a farm on the Witwatersrandt. In 1869 Baines passed over the northern outcrop of the famous conglomerate beds when he was conducting a party of gold prospectors from Durban to Matabeleland. During the period of the annexation (1877-81), an Australian expert, Mr Armfield, was employed by the first administrator, Sir Theophilus Shepstone. He was at work prospecting on the Randt, but the conglomerate beds escaped his hammer. And so it was not until two years' patient and skilful search had been completed by two brothers, Mr H. W. and Mr F. Struben, that the existence of the most valuable and the most permanent gold field yet known to the world was revealed.

After the discovery of the Tati gold field by the German explorer, Karl Mauch, in 1865, the early restrictions upon prospecting were withdrawn by the Transvaal Government, and gold discovery was encouraged In 1872 the subject had become sufficiently important to require the attention of the Volksraad, and the first gold law was passed in that year. This law—the first of successive enactments which were codified by the "Consolidated Gold Law" of 1885—declared the right to all minerals and precious stones to be vested in the state (Note 23). At the same time rewards were offered for the discovery of payable gold fields.

The first gold fields in the Transvaal were in the mountainous regions east and west of the Northern Drakensburg.

In 1873 the Landdrost of Lydenberg reported that gold had been discovered thirty-three miles east of his town, and these Lydenberg fields have continued to be worked up to the present with varying fortune. After the Retrocession (1881) the Transvaal Government adopted the "concession" or "monopoly" principle. It is alleged that they wished to reduce the numbers of the miscellaneous mining population by placing the industry in the hands of a few capitalists. Whether any such intention existed or not, the object in question was not secured. The diggers withdrew to the De Kaap valley, fifty miles south of Lydenberg, where the existence of gold had been reported as early as 1875. In 1886 a rich mine, the Sheba mine, was discovered in this district, and in the following year Barberton, the centre of the De Kaap fields, had attracted a population of 10,000 persons. Since that date Barberton has gradually declined. For both the Lydenberg and the De Kaap fields have been drained of their population by the Randt, which was declared a public gold field in September 1886.

The Witwatersrandt is the ridge of a great stretch of uplands, the "high veldt" of the Transvaal, which runs for 300 miles, almost due east and west, between the valley of the Vaal and the head waters of the Limpopo.

Johannesburg stands on the crown of this ridge at an elevation of 5735 feet above sea level.

It was on these same desolate uplands that the Transvaal flag was raised by the Triumvirate in revolt against the Imperial Government on the 16th December 1880. In 1886 a few prospectors and their workpeople were the sole inhabitants of the Randt. To-day Johannesburg ranks as one of the commercial centres of the world; and for thirty miles along the crest of the ridge the pit-head gears, batteries and surface works of the sixty or seventy companies in active operation, give evidence of the millions of capital which have been invested.

"Johannesburg," says Lord Randolph Churchill, "extends for a considerable distance along a ridge of hills 6000 feet above the level of the sea. Around, wherever the eye reposes, it is arrested by mining shafts, hauling gear, engine houses and tall chimneys. Johannesburg presents a very English appearance, that of an English manufacturing town minus its noise, smoke and dirt. The streets are crowded with a busy, bustling, active, keen, intelligent-looking throng. Here are gathered together human beings from every quarter of the globe, the English possessing an immense predominance. The buildings and general architecture of the town attain an excellent standard, style having been consulted and sought after, stone and bricks the materials, corrugated iron being confined to the roofs, solidity, permanence and progress the general characteristics. The rise of the town has been almost magical." *

The sudden growth of Johannesburg † is the more remarkable when we remember that at first every nail, every plank, every brick, every morsel of food and every drop of drink had to be carried up to the desert plateau, for a hundred miles or more, on ox-waggons. The average pace of the ox-waggon is a mile and a half an hour. To-day, however, the railway has brought Johannesburg within forty-nine hours of Cape Town, and seventeen or eighteen days of London.

Geologists tell us that the granite foundation of South Africa was overlaid by sedimentary accumulations which became quartzose strata; that both granite and horizontal strata were pierced and broken by the intrusion of igneous rocks; that the distorted surface was again covered by horizontal strata, and again broken by fresh intrusions of eruptive masses; and that, finally, the whole system was subjected to a great convulsion which carried the

* " Men, Mines, and Animals in South Africa," p. 58.
† The present population is 102,078. See Note 30.

edges of broken sections of the horizontal strata to the surface, and in places even thrust the granite through the successive layers of sedimentary rocks. Then the face of the whole country was smoothed and softened by the silent passage of the hand of Time.

The Randt basin is a section of the upper series of quartzose strata, broken and dislocated, but preserving

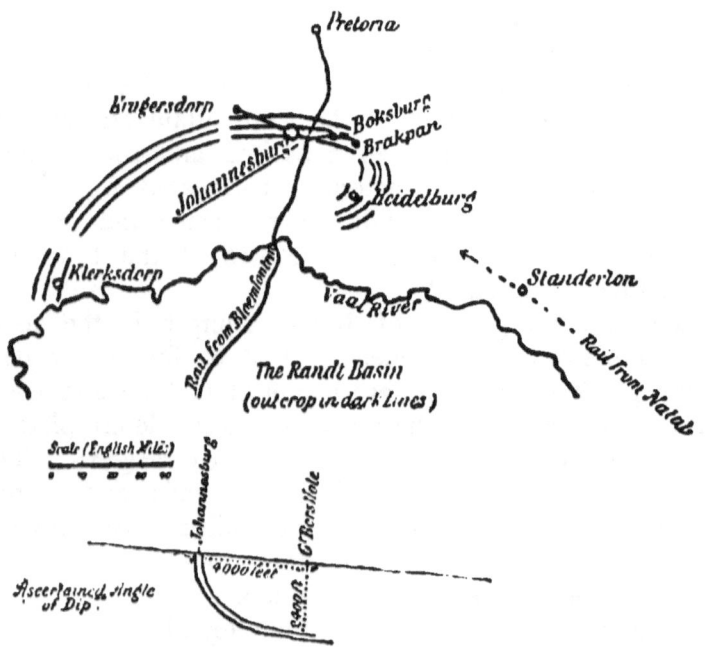

a certain regularity of curvature from its depressed centre to its upturned edges. The sandstones and quartzites are interstratified with beds of conglomerate, and it is these conglomerate or "banket" reefs which carry gold.

The edge of the basin can be traced for some 130 miles on the southward slope. On the northern edge there is an outcrop of half-a-dozen parallel reefs—the Main Reef series—which extends for thirty miles east and

GOLD-MINING

west of Johannesburg. Further east at Heidelburg, and further west at Klerksdorp there are fresh outcrops; and from all these outcrops the reefs dip towards the centre of the basin at angles varying from 80 to 10 degrees.

The thirty miles of the northern outcrop, from Randfontein to Boksburg, is the centre of the mining activity. There are some sixty or more companies at work, and the district is traversed by a railway which runs from the Spring Colliery on the east to Krugersdorp on the west; and thus provides the industry with its supplies of coal.

The character of the ore is such that both the most efficient machinery and the most skilful processes are required for successful gold extraction. Above the water level—which varies in depth from 50 to 150 feet—the ore was a friable conglomerate, which yielded by milling 80 per cent. of its gold. But the supply of free-milling ore was soon exhausted. Below, it is a hard, pyritic conglomerate, yielding only 50 per cent. by mechanical processes; and it is this pyritic ore which constitutes the auriferous supply of the Randt basin.

The crushing of the stamps, therefore, and the concentration of the vanners, are supplemented by chemical processes (Note 24). The "concentrates" are treated by the Plattner or Chlorination process; and the "tailings" by the M'Arthur-Forrest or an equivalent Cyanide process.

The result of this combination of milling, concentration, and precipitation is that 90 per cent. of the gold which the hard pyritic ore carries is successfully recovered.

And now a question of great interest arises: What is the probable area of these auriferous deposits? What is the probable extent of the conglomerate beds? This is a question which can only be answered by experts, and that approximately.

Mr Hamilton Smith, the American mining engineer,

visited the Randt at the end of 1892, for the purpose of reporting to Messrs Rothschild on the prospects of mining at deep levels. He assumes that 50,000 feet of the northern outcrop, that is to say, not quite eleven out of thirty miles of outcrop, extends southwards to an inclined depth of 5200 feet, with an average probable thickness of five feet. He calculates that this extent of conglomerate would contain 100,000,000 tons of ore, of which 3,000,000 tons had been already raised, and that the value of the balance, at a yield of 12½ dwts. the ton, would be £215,000,000. He further assumes that "the many miles" of conglomerate beds outside this area will produce at least half as much more, and concludes, therefore, that the total value of the Randt deposits is £325,000,000, or about £100,000,000 in excess of the total yield of California between 1849 and 1892 (£230,000,000). He also adds that in his opinion the producing power of the mines will be raised in "three or four years" to an output of "five or six million tons of ore per annum," and a yield of £10,000,000 in value. As the yield of the Randt for 1895 amounted to a total of 2,277,635 ozs., valued at £7,839,500, it appears that this forecast will be realised. This output is, of course, independent of the lesser Transvaal fields. Beside the Lydenberg and De Kaap fields, those of Klerksdorp and Potchefstroom have commenced to yield handsomely. These lesser fields yielded 250,000 ozs., or about £850,000 worth of gold in 1895.

A later estimate, that of Mr Theodore Reunert,* puts the value of the auriferous deposits of the Randt basin at £450,000,000.

This estimate proceeds upon the assumption that the reefs which outcrop for thirty miles on the edge of the basin can be worked for one mile across the dip, and have, as before, a payable thickness of five feet. This thirty square miles of conglomerate beds would yield, at the low

* In "Diamonds and Gold in South Africa," p. 193.

GOLD-MINING

grade of 8 dwts. the ton, 130,000,000 ozs., or rather more than the £450,000,000 worth of gold.

The actual evidence of the southward extension of the conglomerate beds, which is a necessary assumption in both these estimates, consists of the results obtained by the borings and shafts already sunk. Vertical shafts have struck the reefs at a depth of 700 feet, and inclined shafts have followed the dip for 1000 feet. The "great bore-hole," starting from a point more than three-quarters of a mile south of the outcrop, found the Main Reef, in June 1893, at a depth of 2400 feet. Here the angle of the dip has changed from 60 to only 16 degrees, and both the thickness and the auriferous character of the reef is maintained.*

This evidence, combined with the fact that the outcrop of the reefs has been traced for 150 miles in all—for there is an outcrop southward of the Vaal River in the Free State—makes us inclined to believe that the actual magnitude and value of the gold deposits of the Randt have been underrated in both these cautious estimates. Indeed, both these estimates are based upon what is admittedly only a partial review of the auriferous resources of the great gold field.†

But the gold deposits of South Africa are by no means confined to the Randt basin.

The establishment of railway communication between Pretoria and Delagoa Bay, now accomplished, is expected

---

* According to the Johannesburg *Star* of June 17th, 1893, 5 ft. 8 in. of the Main Reef was traversed, and assays of the South Reef, previously pierced at a depth of 2343 feet, gave an average yield of 23 dwts. 12 grs. to the ton of ore.

† Since the above was written Mr Hamilton Smith has contributed a fresh article to the *Times* (Feb. 19, 1895), in which he gives the results of observations made from August to December 1894. He says: "From the foregoing statement it is evident that the chances are far greater now than they were in 1892 of my conjectures of that date being realised, and to-day nearly every one conversant with the Randt considers them as being considerably under the mark." A further extract is given in the Notes (25).

to produce renewed activity in both the Lydenberg and the De Kaap fields; and at any time the gold fields of Mashonaland and Matabeleland may leap into competition with the Randt.

In the immediate future, therefore, we may expect to find in South Africa the largest and most reliable contributor of gold that the world has ever possessed.

It will probably merit both these adjectives.

The output of the Randt alone has grown from 34,897 ozs. in 1887 to 2,277,635 ozs. in 1895; rising in value from £125,000 to nearly £8,000,000. The advance of the last year (1895) is about 250,000 ozs., or about £850,000 in value.

If this rate of progress is maintained in the Randt, the Transvaal output will overtake the highest outputs of the United States or Australia, the £15,000,000 and £13,000,000 worth of gold which were respectively won in these countries in 1853. But will this rate of increase be maintained? Apart from the evidence of the extent of the conglomerate beds already given, there is this further consideration which points to the permanency of the Randt output. Whereas the Californian and the Australian fields were indebted for their great initial outputs to alluvial deposits, or rich veins of gold, the Randt output has been drawn from the first from reef mining. The Randt, therefore, has no reason to fear any such rapid decline as accompanied the change from alluvial to quartz mining in both the United States and America.*

* Professor Egleston, in "Metallurgy of Gold, Silver, and Mercury in the United States," says that £210,000,000 out of an estimated total of £235,000,000 worth of gold yielded by California between 1851 and 1861 was drawn from "auriferous gravels." His estimate of the Californian output is higher than Mr Hamilton Smith's (given above), and he puts the total gold production of the world between these years at a higher figure than that of Dr Soetbeer, upon whose tables the figures in the text are based. (*Journal* of Statistical Society, June 1894.

The diminished Australian output of gold remained at (about) £6,000,000 value for the fifteen years 1875-1890; and the diminished output from the United States remained at (about) £6,500,000 value during the years 1882-1892. The Australian output has since been strengthened by discoveries in Western Australia; and the total American output (including the United States, Mexico, and British Columbia) is reported to have amounted in 1894 to more than £9,000,000 in value—a yield which exceeds that of any previous year subsequent to 1870. There is one other important contributor to the world's gold supply — Russia. The Russian output has averaged from £4,000,000 to £5,000,000 in value for the last twenty years, and it is said that prospects of an increased output are entertained.

In view of the long continued decline in the gold outputs of the United States and Australia the appearance of a new and apparently permanent contributor to the world's gold supply is obviously a matter of great commercial importance. From 1700 to 1850 the world's annual gold supply was about £2,000,000 in value. For the twenty-five years, 1850-1875, it averaged £25,000,000. This was the period when both the American and the Australian gold fields were at the height of their productiveness, and it was marked by a great industrial and commercial expansion. During the fifteen years 1875-1890 the world's gold supply fell to an average of £20,000,000. Assuming that America, Australia, and Russia continue to produce not less than a total output of (say) £18,000,000, the Randt's present contribution of £8,000,000 raises the world's annual gold supply to the level of the period 1850-1875. If, however, the Randt's output be increased, or still more, if both the Randt's output be increased and further contributions are added from other South African gold fields, the supply at the end of the century will exceed that obtained during the ten years 1850-1860, the period of the great initial output of the American and Australian fields (Note 25).

No one, I suppose, would deny that this increase in the world's supply of gold will have a beneficial effect upon agriculture, manufactures, and industries.

The prices which were obtained by producers during the normal period 1867-1877 had fallen in 1891 by 28 per cent.* Since then they have reached a still lower level. We need not stop to enquire to what extent this loss to the producer has been modified by the fact that the producer is also a consumer—a consideration which includes the further fact that the workman's wages have an increased purchasing power. It is sufficient for the moment to assume the truth of the statement, which we hear repeated on every side, that this fall in prices is the immediate cause of the present agricultural and commercial depression. Ultimately, no doubt, the producer would again receive a normal value for his produce. Meanwhile he is at a disadvantage. He is at a disadvantage in payments made for all services from those of an employé to the highest professional skill. For these services are estimated by reference to the general wealth of the community—the general capacity of the community at large to purchase them; and this is *ex hypothesi* a higher standard than that of the falling industry. Again, in payments made in respect of loans and debts, either on account of capital or interest; for the capital repaid has now a higher purchasing power, and the interest is paid at a rate fixed when the profits of the industry were greater. Lastly, he is at a disadvantage in payments made to the State. During all this period of falling prices, from 1877 onwards, we have been unconsciously laying an increasingly unfair proportion of the burden of taxation upon our producers. In all these

* Mr A. Sauerbeck's table in Statistical Society's *Journal*, March 1892.

ways the classes which are economically the most important in the community are receiving an inadequate share of the general profits.

Without pretending to trace the working of a process so subtle as the " appreciation " of gold, or the acquisition of an artificial value by money under the present monometallic system, it is impossible not to connect this fall in prices with the absolute decrease of 20 per cent., and the far higher relative decrease in the output of gold shown by the period 1875-1891 in comparison with the period 1850-1875. If this be so—if the remedy for the partial paralysis of our agriculture and of our commerce be an increased supply of gold—we may take heart, for this remedy is surely at hand.

CHAPTER X.

CONFLICT OF NATIONALITIES AND RACES.

ASSUMING the population of South Africa * to be 4,000,000, this total would be composed of 650,000 Europeans and 3,350,000 coloured people. The numerical relationship of the Europeans to the coloured people varies in the several colonies, states, and territories.

In the Cape Colony the Europeans are to the coloured people in the proportion of one to four ; in Natal they are as one to twelve ; in the Free State, as one to two ; in the Transvaal, as one to four ; in the Crown Colony of Bechuanaland, as one to ten ; and in the territories of the Chartered Company, as one to one hundred.

Neither the coloured nor the European population is homogeneous.

The composition of the former is approximately shown by the subjoined table :—

Aborigines (Hottentots and Bushmen)		50,000	
Bantu	Military: *i.e.* Kafirs, Zulus, and allied tribes	2,350,000	3,350,000
	Industrial: *i.e.* Bechuanas, Basutos and Mashonas	700,000	
Mixed Races (Cape "boys")		250,000	
Malays		13,000	

Of the 650,000 Europeans, if we omit to take account of other nationalities, probably 375,000 would be Dutch and 275,000 English. The two sections would approxi-

* As previously defined : Africa south of the Zambesi, omitting the German and Portuguese territories.

CONFLICT OF NATIONALITIES AND RACES 167

mately be distributed as follows :—in the Cape Colony, as eleven to nine; in Natal, equally; in the Free State, as nine to one; in the Transvaal, equally, although, ten years ago, the Dutch were to the English as seven to one.

These three main elements, Bantu, Dutch, and English, are organised into a variety of communities :—

Mode of Government.

Two British Colonies	{ Cape Colony Natal }	Responsible Government.
Two Republics	{ South African Republic (Transvaal) Free State }	Full internal freedom within terms of Conventions.
Native Territories	{ Basutoland Zululand Tongaland }	Officers under High Commissioner.
	{ Transkei Tembuland Griqualand Pondoland }	Officers under Cape Government.
Territories of the Chartered Company	... ...	Administrator for civil, and Deputy Commissioner for military, affairs.

The relationship of these states to England as paramount power, of course, varies very considerably.

In the Cape Colony and Natal the Governor is the "link" by which this relationship is maintained. The political functions of the Governor of a Parliamentary Government have been aptly compared by Lord Dufferin to the duties performed by "the man with the oil can" in tending a piece of machinery. Sir Hercules Robinson, in a speech delivered at Kimberley in 1884, described the more obvious duties of his office in some detail. Those duties, he said, were negative rather than positive. In case of a difference of opinion between the Governor and the Ministry, he could say "No." If the ministers then resigned, the appointment of the person to be entrusted with the formation of a new Ministry rested with him. In case of a disagreement between the Ministry and the Parliament, the Governor must decide whether it is best for the public interests that there should be a new Ministry or a new Parliament.

The Governor acts as a link between the colony and the mother-country in so far as he is himself advised by an Imperial Minister, the Secretary of State for the colonies, in giving advice to the colonial ministry. Moreover, he is in all things political and social the representative of the Sovereign, and as such he exercises the peculiar prerogatives of the Crown.

It must be remembered that the Governor of the Cape Colony fills two distinct and sometimes conflicting offices—those of Governor of the Cape Colony and High Commissioner for South Africa.

In his capacity of High Commissioner he gives effect immediately to the views of the Imperial Government. Through the high Commissionership the forces of the Chartered Company and the territory of Basutoland are kept under the direct control of the Imperial Government. The Government of Zululand is also similarly related to the Imperial Government; for the Resident Commissioner in that country represents the Governor, not the Government, of Natal.

The control which England exercises over the Republics is based partly upon the position of the former as paramount power in South Africa, and partly upon rights definitely reserved by the terms of the successive Conventions.

As paramount power the Imperial Government has (and exercises) the right to interfere in cases where the action of an otherwise independent state would endanger the common interests of the Europeans in South Africa.

Under the Conventions, the ultimate control of the relationships of the two Republics with foreign powers is maintained by special clauses, which render the assent of the Imperial Government necessary to the validity of treaties respectively concluded between the Republics and such foreign powers.*

The fate of Rhodesia is still undecided. At present, an Imperial officer is placed in command of the local forces. The civil administration is left in the hands of the Administrator, who is appointed by the Directors of the Company with the approval of the Secretary of State for the colonies ; but, whereas he can be removed by the Directors only with the consent of the Secretary of State, he can be removed by the Secretary of State immediately and without the assent of the Directors.†

Here, then, is a great country in the making.

Did ever history present a more amazing picture of political complexity? Was there ever a single country, or rather a single province of an Empire, that consisted of such diverse elements and showed so great a variety of political and social organisation?

I speak of South Africa as one country. Am I justified in so doing? Yes, because there exists a principle of unity which cannot be overlooked or forgotten — the paramount power of England. Its present divisions—where such divisions are real and not apparent—are due to the neglect of this principle in the past, and its future progress and ultimate consolidation depends upon the maintenance of this principle in full vigour and in full operation in the future.

But the paramount power of England was not effectively exercised in South Africa until a comparatively recent period —the period of the Bechuanaland Settlement (1884-5). Then for the first time the policy of the Imperial Govern-

* By article IV. of the London Convention the South African Republic is prevented from making treaties without the assent of the Imperial Government with foreign powers other than the Orange Free State. See p. 105, and full text in Appendix.
† Clause III., Agreement of May, 1894.

ment was based upon a consideration of the conditions of South Africa as a whole. Then for the first time the eyes of her Majesty's Government were officially opened to the existence of two facts which had from the first governed the course of South African history, and which, acting in combination, made the administration of South Africa more difficult than that of any other colony or dependency of the Empire. Yet these two facts were plain enough to eyes which were not thus officially blind, being nothing more than the natural desire of the Europeans to possess themselves of fruitful and unoccupied lands, and the natural property of the dark-skinned people, to increase and multiply.

With certain other special conditions of South Africa the Imperial Government had been acquainted from the first. They were aware that the Europeans were not the sole claimants to the soil; that, on the contrary, every step in advance taken by the colonists brought them into more serious conflict with a numerous and courageous race of dark-skinned people; and they were inclined, at least at one period, when the tide of philanthropic zeal ran high in England, to over-estimate the value of the claims advanced by the Bantu both in point of fact and equity. They were aware, too, that the Europeans were themselves divided into two nationalities, and that the Dutch and English colonists were separated by differences of language, customs and character.

A knowledge of these conditions had been forced upon the Imperial Government by the logic of facts. In the one case the eastern frontier of the Cape Colony had been maintained by a series of costly and disastrous Kafir wars; and in the other, a measure acceptable enough to English sentiment, the abolition of slavery, had produced the expatriation of many thousands of the Dutch settlers.

Obviously this was a country which required the

establishment of a strong central power, for such an authority could alone grasp the general conditions, and control the political and social tendencies arising out of them.

What prevented the Imperial Government from assuming the responsibilities and exercising the rights of a paramount power in South Africa was at first the feeling that no adequate return could be expected from the necessary expenditure of moral and material force. I speak now of the period after the great emigration, when it had become apparent that a central authority was necessary to preserve the unity of the separate European communities, and to effectively regulate the relationships of those communities with each other and with the coloured races, but before the commercial importance of the country was recognised. This attitude was maintained—with intervals of spasmodic activity—during the period between the great emigration and the discovery of diamonds—1836-1870. In plain words, it was not thought worth while for England to assume the rôle of paramount power. This was the impression in England. It was an erroneous view, and one which was quite opposed to the best local opinion.

In 1858 Sir George Grey wrote :—

"In recommending a remedy . . . I would urge that experience has shown that the views which led to the dismemberment of South Africa were mistaken ones. That in point of fact, Her Majesty's possessions here are of great and yearly increasing value to the trade and commerce of Great Britain, and may be made valuable to an almost indefinite extent. That it has now been conclusively shown that the people do not desire Kafir wars; that they are fully aware of the much greater advantages they derive from the peaceful pursuits of industry, and from cultivating their valuable exports." *

* Despatch to Sir E. B. Lytton, November 19th, 1858.

Sir George Grey's remedy, of course, was the immediate creation of a central authority by uniting the colonies and now independent Dutch communities, founded by the emigrant farmers, in a federal system.

During this period it would have been comparatively easy to have established this central authority by means of which the paramount rights of England could have been effectively exercised. Subsequently, that is to say, after the discovery of diamonds had produced a material alteration in the attitude of England towards South Africa, the Imperial Government were extremely anxious to apply this "remedy"—federal union—of Sir George Grey. But the difficulties of the situation had then enormously increased.

At the same time mere lukewarmness and shortsightedness on the part of the Imperial Government is not in itself sufficient to account for the very special disasters, and the general ineffectiveness, which has characterised our administration of South Africa up to 1881—the year of the retrocession of the Transvaal. Indeed, after the establishment of the diamond industry the Imperial Government ceased to be lukewarm.

In order to explain this comparative failure we must look deeper.

Up to this date the two authorities which should have unitedly given effect to the power of England were in constant conflict. The cause which lay at the root of the endless "divergencies of opinion" between the home and colonial authorities lay in the simple fact that the information, or rather the data, upon which the respective opinions of Downing Street and Capetown were founded, was different. The home authorities were guided by certain general principles, the colonial by a knowledge of the actual facts of the case acquired locally and impossible to communicate. It is to this conflict between "the man in Downing Street" and "the man on the spot"—whether a civil or military officer—that the disasters suffered by the British arms, and the losses incurred by the British treasury, are directly attributable. It is this conflict, too, which has made South Africa "a grave of reputations" for the colonial administrator.

Let us take some examples:—

After the colony had been cleared of the Kafirs who had swept over the Eastern frontier in 1834-5, Sir Benjamin Durban was of opinion that certain measures were necessary for the future security of the colonists. He proposed to grant lands between the Keiskamma and the Fish Rivers to the settlers who had suffered most in this and the preceding Kafir invasions. The object of this proposal was at once to compensate the sufferers, and at the same time to form "a belt of a dense European population," in advance of the Fish River. He also proposed to locate between the Keiskamma and the Kie a body of loyal Kafirs who were to be at once controlled and protected by a chain of forts occupied by a military force. These measures were reversed by Lord Glenelg's despatch of December 26th, 1835. The Imperial Government were of opinion that the colonists and not the Kafirs were the aggressors, and that future conflicts could be avoided by a recognition of the claim of the Kafirs to the country beyond the Fish River, and they, therefore, ordered the evacuation of the country eastward of that river.

In the year 1858, Sir George Grey was of opinion that the application of the Orange River Free States for the resumption of British authority over them should be favourably entertained, and that a Federal Union might be established between these States and the British Colonies; and that by means of this union the solidarity of the Europeans in South Africa might be regained, and the danger of future conflict between the Dutch and English sections avoided.

The Imperial Government decided "not to assent to any project for the resumption of British sovereignty in any shape over the Orange River Free States." They were of opinion that Sir George Grey's action in endeavouring to reunite the Europeans in South Africa "had so far compromised them, and endangered the success of that policy which they must deem right and expedient in South Africa, that his continuance in the administration of the government of the Cape could be no longer of service to public interests." *

In December 1878, Sir Bartle Frere was of opinion that the necessity for immediate action against Ketshwayo was so great as to render it impossible for him to incur the delay which would have been involved in submitting the terms of his ultimatum to the Imperial Government. He wrote :— †

"The Zulus . . . had violated English territory, slain persons under English protection, and had repeatedly refused the redress which we demanded. Could a final demand for redress on this account be postponed? It seems to me clearly not, with any safety to Natal and its inhabitants."

He adds that this reference would have required a delay of two months. These two months would not have passed without "fresh manifestations of Zulu impatience," or an outbreak in the Transvaal, for " whatever were the chances of Zulu acquiescence, there was no question of the bitter anger with which [the award] was received in the Traansvaal."

The Imperial Government were of opinion that, notwithstanding these circumstances, the delay should have

* Correspondence, etc., relative to recall of Sir George Grey. Printed, April 17th, 1860.
† Despatch, March 1st, 1879. C—2316.

CONFLICT OF NATIONALITIES AND RACES 175

been incurred; and for this "indiscretion" Sir Bartle Frere was partially superseded* and discredited.

Here are three crises in the history of South Africa in which the Imperial Government and their representative are in conflict.

The nett result of these endless divergencies of opinion was, that the colonial administration never became sufficiently stable to acquire and maintain for England the position of a paramount power in South Africa, either during the period when such a position might have been naturally assumed, or afterwards.

The rapid development of the Cape Colony, which succeeded the discovery of diamonds at Kimberley, established the fact that South Africa was a country in which British energy and capital might be profitably invested. Nor was there any question now as to the evils which had resulted from the dismemberment policy, and the necessity for the creation of a central government to remedy them. The indemnity paid to the Free State Government for the trespass committed by the declaration of British authority over the diamond fields, and the numerical increase of the Bantu, together with the reported formation of fresh military systems among them, afforded practical evidence on both points. The Imperial Government, therefore, resolved to take South Africa in hand, and establish, by means of a federal union, the central authority which was the necessary instrument for the exercise of its paramount rights.

But the difficulties were now enormously increased. The Dutch element had advanced in power and solidarity, the natives had multiplied and grown stronger, and there was a danger of collision with Germany. The proposal to unite the colonies and states of South Africa in a federal union was unsuccessful, both when it was advanced under the Imperial initiative of Lord Carnarvon, and again when it was launched under the immediate control of the local

* By Lord Wolseley, as High Commissioner of South-East Africa.

administrator, Sir Bartle Frere. And so the intention to assume the position and responsibilities of a paramount power at this time was defeated. The Imperial Government were earnest enough in making the attempt. They were no longer deterred by any shadowy dread of unknown and unjustifiable responsibilities. Since the time of the Sand River and Bloemfontein Conventions an altogether higher and wider view of the Imperial destiny of England had grown up in the minds of Englishmen and their rulers. The head of the Imperial administration at this time was Lord Beaconsfield, the one man who of all others had done most, by stimulating a sense of national responsibility, to direct the current of the Anglo-Saxon race into a wider and more splendid course. But under compulsion of the exigencies of party politics, Lord Beaconsfield's Government shrank back at the critical moment, from fear of an expenditure of military force and tax-payers' money, which, necessary as it was from the point of view of South African interests, could not be justified in the eyes of an electorate only partially informed of the facts of the case. And the sequel? It is already known to us. An able and conscientious administrator was unjustly discredited; the union of South Africa was indefinitely postponed. The Imperial Government had put its hand to the plough and looked back.

In the Bechuanaland Settlement (1884-5) the Imperial Government for the first time assumed the responsibilities of a paramount power, and in so doing they avoided the mistake of 1854. At this period a fresh expansion of the Europeans beyond the limits of the colonies and states took place. But the communities of Stellaland and Land Goshen were not allowed to grow into independent republics, nor was the relationship between the settlers and the natives left to adjust itself by natural methods—methods which resolved themselves into the gradual extermination, or practical enthralment, of the weaker race. Provision was

CONFLICT OF NATIONALITIES AND RACES 177

made for the inevitable disintegration of the native systems produced by contact with civilisation. Where the chief was strong and the tribe sufficiently cohesive, chief and tribe were protected from premature interference; where the tribal organisation had already broken down, the magistrate was introduced to take the place of the chief. In short, a *modus vivendi* was established under which the settlers and the natives could live peaceably side by side, and mutually benefit each other.

In 1889 the principle was again applied, and the Imperial Government, as paramount power in South Africa, undertook the task of regulating the expansion of the Europeans, and controlling the consequent disintegration, and ultimate civilisation, of the coloured races throughout the whole of the immense region stretching northward to the Congo State. In this case the Imperial Government have delegated the immediate duty of organisation and administration to private enterprise, but even under the present constitution of the Chartered Company they are responsible for the final destiny of this great accession to the Empire.

The purpose of this retrospect is to advance the contention that the conflict of races and nationalities in South Africa is not alone sufficient to account for the unhappy separation of the Europeans, or the cruel and costly process by which the supremacy of the Europeans has been established over the native races. And the inference I wish to suggest is hopeful, but not unduly optimistic. It is that if the main cause of these evils be that which I suggest, the repetition of these evils can be checked, if not altogether prevented, in the future.

The nationality difficulty of course exists, and the native question exists; but neither of these are insoluble problems.

There is no inherent divergency between the Dutch and English character sufficient to prevent the amalgama-

M

tion of the two peoples. The Dutch in South Africa have won the admiration of authorities as distinct as the late Mr J. A. Froude and Mr Selous. Mr Froude says of the Boers that they "of all human beings now on this planet, correspond nearest to Horace's description of the Roman peasant soldiers who defeated Pyrrhus and Hannibal."* And Mr Selous has found "no people in the world more genuinely kind and hospitable to strangers than the South African Dutch in the Transvaal, the Free State, or the Cape Colony"; and is sure that since they "possess in such an eminent degree so many of the qualities that Englishmen profess to admire, the two races would, with a better knowledge of one another, soon shake off their mutual prejudices, and agree to work together for the common good and advancement of the best interests of South Africa." † These are weighty opinions, but, apart from any such individual testimony, a study of South African history shows us that the "awkwardness" of the Franco-Dutch settlers and their descendants is due far more to circumstances than to nationality.

At the beginning of the century, when England assumed the administration of the Europeans in South Africa, these people had been cut off for more than a hundred years from European influence, that is to say, from civilisation. From that time onwards the quarrel of the Boers has been against the Government as such, and not against individual Englishmen. Pringle relates ‡ how "Groot Willem" Prinslo "came forth very good-humouredly to shake hands, and drink to the better acquaintance" of the very party of Albany settlers who were about to take possession of the lands from which this Prinslo and other Dutchmen had been dispossessed

* "Oceana," ch. iii. p. 37.
† " Travel and Adventure in Africa," p. 7.
‡ " Narrative of a Residence in South Africa."

CONFLICT OF NATIONALITIES AND RACES 179

in consequence of their share in the "wicked and foolish" Bezeidenhout rebellion. Such instances might be multiplied almost without end. A remarkable application of the principle was made by Sir Evelyn Wood in his telegraphic despatch to the Secretary for the Colonies immediately after the cessation of hostilities in the Transvaal Revolt: "Uneducated men mistrust Governments, but trust persons, therefore Roberts should go himself to Transvaal to get known by the people."* The expatriation of the Boers again removed a large section of the Dutch population from the influences of civilisation; and the non-interference, or dismemberment, policy perpetuated this isolation. It is not surprising, therefore, that in South Africa to-day there should be a certain antipathy between the "old," and the new "colonists," which is quite independent of any difference of nationality. These old colonists who have been thus cut off for two centuries from civilisation are, from a consciousness of their own deficiencies, slow and cautious; distrustful, if not actually resentful, of the changes which are being forced upon them. The new colonists, who come fresh from the industrial centre of the world, are naturally more enterprising, and they manifest a certain impatience towards these men who cling so tenaciously to the soil which they do so little to improve. But this antipathy is being broken down. The moral intervals upon which it is based are being diminished by the action of two powerful levelling agencies—education and the railway.

Mr Rhodes has, from the commencement of his career, grasped the fact that what divides the Europeans in the Cape Colony, and generally in South Africa, is not nationality but education; and additional merit belongs to his public services, because the appeal for support to carry out his measures has been addressed to all enlightened men

* C—2858.

irrespective of nationality. By this policy he had, until the date of the Jameson incursion, produced a partial union of the Dutch and English parties in the Cape.

The question which lay at the root of the original separation of the Europeans in South Africa was the question of slavery. The same cause threatened to rend apart the United States of America, but there its operation was prevented, and the national unity was maintained, at the cost of a civil war. The question has disappeared in this acute form, for, apart from the Conventions, no European community could venture to maintain an institution which has been condemned by the moral sense of the whole civilised world. But the question of the treatment of the natives, in the form of the admission or not of the coloured people to political and civil rights, still constitutes the main cause which tends to maintain the separation of the Dutch and English. In the republics the coloured people are entirely excluded from political, and partially excluded from civil, rights. In the British colonies the principle of political equality, irrespective of colour, is established. Nor is the significance of this difference affected by the fact that both in Natal and the Cape Colony limitations have been introduced to prevent the abuse of such privileges, for these limitations are the result of practical experience, and as such they commend themselves to all reasonable persons. In Natal a native must have lived for seven years exempt from the control of the native laws before he can avail himself of the several qualifications which otherwise entitle him to take part in the government of the colony. Similarly in the Cape Colony the application of the general terms of the franchise to the native population is limited by the two provisos—that no person is entitled to be registered as a voter on account of sharing in any native communal or tribal occupation of lands, nor unless he is able to sign his name, and write his occupation and address. Also in the ·Cape Colony—where alone in

CONFLICT OF NATIONALITIES AND RACES 181

South Africa the work of civilising the natives has sufficiently advanced to make the question of immediate importance—the distribution of seats is so arranged as to counterbalance the enormous numerical superiority of the coloured races, a superiority which might otherwise constitute a serious menace to the well-being of the community in the future (Note 26). Thus in the Eastern Province, which contains the great mass of the native population (inclusive of the Transkei territories), a member of the Legislative Council is apportioned to mixed constituencies containing an average of respectively 227,492 coloured people and 18,065 Europeans; and a member of the House of Representatives is similarly apportioned to 56,873 natives and 4516 Europeans. Whereas in the colony as a whole, the average population represented by a single member of the Legislative Council or House of Representatives is, respectively, 69,352 and 20,076.* And, as a matter of fact, there are few constituencies in which the native vote has any weight. The Malays in and about Capetown, the Hottentots of the Kat River Settlement, and the Kafirs at King Williamstown, Fort Beaufort, and Alice, alone command the attention of a Parliamentary candidate. In the Transkei, where the natives are practically untouched by civilisation, the grant of representatives has been received with stolid indifference. "I do not think any political impression whatever," says Mr H. G. Elliott, Chief Magistrate of Tembuland, "has been produced upon the native population of this territory by the return of a member to the House of Assembly. I am confident that not five per cent. know the meaning of it, and not one per cent. care anything about it, and that the balance only wish to be left as they are." †

Here we have approached another aspect of the Native Question of South Africa. What will be the nature of the

* Tables of Director of Census (1891).
† Report in Cape Blue-book on Native Affairs, 1889.

relationship—numerical, social, and political—which will be ultimately established between the natives and the Europeans? The task of organising, controlling, and educating the dense mass of rapidly increasing Bantu which lies between the Cape Colony and Natal has been assumed by the Cape Government, and it constitutes a problem of which it is hard to over-estimate either the intrinsic difficulty, or the importance to the civilised world.

There is, however, this consideration, which is of a reassuring character. In the past the great disasters due to the presence of the Bantu peoples have arisen from movements which have taken place among tribes beyond the control of the European Governments. Such movements have been of two kinds—the formation of military systems by ambitious and energetic chiefs, and the consequent displacement of native populations. Formerly, the European Governments, even when such movements were known to them, were unable to interfere until the evil was full grown and some unmistakable act of aggression had been committed, because these native tribes and their chiefs were regarded by the Imperial Government as independent powers, and had to be treated as such. Henceforward, we may hope that such disasters will not be repeated. For the withdrawal of the white police, which gave the Matabele their opportunity, is a special cause which is not likely to occur again. And now from the Zambesi to Capetown there is a network of European Magistracies, with officials whose duty it is to watch and report the earliest signs of danger.

The Secretary for Native Affairs is the minister who is specially charged with the difficult task of securing the peaceful development of the native population within the colonial boundary.

Mr Rhodes, who, until his resignation, occupied this position in addition to the premiership, has endeavoured to solve the problem by the Glen Grey Act (1894) (Note 27).

In introducing this important measure Mr Rhodes said that in the Transkei there were 600,000 Bantu, that in about twenty years there would be 1,200,000, and that the Transkei could not support such a population as this. He also made the interesting statement that he was personally responsible for some 2,000,000 African natives. As Managing Director of the Chartered Company he was responsible for half a million natives north of the Zambesi and half a million south of the Zambesi; and as Secretary for Native Affairs he was responsible for one million natives in the Cape Colony. He aimed, therefore, at the introduction of a system which could be applied ultimately throughout South and Central Africa. It should also be noticed that Mr Rhodes is strongly opposed to the encroachment of Europeans upon the native territories, or to anything which might lead to the mixing of the two races.

The objects and methods proposed by the Glen Grey Act are these—

The overcrowding of natives upon the land is to be prevented by the substitution of a system of allotments, with rights of commonage, held under a regular title by the head of a family and descending to the eldest son by the law of entail, in place of locations held under communal tenure.

The minds of the natives are to be occupied and their faculties developed by the establishment of a simple system of local government, consisting of village and district councils. Mr Rhodes points out that, by the control of civilised governments, the employment furnished by war and councils of war has been taken away, and nothing has so far been substituted in its place. By these means, however, the natives will be able to occupy themselves with matters "like bridges, roads, education,

plantation of trees, and various local questions." * They
are also to be allowed to tax themselves for these local
purposes. In this way the Transkei will be able to pay
the cost of its own development. Mr Rhodes estimates
that in Fingoland a tax of ten shillings per allotment will
produce £9000 per annum.

In order to provide a "gentle stimulus to come forth
and find the dignity of labour," the idle young males,
that is to say, those who have no white employers, are
to pay a labour tax of 10s. per head. The proceeds of
this tax are to be devoted to industrial schools and training, and so "the neglect of labour will provide a focus
for instruction in labour." By this means, also, the labour
market of the colony will be replenished, and the prospects
of agriculture materially improved.†

The "liquor pest" is to be removed. Power is given
to the District Councils to close the canteens, but the
several districts must tax themselves to raise funds for
compensating the canteen-holders.

To prevent disturbances it is proposed to apply the
bill gradually. At first its application was limited to
the Glen Grey area and to Fingoland; and its subsequent
extension depended upon the results observed in these
districts.‡ The ultimate success of the measure, of course,
can only be demonstrated by time and experience; but
in breadth of principle it is a great advance upon any
previous native legislation; and it is an experiment which
will be closely watched.

Fortunately South Africa is by no means deficient in
public men. The difficulties of the situation have formed
an excellent training school in politics, for in no other

* Report in the Cape Weekly *Argus*, July 26, 1894.
† Mr Rhodes compares the wages of the coloured labour in the Cape
Colony—2s. and 2s. 6d. a day—with those of coloured labour in Egypt
and the Niger Protectorate, where it is respectively, 2d. and 4d. a day.
‡ It has since been announced that the Government have extended
the Act to three new districts.

colony or dependency of the Empire do more various or more important problems arise. And these difficulties have produced public men of commensurate ability. Apart from Mr Rhodes, the names of Sir Henry de Villiers, the late President Brand, and Mr Hofmeyr at once present themselves.

It is to such men and others like them that the consolidation of the Europeans and the education of the natives —the two great tasks which lie before the Europeans in South Africa—must be entrusted.

One thing at least we may expect and require, that in the future the progress of South Africa may not be hindered by any such grave divergencies of opinion between the Imperial and Colonial authorities as have happened in the past. The possibility of such divergencies unhappily exists, but the danger of their occurrence has been largely diminished by the establishment of cable communication,* and by the increased and increasing speed of the ocean-going steamships which bridge the interval between England and her daughter States, and make it possible for the representatives of the Colonial and Imperial Governments to meet in frequent conference.

And when the schoolmaster and the railway have done their work; when the old sores have been healed, and the old antipathies forgotten, what will be the character of the Africander race? It should be courageous, strenuous, and patriotic: for it will need these qualities to fulfil its destiny. Courage to maintain its supremacy over the coloured races nurtured in its borders; strenuousness to overcome the natural deficiencies, and use to the full the natural advantages of the land of its adoption; and an intense patriotism to keep itself free from the insidious effects of constant association with a race lower than itself in the scale of humanity.

* This was done in June 1880, after Isandlhwana.

CHAPTER XI.

SOUTH AFRICAN LITERATURE.

IN proposing to discuss South African literature as a part of South African life—that is to say, of the life of the English colonists—we are confronted at the outset by a difficulty. The political unity of the Anglo-Saxon race has been lost, but its literary unity is unquestioned. Shakespeare and Milton belong as much to the United States of America, or the commonwealth of Australia, as to England: the literary heritage of which they form part is a common possession of the English under whatever sky they live. In the face of this obvious fact, must not any distinction which is drawn between writers in England and writers beyond the seas be purely artificial, or one which would most suitably be considered among distinctions which are based upon conditions which are merely part of the personality of the author?

On the other hand, we must remember that this very Elizabethan and Stuart literature was itself the outcome of a period of national expansion, similar in character to the Victorian expansion, though it was infinitely less rapid and far-reaching. In spite, then, of this difficulty, we must try to form some definite conception of colonial or extra-insular literature. This conception will be more of the nature of a working hypothesis than a definition, but without something of the kind, however tentative, we shall not be able to make any advance at all in the enquiry we have in hand. It will clear the ground a little if we decide first of all what a work of this class is not.

In order, then, to be included in this class it is not necessary that the novel or poem, as the case may be, should be the work of a "colonial-born" author. That requirement would exclude from our list such characteristic novels as those of Marcus Clarke, the author of "For the Term of his Natural Life," and of Mr Thomas Alexander Browne, the author of "Robbery under Arms," and such characteristic poetry as that of Adam Lindsay Gordon. All of these authors would be disqualified by this test, although one of them, Mr Browne, was only three years old when he reached Sydney, and the other two arrived in Australia before they were twenty-one.

Nor is it sufficient that the work should show a special knowledge of the locality in which the scene is laid, or of the social and material conditions which govern the action of the persons. For that would include the "historical novel" and the "novel of adventure" as such.

What gives individuality to authors of the class we are proposing to consider is the capacity to reproduce the spirit, and not merely the letter of colonial life, or better, of the life of the English outside of England. In its broadest aspect this will be the life of the Anglo-Saxon race, when the blood of its sons is stirred with strife, and their faces are flushed with victory over the forces of nature and alien races, or their teeth set tight in defiance of the inevitable. The fiction which reflects this life is marked by a note of freedom with which is associated a certain natural materialism, born of cloudless skies and virgin lands; its poetry, by a fierce realism which glories in the worst, whether that worst be the result of physical conflict or mental anguish. For in this struggle our race is at its best and at its worst; and the eyes of the spectators are quickly opened to the realities of existence.

In two such characteristic works as "Robbery under Arms," and "The Story of an African Farm," the leading motive is a revolt against society. The former is a book of action, and in it the will of society is defied in its external form of law : the latter is a book of thought, and the revolt here is against "convention," that is to say, the rules by which society regulates its inner life, and which are based upon no definite physical sanction. The wider charity which makes both these authors recognise, and emphasise, an underlying morality in immoral action, is a reflex of the wider social and material conditions of colonial and extra-insular life. In England men are enclosed in grooves, in the Australian colonies an efficient democracy has produced a fusion of ranks, in India and South Africa, and in other countries which present a career, the personal element is more powerful, and in all the material of social life is less closely compacted.

In extra-insular poetry there is also a distinctive note, and, although such poetry is, naturally, to a large extent concerned with the imperial aspects of the life of the English, this characteristic feeling is not dependent upon subject. Tennyson deals with the imperial destiny of England—

"The loyal to their crown
Are loyal to their own far sons, who love
Our ocean-empire with her boundless homes
For ever broadening England, and her throne
In our vast Orient, and one isle, one isle
That knows not her own greatness : if she knows
And dreads it we are fall'n." *

Matthew Arnold is characteristically touched by the pathos of the situation ; by the contrast between the toiling millions and the splendour of the political edifice they are unconsciously erecting ; an edifice too splendid for them to understand, and one in which neither they nor their children will dwell. Under the influence of this thought, England becomes the " Weary Titan," who already staggers under the burden of empire.

* Dedication to the Queen : *Idylls of the King*.

But the spirit in which these utterances are conceived is quite distinct from the spirit which pervades the poetry which, in default of a better name, I call extra-insular, when it is concerned with the like subjects.

Take, for example, Tennyson's *Defence of Lucknow*, and in particular the two lines—

"Handful of men as we were, we were English in heart and limb,
Strong with the strength of the race to command, to obey, to endure;"

and compare it with Mr Rudyard Kipling's *Ballad of East and West*, in which the same pride of race is set forth in a more subtle and triumphant form—a form in which the comparison is expressed by emphasising points not of contrast, but of similarity, and at the same time suggesting a wide field of superiority. In the pursuit of the stolen horse the reckless daring that matches the temper of the chief of the Border thieves is shown by the "Colonel's son"; the honourable reluctance to slay an enemy who is completely in his power comes from Kamal. And so, Kamal the Border chief not only surrenders the favourite horse, but sends his son "to eat the white Queen's meat," and become a "man of the Guides"—

"Oh, East is East, and West is West, and never the twain shall meet,
Till earth and sky stand presently at God's great judgment seat;
But there is neither East nor West, Border, nor Breed, nor Birth,
When two strong men stand face to face, tho' they come from the ends
    of the earth!"

That is a verse which could only have been written by a man who is sensitive to influences which pulsate but faintly in our island air, who has been born in a day of Ilbert Bills; a day when the native press of India surrounds the page which contains an account of the farewell ceremonies of a popular Viceroy with a band of gold; a day in which an Indian gentleman represents a metropolitan constituency in the House of Commons.

Or compare the "grand air" of the verse—

> "We sailed wherever ship could sail,
> We founded many a mighty state,
> Pray God our greatness may not fail
> Through craven fear of being great."

with the fierce realism which characterises Mr Rudyard Kipling's presentation of the ocean predominance of England in his poem *The English Flag*. Here, in answer to the poet's invocation, the four winds declare, each in their turn, what *they* know of the flag, which is so little known, and so lightly esteemed, by the English in England. The same quality runs through the whole poem, but perhaps it shows most clearly in the reply of the West Wind—

> "The West Wind called:—"In squadrons the thoughtless galleons fly
> That bear the wheat and cattle lest street-bred people die.
> They make my might their porter, they make my home their path,
> Till I loose my neck from their rudder and whelm them all in my wrath.
>
> I draw the gliding fog-bank as a snake is drawn from the hole,
> They bellow one to the other, the frighted ship bells toll,
> For day is a drifting terror till I raise the shroud with my breath,
> And they see strange bows above them and the two go locked in death.
>
> But whether in calm or wrack-wreath, whether by dark or day,
> I heave them whole to the conger or rip their plates away,
> First of the scattered legions, under a shrieking sky,
> Dipping between the rollers, the English Flag goes by.
>
> The dead dumb fog hath wrapped it—the frozen dews have kissed—
> The naked stars have seen it, a fellow star in the mist.
> What is the Flag of England? Ye have but my breath to dare,
> Ye have but my waves to conquer. Go forth, for it is there."

Now, let us glance for a moment at the work of Adam Lindsay Gordon. The subject is a very commonplace one, but I think we can recognise a distinctive value in the poem; that, in short, it possesses the characteristic feeling which separates it, and poems of this class, from the general mass of English poetry. It is the death of

SOUTH AFRICAN LITERATURE

the outcast in the Australian bush. As *The Sick Stockrider* looks back he forgets the material hardships of the past, and remembers only its pleasures—

> "'Twas merry in the glowing morn, amid the gleaming grass,
> To wander as we've wandered many a mile,
> And blow the cool tobacco cloud, and watch the white wreaths pass,
> Sitting loosely in the saddle all the while.
> 'Twas merry 'mid the blackwoods when we spied the station roofs,
> To wheel the wild scrub cattle at the yard,
> With a running fire of stock-whips, and a fiery run of hoofs;
> Oh, the hardest day was never then too hard!"

Then he faces the present—

> "Let me slumber in the hollow where the wattle blossoms wave,
> With never stone or rail to fence my bed;
> Should the sturdy station children pull the bush flowers on my grave,
> I may chance to hear them romping overhead.
> I don't suppose I shall tho', for I feel like sleeping sound;
> That sleep, they say, is doubtful. True; but yet
> At least it makes no difference to the dead man underground,
> What the living men remember or forget.
> Enigmas that perplex us in the world's unequal strife
> The future may ignore or may reveal,
> Yet some as weak as water, Ned! to make the best of life,
> Have been to face the worst, as true as steel." *

Among South African authors two names are pre-eminent, Thomas Pringle and Olive Schreiner. Both of these authors have made contributions to English literature of permanent value, and both satisfy, though in different ways, the conception of colonial, or extra-insular, literature which I have tentatively advanced.

Pringle was born at Kelso in 1789. He came to South Africa as the leader of the "Scotch party" in the Albany Settlement of 1820. Afterwards he removed to Capetown, and took part in the struggle for the freedom of the colonial press which signalised the arbitrary administration of Lord Charles Somerset. Subsequently, in 1826, he returned to England, and became the secretary of the Society for the Abolition of Slavery. He died on

* This is the original stanza.

December 5th, 1834, little more than a year after the efforts of the society had been crowned by the passing of the Abolition Act.

Pringle, therefore, was only a very short time—some six years—resident in South Africa, but his characteristic work is South African. His inspiration, with few exceptions, comes from the Karoo, from the barren ranges and deep valleys of Kaffraria, and from the life of the settlers and the coloured people. His best known poem is *Afar in the Desert*, and of this poem Coleridge has written, with what at this period of time seems disproportionate warmth, "I do not hesitate to declare it among the two or three most perfect lyrics in our language." To us the merit of the poem lies in the descriptive power which it reveals. As a picture of the Karoo it is singularly true both in expression and feeling, but the lyric exaltation is not there.

"Afar in the desert I love to ride,
With the silent Bush-boy alone by my side:
Away—away—in the wilderness vast,
Where the White Man's foot hath never passed,
And the quivered Coranna or Bechuan
Hath rarely crossed with his roving clan:
A region of emptiness, howling and drear,
Which man hath abandoned from famine and fear;
Which the snake and the lizard inhabit alone,
With the twilight bat from the yawning stone;
Where grass, nor herb, nor shrub takes root,
Save poisonous thorns that pierce the foot;
And the bitter-melon, for food and drink,
Is the pilgrim's fare by the salt lake's brink:
A region of drought where no river glides,
Nor rippling brook with osiered sides;
Where sedgy pool, nor bubbling fount,
Nor tree, nor cloud, nor misty mount,
Appears, to refresh the aching eye:
But the barren earth, and the burning sky,
And the blank horizon round and round,
Spread—void of living sight and sound."

Otherwise the poetic value of his work is not high.

Traces of the influence of Scott, his poetic master, are everywhere apparent. Perhaps the best individual poem is the *Song of the Wild Bushman.*

> " My yoke is the quivering assagai,
>   My rein the tough bow-string;
> My bridle curb is a slender barb—
>   Yet it quells the forest king.
> The crested adder honoureth me,
>   And yields at my command
> His poison bag, like the honey bee,
>   When I seize him on the sand.
> Yea, even the wasting locust swarm,
>   Which mighty nations dread,
> To me nor terror brings nor harm—
>   For I make of them my bread."

Here and there we find isolated couplets which are powerful: such, for example, as the lines in the *Caffer Commando*—

> " For England hath spoke in her tyrannous mood,
>   And the edict is written in African blood."

Or those in *Evening Rambles*—

> " And the aloe rears her crimson crest,
>   Like stately queen for gala drest."

It is the descriptive merit which appears in these last lines—and in the poem of which they form part—which gives his poetry its value. We have seen it in the picture of the desert; it is equally noticeable in his description of the bare, serrated ridges which are characteristic of the South African mountain ranges—

> " Sterile mountains rough and steep,
>   That bound abrupt the valley deep,
>   Heaving to the clear blue sky
>   Their ribs of granite, bare and dry,
>   And ridges by the torrents worn,
>   Thinly streaked with scraggy thorn."

It is present, too, in his cameos of the natives. In *The Hottentot*—

"Mild, melancholy, and sedate, he stands,
Tending another's flock upon the fields,
His fathers' once, where now the white man builds
His home, and issues forth his proud commands."

And in *The Caffer*—

"Lo ! where he crouches by the cleugh's dark side,
Eying the farmer's lowing herds afar ;
Impatient watching till the evening star
Lead forth the twilight dim, that he may glide
Like panther to the prey. With free born pride
He scorns the herdsman, nor regards the scar
Of recent wound—but burnishes for war
His assagái and targe of buffalo-hide."

Mrs Cronwright Schreiner, the authoress of "The Story of an African Farm," is the daughter of a Lutheran minister at Capetown. One of her brothers, Mr Advocate Schreiner, after graduating at the Cape University, proceeded to Cambridge, where, in 1882 I believe, he was placed by the examiners first in the first class of the Law Tripos, and afterwards elected a fellow of Downing. Quite recently he served for some time as Attorney-General in Mr Rhodes' ministry. At the time the "Story of an African Farm" was written, now fifteen years ago, Olive Schreiner was exceedingly young ; and she was actually living among the surroundings which are so faithfully reproduced.

The key to the book is to be found in a remark which the boy Waldo makes, when the children are discussing the history of Napoleon : "The brown history tells only what he did, not what he thought."

It is a book of "thought." In its external aspect the first part is a study of child-life, and the second an essay in woman's rights ; while the whole contains a picture of the growth of a soul—of a woman's soul—closely associated with the philosophic conception of the growth of the kosmos, or gradual enlargement of the area of the sense-perceptions both of the race and of the individual. Its faults of structure, its incompleteness, its strange gaps, seem to reflect the physical characteristics of the Karoo, and the social and material conditions under which it was written.

A youthful, and therefore impressionable, but well-stored mind, was suddenly thrown back upon itself by a singular monotony of physical and social surroundings. To these conditions are due the unusual union of introspective analysis, with vivid, almost photographic presentation of character, and of certain aspects of nature. Moreover, under these conditions, certain states of mind, which are ordinarily forgotten, or passed over, both in real life and in the delineation of that life by the novelist, assume a substantive and definite form. People who live in cities, or within the reach of city influences, do not pay much attention to "dreams" and "reveries"; but there is an actual predominance of dreams and reveries and communings with nature in Olive Schreiner's work.

Of the value of the thought which this book contains in relation to the development of woman it is sufficient to say that in "Lyndall" we have the immediate prototype of the heroine of a large class of recent novels. In reviewing these novels collectively under the title of "The Novel of the Modern Woman," a sympathetic critic* says, "Who could have foreseen that the new, and in many respects the most distinctive note of the literature of the last decade of the nineteenth century, would be sounded by a little chit of a girl reared in the solemn stillness of the Karoo, in the solitude of the African bush? The Cape has indeed done yeoman's service to the English speaking world. To that pivot of the empire

* Mr Stead, in the *Review of Reviews*, July 1894.

we owe our most pronounced type of the imperial man and of the emancipated woman."

Not the least valuable for us is its faithful and vivid portrayal of rural life in the Cape Colony, and in particular of the character of the Boer.

To begin, let us observe how nature is drawn in its most characteristic aspect in South Africa.

First the long period of drought—

"From end to end of the land the earth cried for water. Man and beast turned their eyes to the pitiless sky, that, like the roof of some brazen oven, arched overhead. On the farm, day after day, month after month, the water in the dams fell lower and lower; the sheep died in the fields; the cattle, scarcely able to crawl, tottered as they moved from spot to spot in search of food. Week after week, month after month, the sun looked down from the cloudless sky, till the Karoo bushes were leafless sticks, broken into the earth, and the earth itself was naked and bare; and only the milk bushes, like old hags, pointed their shrivelled fingers heavenwards, praying for the rain that never came." *

Then the torrential rain—

"Outside the rain poured; a six months' drought had broken, and the thirsty plain was drenched with water. What it could not swallow ran off in mad rivulets to the great 'sloot' that now foamed like an angry river across the flat. Even the little furrow between the farmhouse and the Kraals was now a stream, knee-deep, which almost bore away the Kafir women who crossed it. . . . The fowls had collected, a melancholy crowd, in and about the waggon-house, and the solitary gander, who alone had survived the six months' want of water, walked hither and thither, printing his webbed foot-marks on the mud,

* P. 12. Ed. of 1894.

to have them washed out the next instant by the pelting rain." *

And afterwards the "princely day" which follows the breaking of the drought—

"The long morning had melted slowly into a rich afternoon. Rains had covered the Karoo with a heavy coat of green that hid the red earth everywhere. In the very chinks of the stone walls dark green leaves hung out, and beauty and growth had crept even into the beds of the sandy furrows and lined them with weeds." †

Then there is the farmhouse on the Karoo and its inhabitants. In spite of the strangeness of the surroundings, how familiar the author has made it all; and how well we seem to know the chief personages of the story. Tant' Sannie, the Boer woman, with her grossness of person and language; Em and Lyndall, the two little English girls whose dead father married Tant' Sannie to provide them with a protector; the kindly old German overseer and his son Waldo; the vagabond Englishman who supplants him: Greg, who takes half the farm off Em's hands when she has grown up; even the Hottentot maids and the Kafirs, the Boer visitors, and the strangers who come and go—all assume reality under the deft portraiture of Olive Schreiner.

Tant' Sannie does not occupy much space upon the canvas, but the figure is distinct and vigorous. As she sits in her elbow chair, sipping her coffee, with her feet comfortably resting upon the wooden stove, and her Hottentot maid in attendance, she seems to personify the Africander Dutch in every inch of her huge frame. Apart from her external appearance she displays the typical mental attitude in its two characteristic traits—she is superstitious, and averse to change. For this gross creature, in spite of her violent language and material philosophy, "was a firm believer in the chinks

* P. 270. † P. 334.

in the world above, where not only ears, but eyes, might be applied to see how things went on in this world below. She never felt sure how far the spirit world might overlap this world of sense, and, as a rule, prudently abstained from doing anything which might offend unseen auditors."*

Equally characteristic is her reproval of Em for using soda, instead of milk-bushes, to make soap.

"Not that I believe in this new plan of putting soda in the pot. If the dear Father had meant soda to be put into soap, what would he have made milk-bushes for, and stuck them all over the 'veld' as thick as lambs in the lambing season?"

And again :—

"'*My* mother boiled soap with bushes, and I will boil soap with bushes. If the wrath of God is to fall upon this land,' said Tant' Sannie, with the serenity of conscious virtue, 'it shall not be through me. Let them make their steam-waggons and their fire-carriages : let them go on as though the dear Lord didn't know what he was about when he gave horses and oxen legs—the destruction of the Lord will follow them. I don't know how such people read their Bibles. When do we hear of Moses or Noah riding in a railway?'" †

The grotesque use of Biblical phraseology is one of the results of the long isolation of the Boers from civilising influences. Neither Tant' Sannie's language nor her demeanour is overdrawn : on the contrary, both can be matched by a discussion which took place, less than two years ago, in the Transvaal Volksraad, when a proposal to co-operate with the Governments of the Free State and Cape Colony in destroying the locusts was violently opposed on the ground that the locusts "were a plague sent by God, as in the days of King Pharaoh."

* P. 83. † Pp. 336-7.

Of the other characters, and of the story into which their several fortunes are woven, I can only speak very briefly.

The first of the two parts into which the book is divided is, as I have already said, a study of child-life in a South African setting: of the life of Waldo, the German boy, and of the two little English girls, Em and Lyndall. Em is to have the farm when she is seventeen, but Lyndall will have nothing, and therefore she makes up her mind to go to school. In reply to Em's pitying generosity, she says—

" 'I do not want your sheep; I want things of my own. When I am grown up,' she added, the flush on her delicate features deepening at every word; 'there will be nothing that I do not know. I shall be rich, very rich, and I shall wear not only for best but every day a pure white silk, and little rosebuds like the lady in Tant' Sannie's bedroom.' " *

The life of the great world is borne in upon these children in a curiously distorted fashion through the sole medium of books. They have read of Napoleon, and in discussing his life Lyndall says—

" 'I have noticed that it is only the made-up stories that end nicely; the true ones all end so.'

" As she spoke the boy's dark, heavy eyes rested on her face.

" 'You have read it, have you not?'

" He nodded. 'Yes; but the brown history tells only what he did, not what he thought.'

" 'It was in the brown history that I read of him,' said the girl; 'but I know what he thought. Books do not tell everything.'

" 'No,' said the boy, slowly drawing nearer to her, and

* P. 14.

sitting down at her feet, 'what you want to know they never tell.'" *

It is this inner life that is described, and the gradual awakening of the conscious being: its agonies and disappointments, and its final compromise, when "this thing we call existence" is realised to be no longer "a chance jumble," but "a living thing, a *one*."

"And so it comes to pass in time that the earth ceases for us to be a weltering chaos. We walk in the hall of the universe, our soul looking up and round reverentially. Nothing is despicable—all is meaning-full; nothing is small—all is part of a whole, whose beginning and end we know not. The life which throbs in us is a pulsation from it; too mighty for our comprehension, not too small.

"And so it comes to pass at last, that whereas the sky was at first a small blue rag stretched out over us, and so low that our hands might touch it, pressing down on us, it raises itself into an immeasurable blue arch over our heads, and we begin to live again." †

The second part is occupied with the tragedies of their lives, mainly that of Lyndall. Into these I have not time to enter now; yet neither as children, nor afterwards, are they characters that are likely to be forgotten. There is Waldo, with his "silky black curls" and uncouth movements, with his infinite yearnings after the unseen, and his infinite anguish in the material world. And Em and Greg—well, they are Em and Greg. These homely diminutives sufficiently indicate the comparative commonplaceness of their respective characters and fortunes. And Lyndall, how could we forget Lyndall, with her frailty of person and strength of will, with her worldly philosophy and unworldly action? Lyndall is the favourite child of the author. She is endowed with a personal charm that nothing can dispel—not even the equivocal position in

* P. 18.   † P. 52.

which she has at last placed herself. We are never told in so many words in what her beauty consists, but we know that her face had that highest form of beauty, beauty of expression, "the harmony between that which speaks from within, and the form through which it speaks."

I have spoken of the incompleteness, of the strange gaps, which characterise the work. This deficient construction, the absence of any subordination of the parts to the whole, or of the lesser characters to any central action, is nowhere more conspicuous than in the treatment of Lyndall's "stranger."

On this point the author has explained herself in the preface to the second edition.

"Human life," she says, "may be painted according to two methods. There is the stage method. According to that, each character is duly marshalled at first, and ticketed; we know with an immutable certainty that at the right crisis each one will reappear, and act his part, and, when the curtain falls, all will stand before it bowing. There is a sense of satisfaction in this, and of completeness. But there is another method—the method of the life we all lead. Here nothing can be prophesied. There is a strange coming and going of feet. Men appear, act and re-act upon each other, and pass away. When the crisis comes the man who would fit it does not return. When the curtain falls, no one is ready. When the footlights are brightest they are blown out; and what the name of the play is no one knows. . . Life may be painted according to either method; but the methods are different. The canons of criticism that bear upon the one cut cruelly upon the other."

Well, the author ought to know how her book was written, but, apart from this, the book tells its own story. She has written it so because it actually happened so. Constructively it is not, it was never intended to be, a work of art: it is a bit of real life, a record of experience, a human document. Lyndall's stranger is indicated in this shadowy form because it was only in this shadowy form that he existed in the author's mind. The Boer woman, Em, Greg, Waldo, the coloured people—all these she has actually seen, and she has drawn them as she saw them: the stranger she has imagined, and his picture contains just so much as could assume substance in her mind.

There is another branch of South African literature upon which I must say a word.

It is somewhat remarkable that, while colonial fiction and colonial poetry is read in England, no account is taken of the skill exhibited in political essay-writing. And yet the success achieved by colonial writers is more general, and relatively higher, in this than in any other branch of letters. It would be strange if this were otherwise, for as Amiel, the Genevan, has pointed out, democracy tends to develop the individual upon political lines. "On things," he says, "its effect is unfavourable, but on the other hand, men profit by it, for it develops the individual by obliging everyone to take an interest in a multitude of questions." Among works of this class in South Africa we have Cloete's "Five Lectures on the Emigration of the Dutch Farmers," and the late Judge Watermeyer's "Three Lectures on the Cape of Good Hope under the government of the Dutch East India Company." The difficult circumstances under which the colonisation of South Africa by the Europeans has been effected present a wide field to the historian, and, apart from the monumental work of Mr Theal, we find a group of colonial writers who have devoted themselves to the useful task of recording the work of past generations of colonists for the benefit and instruction of the present.

In this connection it is necessary to make some mention of the Cape University. The University of the Cape of Good Hope was incorporated in 1873, and obtained its charter in 1877. It is the crown of a remarkably complete and effective system of national education; and although its teaching staff is distributed among the various colleges, there is a sufficient amount of academic work to be transacted at its head-quarters at Capetown to render the University circle a distinct stimulus to the literary enterprize of the colony.

But the work of Olive Schreiner stands out conspicuous, if not unique, not only in South Africa, not only throughout the British Colonies, but throughout the English-speaking world. If we ask to what special element this pre-eminence is due, we can find the answer in that remarkable chapter which contains the Allegory of the Search for Truth.*

"The attribute of all art, the highest and the lowest, is this—that it says more than it says and takes you away from itself. It is a little door that opens into an infinite hall where you may find what you please. Men, thinking to detract, say, 'People read more in this or that work of genius than was ever written in it,' not perceiving that they pay the highest compliment."

It is this attribute of art that is conspicuous in "The Story of an African Farm." Its literary merit is due, not to its realism, not to its discussion of a social problem, but to its suggestiveness; in short, to its possession of this highest quality of art, to speak directly to the mind, not by reason but through the imagination.

* Part II. ch. 2.

CHAPTER XII.

The Chartered Company and Mr Cecil Rhodes.

FOLLOWING the precedent established by Napoleon, when — now a hundred years ago — Péron, the naturalist, was sent to report upon the Antipodean settlement of Botany Bay, the French Government have lately despatched Monsieur Lionel Décle on a scientific mission to Africa. With the general results of the observations made by the explorer during his journey from Capetown to Uganda we are not specially concerned: he has however, with the aptitude of the French mind for rapid generalisation, provided us with a happy phrase to characterise the field of the Chartered Company's operations— " The pick of Central Africa on both sides of the Zambesi." But we are dealing with a country which is not only physically but historically attractive. Apart from the interest which attaches to the scene of a great colonising effort, the territories now opened up by the Company possess two strong claims upon our attention, the great River Zambesi and the ruins of Zimbabwe.

The special objective of the Company's operations * is the high plateau which stretches for 300 miles, at an

* The Company's "field of operations" extends from the Molopo River to the Congo State, over an area of 750,000 square miles. Matabeleland and Mashonaland have been provided with an administrative system similar to that of a Crown Colony; and the Company assume the administration of the country north of the Zambesi (except Nyasaland) under the Agreement of November 4th, 1894. Under the Charter the Company have the sole right to obtain concessions of land and minerals in the Bechuanaland Protectorate. The military forces of the Company are under the direct control of the Imperial Government. But see Chapter XIV.

elevation varying from 4000 to upwards of 5000 feet, in a north-easterly direction from Buluwayo to Umtali, and forms the watershed of the Zambesi on the north, and the Sabi and Limpopo on the south. It is here in the uplands of Matabeleland and Mashonaland that the political and social interest, the colonising interest in fact, centres.

Northward our attention is attracted by the Zambesi, a river second only to the Nile among the rivers of Africa in geographical significance.

The interest of the Zambesi culminates in the Victoria Falls. Here, at a point midway in its eastward course, when its stream is more than a mile broad and its waters so placid that they assume the appearance of a lake, the Zambesi encounters a strange obstacle. A rock-bound channel, 400 feet deep and 300 feet wide, stretches across the whole breadth of its stream and then doubles sharply backwards, leaving a wedge-shaped platform of rock level with the surface of the upper waters. Into this channel the Zambesi flings its waters down the perpendicular wall of rock. The effects which accompany this physical *tour de force*—the thunderous noise with which the waters fall over the precipice and crash together in the narrow channel; the chromatic brilliancy of the play of sunlight upon spray-clouds; the glimpses of the island-studded palm-fringed river seen through the shifting curtain of mist at dawn or sunrise, when every chromatic value is raised to a point of brilliancy reached only during the rapid approach or rapid withdrawal of the tropical sun—can be imagined but not described.

The regions in which the historic interest centres lie eastward of the Mashonaland plateau. The venerable ruins on the Lunde River and at Zimbabwe record the scene of the Semitic colonisation undertaken, probably under Phœnician auspices, in the era of King Solomon.

Its object was, of course, commercial: to work the gold mines, to trade with the natives in ivory and ostrich feathers. The ruins of the temple-fortress of Zimbabwe lie 20 miles east of Fort Victoria. The methods of building, the scientific and religious motives of the architectural design, clearly indicate the presence of a race superior in civilisation to any native African people. This superior race is identified by Mr Theodore Bent with the Sabeaans,* and their sphere of operations with the Ophir of the Bible.

On the coast, in a line due east from Zimbabwe is Sofala, the first point of Africa south of the Equator occupied by the Europeans. These earliest European colonists were the Portuguese; but here in Africa, as in India, they had been forestalled by the Arabian merchants. In 1497 Vasco da Gama, in the course of his voyage to India, found Arab traders established on the east coast of Africa; and when, in 1505, Alvarez occupied Sofala, it is mentioned that two Arab dhows were lying there ladened with gold.†

The existence of the Zimbabwe ruins was known to the Portuguese, and the district in which they were situated was termed Monomotapa, but in Mr Bent's opinion the Portuguese themselves never penetrated so far inland, and their information was based upon the reports of the Moorish traders. The first European who saw the Zimbabwe ruins was the German explorer, Karl Mauch. The discovery took place in 1871, but, unfortunately, he maintained that "the fortress on the hill was a copy of King Solomon's Temple on Mount Moriah, that the lower ruins were a copy of the palace which the Queen of Sheba inhabited during her stay at Jerusalem, and that the trees in the middle of it were undoubtedly almug trees." ‡ Karl Mauch

---

* " Ruined Cities of Mashonaland," p. 195.
† *Idem.* pp. 196-7.
‡ *Idem.* p. 209.

THE CHARTERED COMPANY 207

suffered for his enthusiasm. His picturesque statements excited incredulity and the work of scientific exploration was delayed for twenty years, when it was undertaken by Mr Theodore Bent under the joint auspices of two * London societies and the Chartered Company.

The original inhabitants of the Mashonaland plateau are a tribe of industrial Bantu. The Mashonas are without military organisation, live in open villages, and have made some progress in the arts. Interesting evidence of the character of these people is afforded by a description of a visit to one of their villages which was lately read by Mr Frank Surridge at a meeting of the Colonial Institute.† Mr Surridge was chaplain to the pioneer force which occupied the country in 1890; and his account, therefore, is valuable, because he describes the people while they were still untouched by European civilisation. He tells us that the inhabitants of the village fled on the appearance of "a white stranger with a huge camera and tripod," and that he was left in possession of the chief's kraal. He continues, "Moving about through the quaint little houses, we may see signs of their industry. There stands the smith's forge, of a very primitive type of their own designing, but sufficient to produce some splendidly finished specimens in wrought iron, such as assagais, reaping implements, and knives. At another place may be seen the miniature arsenal, where the native men had been occupied in the manufacture of their own gunpowder. Another man may be bestowing some time and labour in carving a charm in ivory or a pillow in wood. Others may be occupied in cotton-spinning or mat-making. And last, but not least, there might be seen the native brewer labouring at his trade, and producing what is generally known as Dtchuala, or beer very small in character. Around the village there is some agricultural

* The Royal Geographical and the British Society for the advancement of Science. Mr R. Swan was associated with Mr Bent.
† Reports, vol. xxii. p. 462 (July 1891).

land; the women are the labourers, and gather in their harvests of corn, rice, tobacco, sweet potatoes, pumpkins, and monkey nuts."

But the plateau is not exclusively occupied by the Mashonas. The southern portion is in possession of a very different people, the Matabele. The Matabele Zulus, it will be remembered, retired northwards beyond the Limpopo, after the defeat of Moselekatse by the Boers under Hendrik Potgeiter. Shortly after that event, about the year 1840 according to Mr Selous, this warlike people, under Umziligazi, the son of Moselekatse and father of Lobengula, overran Mashonaland. Following the usual methods of the military Bantu, they exterminated the inhabitants of that portion of the country which they selected for occupation, and reduced the survivors to slavery or vassalage. Since this conquest to the date of Lobengula's death the Matabele king has maintained his supremacy over his Mashona subjects by sending his *impis* among them once a year for the purpose of indiscriminate murder and plunder. It was an interference with this native custom that caused the outbreak of hostilities between Lobengula and the Company. (Note 28.)

Such, then, in brief outline, are the characteristic features of Charterland.

The Mashonaland plateau, the immediate objective of the Company, was known from the accounts of hunters and explorers—and these accounts have since been verified—to be temperate in climate, well-watered, and well-wooded. It was a country where, to use Mr Selous' words written originally in 1883, " European children would grow up with rosy cheeks, and apples would not be flavourless." * There was also presumptive evidence of the presence of gold in the remains of ancient workings which had been discovered, and in the practice of the natives who were known to obtain alluvial gold by primitive methods from the Mazoe and its

* " Travel and Adventure," p. 79 and note.

THE CHARTERED COMPANY

tributary streams. To-day the gold resources of Mashonaland are broadly stated to consist of "2000 miles of mineralised quartz,"* and in addition to gold the existence of ample deposits of coal and iron in juxtaposition has been ascertained.

The occupation of this country might legitimately have been undertaken by the Imperial Government; for is not England both the paramount power in South Africa, and the greatest colonising nation in the world? As a matter of fact, this obvious and salutary task was left to be accomplished by private enterprise, we might almost say by a single individual.

The acquisition of the interior of South-Central Africa by Mr Cecil Rhodes and his associates is probably the most successful application of the resources of civilisation to a commercial enterprise yet placed on record.

A mere narrative of the successive steps by which the occupation has been accomplished is sufficiently impressive.

By a proclamation of the High Commissioner of March 23rd, 1885, the 22nd parallel of south latitude was fixed as the northern boundary of the Bechuanaland Protectorate, and the British sphere of influence was shortly afterwards extended northwards to the Zambesi. By thus fixing the boundary of the Protectorate it was supposed that the northward expansion of the South African Republic would be checked, for a band of red was placed between the Transvaal border and the interior of Africa. Notwithstanding this precautionary measure, it became known in 1887 that the Boers contemplated the establishment of a northern colony. Fortunately the Boers were watched by vigilant eyes in the Cape Colony, and this forward movement was anticipated by the conclusion of a treaty of "peace and amity" between Great Britain and Lobengula. Under the terms of this treaty, which was

* Company's Report, $\frac{AM}{4}$ p. 1c.

O

executed early in 1888, the Matabele king bound himself not to enter into correspondence with any foreign power without the knowledge and consent of the High Commissioner. On October 30th in the same year Mr Rochfort Maguire and two others obtained a concession of the right to work minerals in Lobengula's territory.

The immediate object of the Association which afterwards became the British South Africa Company was to give effect to this concession. The owners of the Rudd concession transferred their rights to the founders of the Company, and the founders of the Company undertook in return to find the necessary capital, and to share the nett receipts arising from the operations of the future Company in South Africa with the concessionaires.*

On April 30th, 1889, proposals for the formation of a Company to develop the Bechuanaland Protectorate, and the territories lying to the north, were submitted by the Association to the Imperial Government. The objects of the proposed Company were shortly stated to be these :—

1. To extend northwards the railway and telegraph systems in the direction of the Zambesi.
2. To encourage emigration and colonisation.
3. To promote trade and commerce.
4. To develop and work mineral and other concessions under the management of one powerful organisation, thereby obviating conflicts and complications between the various interests that had been acquired within those regions, and securing to the native chiefs and their subjects the rights reserved to them under the several concessions.

At the same time the Association declared its intention to petition for a Royal Charter, on the ground that the

* "Report," 1889-92, p. 2. This original arrangement was afterwards converted (in November 1893) into a half share of the increased share capital of £2,000,000.

undertaking "could not be considered as likely to be remunerative for some time," and that "the sanction and moral support" of the Imperial Government was "necessary to the due fulfilment" of the objects proposed.*

In complying with this request the Imperial Government were influenced by two considerations. In the first place, the operations of a Company incorporated by Royal Charter would be more easily controlled than those of a Company formed under the provisions of the Joint Stock Companies Acts; and in the second, Lord Knutsford, the Secretary for the Colonies, was of opinion that such a Company could, generally, "relieve Her Majesty's Government from diplomatic difficulties and heavy expenditure," and, in particular, render valuable assistance to Her Majesty's Government in South Africa by undertaking the administration of the Bechuanaland Protectorate.†

The British South Africa Company obtained its Charter on the 29th of October 1889. Arrangements were at once made by Mr Rhodes, the Managing Director in South Africa, for the extension of the railway northwards from Kimberley; and at the same time a police force sufficient for the occupation of the country and the protection of the settlers was enrolled and organised.

The actual occupation was effected by the famous Pioneer Expedition which left the camp on the Macloutsie River on June 28th, 1890, and reached Fort Salisbury, a distance of 400 miles, on the 12th of September. The Pioneeer Force consisted of 200 Europeans and 150 native labourers: it was organised by Mr Frank Johnson, and conducted by Mr F. C. Selous: the Pioneers were accompanied by the newly-organised police. The police force started 500 strong, but their numbers were gradually lessened as the forts and stations were successively established and garrisoned. The command

* *Idem.* p. 2.
† Letter from Colonial Office to Foreign Office, *Idem.* p. 3.

of the entire expedition was entrusted to Colonel Pennefather. In the course of this march a "serviceable road, 400 miles long," the Selous Road, was constructed by the Pioneers, who cut paths through the forests, rendered the rivers fordable, and spanned the streams with corduroy bridges; and forts with intermediate stations were erected and garrisoned at Tuli, Victoria, Charter, and Salisbury. The cost of the expedition, exclusive of grants of land and mineral rights to the Pioneers, was £89,285, 10s. od. Moreover, the occupation of Mashonaland was effected "without the loss of a single life, and without the necessity of firing a shot."*

On the 29th of September the force was disbanded at Salisbury, the Pioneers dispersed to search for gold, and the administration of the country thus occupied by some 1000 Europeans was assumed by Mr A. R. Colquhoun.

Shortly afterwards the Company's Police found themselves in collision with the Portuguese authorities in Manica at Massi Kessi. The Portuguese, although they had been in possession of certain points on the south-eastern littoral of Africa since the occupation of Sofala in 1505, had never established an effective control over the natives in the interior. It was not anticipated, therefore, that any obstacle would be presented by this shadowy territorial claim to the establishment of free communication between Fort Salisbury and the coast.

Ultimately, further conflict was avoided by the arrangement of a *modus vivendi* on the 11th of November; and the terms of this arrangement were embodied in the Anglo-Portuguese Convention of June 11th, 1891. By this treaty the territorial claims of Portugal were recognised, but the nominal possession by this power of the littoral belt was not allowed to interfere with the development of the interior country. In return for the definite recognition of her territorial rights by Great Britain, Portugal under-

* *Idem.* p. 7.

THE CHARTERED COMPANY   213

took to construct or allow the construction of a railway from Beira to the interior, and to limit the duties levied upon goods in transit across the Portuguese territories between the East Coast and the British Sphere to a maximum of 3 per cent. At the same time the free navigation of the Zambesi was secured.

The unexpected opposition of the Portuguese had an adverse influence upon the Mashonaland Settlement. By preventing the immediate establishment of communication between Salisbury and Beira, the Portuguese compelled the Company to draw their supplies by the long overland route, and the prices of stores and provisions were abnormally raised by this enormous cost of carriage. The 1500 settlers, in Mr Rhodes' words,* "went to work to find their reefs, but they were removed 1700 miles from the coast, and their food cost them £70 a ton." At the same time the difficulties of the situation were increased by the unusually heavy rains which fell during the season of 1890-1. This latter circumstance had the further effect of causing the retirement of the Company's first administrator, Mr Colquhoun; and the appointment of Dr Leander Jameson as his successor.

When Dr Jameson assumed the control of the Settlement, towards the end of 1891, the affairs of the Company had reached something like a crisis.

The settlers were discontented, for fever was prevalent and food at famine prices. The police force, originally 500 strong, had been raised to 650, in order that the Company might successfully co-operate with the Bechuanaland Border Police in preventing a threatened "trek" from the Transvaal. The accounts of the Company showed an annual expenditure of £250,000, while the revenue available for administrative purposes was practically nothing.

Dr Jameson, however, proved equal to the occasion.

* Company's Report of *Annual Meeting*, 29th November 1892.

"If you will give me £3000 a month, I can pull through," he said, when Mr Rhodes "talked matters over" with him.* In the following year the police were disbanded with the exception of 40 men, and a volunteer force of 500 men at £4 a head was substituted in their place. At the same time, as every able-bodied man in the country was liable to burgher duty, arrangements were made for equipping a total force of 1500 men if necessity arose.

This necessity came sooner than was foreseen. As the Company has been in effect charged with directly provoking hostilities with a view to the destruction of the Matabele system, a statement made by Mr Rhodes at the second annual meeting of the shareholders, held on the 29th November 1892, is significant. Mr Rhodes then said: † "Our differences with the Portuguese are over, and we are on most friendly terms with Lobengula. The latter receives a globular sum of £100 a month in sovereigns, and he looks forward with great satisfaction to the day when he will receive them. I have not the least fear of any trouble in the future from Lobengula."

Although Dr Jameson and the officers of the Company have been "clearly exonerated" by an exhaustive and impartial enquiry made by the Imperial Government into the "origin and conduct" of the Matabele War, this statement, made little more than six months before the actual outbreak of the war, retains its significance. It is incredible that Mr Rhodes should have made this definite, and, as it proved to be, optimistic statement, if a struggle with Lobengula had been at that time even remotely contemplated. On the contrary it appears that the recognition and maintenance of Lobengula's authority was part of the Company's programme.

The necessity of abandoning this attitude was forced upon the Company by the action of the Matabele king.

* *Idem.* † *Idem*, p. 7.

THE CHARTERED COMPANY

It is an old story in South Africa. The savage cannot dissociate peace from weakness. When Lobengula saw the white men quietly going about their business, and scrupulously avoiding any aggressive action against himself and his people, he drew his own conclusions, and, under the influence of these conclusions, he became himself emboldened and aggressive. And then, in Mr Rhodes' words,* "We either had to have that war, or leave the country. I do not blame the Matabele," he added, "their system was a military system; they once a year raided the surrounding people, and such a system was impossible for our development."

In the course of this annual raid upon the Mashonas a Matabele *impi*, "about 300 strong," and itself "a detachment of a much larger body," entered Victoria on the 18th July 1893.

"As the lives of the settlers were in danger, Dr Jameson gave the Matabele ample notice to leave the neighbourhood of the township, and on their refusing to do so and continuing their raids, he ordered the mounted police, about thirty-eight in number (under the late Captain Lendy, R.A.), to eject them. The Matabele fired on the police, but they were driven out and pursued for some miles, about thirty of them being killed. It was hoped that this would be a sufficient lesson for them, but such was not the case. Messages were immediately sent to Lobengula, and every effort was made to obtain a peaceful solution of the difficulty; but Lobengula despatched a defiant message in answer to one also sent by Sir Henry Loch, Her Majesty's High Commissioner, refusing to treat until the Company had delivered up to him the Mashona men, women and children who had taken refuge in Victoria." That is the official account of the origin of the Matabele War contained in the Company's Report.†

* Company's Report, $\frac{AM}{4}$ p. 6.
† B. p. 17.

The actual events of the war are too recent to require narration in detail. When once it became evident that a contest was inevitable, both Mr Rhodes at Capetown and Dr Jameson at Fort Salisbury acted with prescience and promptitude. Dr Jameson organised and equipped the scattered settlers, who volunteered almost to a man, and concentrated his available forces, both European and native, at Fort Salisbury, Victoria, and Tuli. Mr Rhodes placed £50,000 to the credit of the Company, and informed the High Commissioner that the Company would need no assistance from the Imperial Government. At the same time he sent up horses from the Transvaal, and forwarded supplies to Palachwe, Macloutsie, and Fort Salisbury.

The columns despatched from Salisbury and Victoria for the capture of Buluwayo numbered 1227 men, and of these 672 were Europeans.* They effected a junction at Indaima's Mount, a point sixty miles equi-distant from Forts Charter and Victoria, on the 16th of October, that is to say, about a fortnight after Dr Jameson had been authorised by the High Commissioner "to take all steps he considered necessary to provide for the safety of the lives and property of the settlers under his administration." The force was commanded by Major P. W. Forbes, but both the administrator, Dr Jameson, and the Company's senior military officer, Major Sir John Willoughby, accompanied the columns. From this point they advanced along the plateau, where the country was comparatively open, in a south-westerly direction upon Buluwayo. On the 24th and 25th of October they were attacked by 5000 Matabele on the Shangani River, and on the 1st of November, in the neighbourhood of the Imbembezi, they were again confronted by a force of 7000 Matabele which included Lobengula's finest regiments. In both cases the Company's force fought in laager, and thus protected,

* P. 18.

THE CHARTERED COMPANY 217

they repulsed the Matabele rush with heavy losses. On the 4th of November Buluwayo was occupied. A month later, Major Allan Wilson and thirty-five others, forming part of a patrol 300 strong despatched to secure the fugitive Lobengula, were surrounded and cut off on the Shangani River. The story of their death, told subsequently by the Matabele, has added another, but not a new page to England's book of memories. By the 22nd of December the columns had been disbanded, and the country was then thrown open to the volunteers for prospecting and settlement.

In these operations the Mashonaland force lost 80 killed, of whom 49 were Europeans; and 45 wounded, of whom 12 were Europeans. The Southern force, which had advanced simultaneously upon Buluwayo from Tati, and which consisted of the Bechuanaland Border Police, under Major Gould-Adams, together with the Tuli column, lost, out of a total of 445 Europeans, 4 men killed and 10 wounded.*

The Matabele War expenditure appears in the Company's accounts as £113,488, 2s. 11d.

At such cost and by such swift methods was the conquest of Matabeleland accomplished.

But the Matabele War was an episode—unfortunately not the only episode—in the progress of operations which are essentially commercial and pacific in their intention.

The first section of the Bechuanaland Railway, or Main Trunk Line of Africa, extending from Kimberley to Vryburg, was opened on the 3rd of December 1890: and the second section, from Vryburg to Mafeking, on the 3rd of October 1894. And, since the beginning of the present year (1896), nearly 180 miles of railway has been laid northward from Mafeking. Palapye, a distance of 300 miles in the direction of Buluwayo, will be reached early in 1897, and Buluwayo by the end of the year.

* Pp. 24-26.

The East Coast, or Beira Railway, was carried from Fontesvilla, a place 45 miles up the Pungwe River, to the 75th mile-stone on the 19th of October 1893, and then forward to the present terminus, Chemoio, a distance of 118 miles inland. The section (about 55 miles) to the Portuguese boundary will be completed by the end of 1896; and the line will then be carried forward without delay to Umtali and Salisbury.

The telegraph has advanced further and more rapidly than the railway. It reached Fort Victoria in December 1891, and Fort Salisbury, a distance of 819 miles from Mafeking, on the 17th of February 1892.

From this point it is proposed to carry the line forward to Wady Halfa, and thus establish direct telegraphic communication between Cairo and Capetown. At the present it has reached Zomba in the Nyasaland Protectorate. The break between Tete on the Portuguese frontier and Salisbury will, if the conditions of labour are favourable, be completed by the end of 1896. It will then advance northwards to Fort Johnston, to Katonga, at the head of Lake Nyasa, and to Abercorn; and, unless unforeseen difficulties occur, will reach Lake Tanganyika in September 1897.

This project is a favourite scheme with Mr Rhodes. "If this telegraph is made," he said,[*] "there will be an end to the slave trade, and it will also give us the keys to the Continent. I repeat that I have no doubt about the success of the project, which is a much easier undertaking than amalgamating the Kimberley diamond mines, or governing the Cape Colony."

Meanwhile the internal development of Mashonaland has not been neglected. Roads have been constructed, telegraphic and postal communication established, public buildings erected in the towns, and the machinery of administration has been completed. Buluwayo, the

[*] Second Annual Meeting, p 12 (November 19th, 1892).

THE CHARTERED COMPANY 219

youngest of the four or five towns with any considerable European population, has far outgrown the rest. In less than a year, that is to say, in September 1894, this place was converted from the home of a savage tribe into a town of 2000 inhabitants, housed to a large extent in brick buildings, and reading one or other of the two weekly newspapers already issued in type. While outside the town as many more were engaged in prospecting on the various gold fields.* With the growth of Buluwayo the success of the Chartered Company's enterprise, as a colonising experiment, may be said to be assured.

At a recent meeting of the Company,† Mr Rhodes spoke definitely on this point. "I have been through the country, and from an agricultural point of view I know it is a place where white people are going to settle. ... I would as soon live there as in any part of South Africa."

Looking at Mashonaland from this point of view, as a new field for British emigration, an important consideration arises. What effect will the commercial basis upon which this country has been developed have upon the settlers? In other words, how are the shareholders of the Company to get a return for their capital without unduly burdening the inhabitants?

The method in which this is to be done constitutes what Mr Rhodes calls his "patent." In the same speech he says:—

"I have once said before that out of licences and the usual sources of revenue for a government you cannot expect to pay dividends. The people would get annoyed if you did; they do not like to see licences spent in dividends—those are assets which are to pay for any public works and for good government. We must, there-

* $\frac{AM}{4}$ p. 23.
† P. 9 (January 18th, 1895).

fore, look to our minerals to give us a return on our capital, which, you must remember, is £2,000,000." *

In the earlier speech to which he here refers, he explains how the idea occurred to him, and how the method will work. In that speech he said :—†

"My experience of the past is that, just as *qua* Government so *qua* a Company—we cannot expect to do more than balance revenue and expenditure from land, customs, and assisting in other matters connected with developing the general natural resources of the country. Therefore, when we created the Charter, we had to consider by what means a return could be given to the shareholders, and I remember thinking out the various ways of making a return to those who had risked their capital in the undertaking. It has always struck me that, if it were possible for the Government of a country to share in the discovery of the minerals, a very fair return would accrue. For instance, I have been a miner at Kimberley, on the discovery of the diamond fields, and I was allowed to mark out one claim. It has always struck me afterwards, when I had become engaged in the politics of the country, that if I had been allowed to mark out five claims, no one would have been hurt if I had pegged out two and a half for myself and two and a half for the Government. The same thought had occurred to me when I went up to Witwatersrand and saw that marvellous gold field, where the terms were that they could each mark out one claim. It had occurred to me that, supposing the law had been that each of them could mark out ten claims— five for themselves and five for the Government—it would not hurt the prospectors, and it would have meant wealth to the Government of the country. The only objection to the idea was that it was a perfectly new one. At any rate, we thought we would try it in Mashonaland, and it

* Since increased.
† Second Annual Meeting, p. 9 (November 1892).

THE CHARTERED COMPANY

was the law of the country that 50 per cent. of the vendor scrip went to the Charter."

The success, therefore, of the Chartered Company as a commercial undertaking depends upon the discovery of payable gold deposits.

The general prospects of gold mining in Matabeleland, Mashonaland, and Manicaland have been ascertained through the report of Mr J. H. Hammond, the consulting Engineer to the Gold Fields of South Africa Company. From this report,* dated November 5th, 1894, it appears that (1) the ore deposits are "true fissure-veins"; (2) that veins of this class are universally noted for their permanency," but "permanency" does not "necessarily imply the occurrence of pay-shoots of commercial value"; (3) on the other hand, "it would be an anomaly in the history of gold-mining if, upon the hundreds of miles of mineralised veins, valuable ore shoots should not be developed as the result of future work."

Up to the time of the native insurrection, gold mining was in progress round Buluwayo in Matabeleland; and in Mashonaland in the districts of Salisbury, Mazoe, Umtali, Lo Magunda, Umfuli, and Victoria. As regards results, the Gold-fields of Mashonaland Company showed an output (for three months only) in 1894 of 385 ozs., and up to July 1895, of 1943 ozs. The Mashonaland Central Company also obtained a crushing of 560 ozs. Mining as well as farming has been brought to a standstill by the insurrection, but after the railways have been completed, and both food and mining plant can be brought up at reasonable cost, industrial enterprize will be renewed.

This, then, is the method by which Mr Rhodes intends, in his own phrase, to "combine the commercial with the imaginative," to pay dividends, and extend the empire.

Let me close this account of the operations of the Chartered Company by Mr F. C. Selous's description

* B. p. 72.

of the state of affairs which he found at Buluwayo, on his return to Rhodesia in the autumn of 1895.

"In short, at this time—the autumn of 1895—everything was apparently *couleur de rose* in Matabeleland. Properties, whether farm lands, building sites in town, or mining claims, went up to very high values, whilst almost every one believed that within a year Buluwayo would contain a population of 5000 souls, and that the town itself would receive a plentiful supply of water from the reservoirs already in course of construction, and be lighted by electric light. In fact, all was mirth and joy and hope in the future; for what was to hinder the ever increasing prosperity of the country? Much good work had already been done on many of the reefs, and on the whole the promise was distinctly good. Then, again, after a probation of eighteen months, the country had been pronounced favourably upon by Dutch and Colonial farmers, especially for cattle-ranching, whilst many predicted that much of the high veld would carry sheep."*

This prospect of security and assured prosperity was rudely destroyed by two events which have now to be related—the Revolt of the Uitlanders in the Transvaal, and its sequel, the insurrection of the natives in Rhodesia.

* Sunshine and Storm in Rhodesia, F. C. Selous, p. 5.

CHAPTER XIII.

THE REVOLT OF THE UITLANDERS.

WHEN the Boer Government was restored in 1881, there were two classes of inhabitants in the Transvaal, whose interests the Imperial Government desired to protect — the natives and the British residents. The general restrictions imposed upon the internal freedom of the Boers with this object in view are now embodied in the Convention of London, which, in 1884, replaced the Pretoria Convention of 1881. With the natives we are not now concerned. British residents who had entered the country during the period of annexation (1877-1881), were exempted from "all compulsory military service whatsoever." It was also sought to secure equal civil and political rights for any Englishmen who might subsequently settle in the country. By Article XIV. (replacing Article XVI. of the original Convention) :—

"All persons, other than natives, conforming themselves to the laws of the South African Republic (*a*) will have full liberty, with their families, to enter, travel, or reside in any part of the South African Republic; (*b*) they will be entitled to hire or possess houses, shops, and premises; (*c*) they may carry on their commerce either in person or by any agents whom they may think fit to employ; (*d*) they will not be subject in respect of their persons or property, or in respect of their commerce or industry, to any taxes, whether general or local, other than those which are or may be imposed upon citizens of the said Republic."

It must be concluded that this article is not legally

sufficient for the purpose in question; but a reference to the proceedings of the Commissioners by whom the form of the Boer Government was fixed will conclusively show what was their intention. In these proceedings the following colloquy is duly recorded in the blue-book as taking place between Mr Kruger and the Commissioners.

"Sir H. Robinson: Before annexation, had British subjects complete freedom of trade throughout? Were they on the same footing as citizens of the Transvaal?

Mr Kruger: They were on the same footing as the burghers. There was not the slightest difference in accordance with the Sand River Convention.

Sir Hercules Robinson: I presume you will not object to that continuing?

Mr Kruger: No; there will be equal protection for anybody.

Sir Evelyn Wood: And equal privileges?

Mr Kruger: We make no difference as far as burgher rights are concerned. There may, perhaps, be some slight difference in the case of a young person who has just come into the country."

Moreover, when Swaziland became part of the territory of the South African Republic, under the Swazi Convention of 1894, the Imperial Government, warned by the inadequacy of the Pretoria Convention, introduced definite stipulations, which secure for the Uitlander in that territory the very rights which are denied to his brother Uitlander in the Transvaal.

It was also sought to secure equal privileges for British trade by Article XIII., which prevents the imposition of discriminating duties against British imports, or the maintenance or imposition of any prohibition "on the importation into the South African Republic of any article coming from any part of Her Majesty's dominions, which shall not equally extend to the like article coming from any other place or country." And when the Vaal Drifts were closed

THE REVOLT OF THE UITLANDERS

in October 1895, the action of the Republican Government was successfully contested by the Imperial Government on the ground that it was a breach of the Convention.

It is due, therefore, to a mere technical error that the Government of the South African Republic have been able to pursue the course of repressive legislation which has reduced the Uitlanders to their present position. The details of their grievances are fully set out in the manifesto of the National Union, issued on the 26th December 1895, and in Mr Chamberlain's despatch of the 4th February 1896.* The general attitude of the Transvaal Executive is expressed in the phrase which President Kruger is reported to have used: "When the floods rise we build the banks higher."

The successive alterations in the franchise laws which have been conceived in this spirit are as follows.

In 1881 the British immigrant could obtain the franchise after two years' residence. In 1882 the period of residence was raised to five years. In 1890 a Second Chamber was created, to which the Uitlander had access under certain restrictions. But this second chamber was invested with none of the powers of an effective legislative body. It can merely recommend legislation on certain matters to the Raad. At the same time as this specious concession was made the period of residence was again raised. Ten years was now required as a qualification for the right to elect members of the Raad, and fifteen as a qualification for the membership of that body. In 1893 a law was passed by the Raad, enacting that a Uitlander could only obtain the franchise after ten years' qualification for the membership of the Second Chamber. As he could not secure this qualification until he was thirty years of age, it followed that no Uitlander under the age of *forty* could obtain the franchise. Moreover, although he must have submitted to the liability for compulsory drill, and compulsory service in

* C—7933.

the field if required, he would still be prevented from exercising the right of voting for the offices of President and Commandant-General.

From this exclusion of the Uitlanders from any share in the Government of the Republic has arisen the present strange and anomalous situation. The British inhabitants, forming an actual majority (note 30) of the people of the Transvaal lie at the mercy of an ignorant and notoriously hostile rural community represented by a bare majority of the twenty-four members of the Raad. The children of this population, which pays, according to Mr Chamberlain, eighteen- or nineteen-twentieths of the total revenue of the state, are growing up in ignorance because the Government refuse to recognise any other medium of instruction than the Dutch language. Public notices are communicated to this British population in Dutch; the legal records of commercial transactions, to be valid, must be written in Dutch; in the courts of law Englishmen must plead in Dutch, and give evidence in Dutch through an interpreter. A great industry—the gold industry—with which the industrial prosperity of the Transvaal is bound up, and on which the commercial development of South Africa depends, is fettered by a fiscal system which offends against economics as flagrantly as it does against justice, and by administrative methods which are both ineffective and immoral.

But President Kruger and the Raad have had certain direct dealings with the National Union and the people of Johannesburg which must be recorded.

In 1894 a petition for reforms, signed by 13,000 men, was addressed to the Raad. It was received with "contemptuous laughter and jeers." In 1895 a similar petition, signed by 38,000 men, was rejected. On this occasion one of the members expressed the opinion that if the Uitlanders wanted the franchise they would have to fight for it.*

* Mr Otto. He said:—"Come on if you want to fight. I say, come on and have it out—the sooner the better. I am prepared to

THE REVOLT OF THE UITLANDERS

Moreover, it must be added that in 1892 President Kruger gave a written pledge to introduce a measure which should extend the franchise to "trustworthy persons." The fulfilment of this pledge consisted in the restrictive legislation of 1893, under which, in Mr Chamberlain's words, the Uitlander "can now never hope to attain these rights *in full*, and their partial enjoyment is only conceded after a term of probation so prolonged as to amount, for most men, to a practical denial of the claim. If he omits to obtain any kind of naturalization for himself, his children, though born on the soil, remain aliens like himself." Well may Mr Chamberlain add that "The feelings of intense irritation which have been aroused" by the original grievances "have not been lessened by the manner in which remonstrances have been met."*

In order to complete this survey of the events previous to the Revolt an account of Lord Loch's action, in June 1894, must be included.

At this date Lord Loch visited Pretoria to discuss matters in connection with the Swazi Convention and the exemption of British subjects from the operation of the Commando laws. It appears from his statement in the House of Lords † that on this occasion he was requested by the residents of the Randt to visit Johannesburg. On the 26th June, however, President Kruger addressed a letter to him, in which he begged him not to take this step. In the reply, dated June 27th, in which Lord Loch acceded to this request, he pointed out that the 40,000 British subjects in the Transvaal appeared to him to have "some very real and substantial grievances." At the same time, he received a deputation of Randt residents, and from these twelve gentlemen he learnt that a resort to

---

fight you, and I think every burgher of the South African Republic is with me. I say to-day that the people who signed the memorials are rebels."

* Despatch of Feb. 4th. † May 1st, 1896.

force was in contemplation. In reply to this information, Lord Loch pointed out the folly and danger of such a course. Subsequently, upon his return to Cape Town, and in view of the continued agitation at Johannesburg, he felt it to be his duty as Her Majesty's High Commissioner to take certain steps, which included the "assembly at certain points of British Imperial Bechuanaland Police." He continued :—

"My intention was that, if disturbances had arisen in Johannesburg—disturbances resulting from the administration extended by the Republic towards the Uitlanders in that city—it would have been my duty, I considered, to have informed President Kruger that he would be held responsible for the safety of the lives and property of British subjects. I should have further considered it to be my duty to have informed President Kruger that if he had failed in providing the necessary protection of the lives and property of British subjects in Johannesburg, I should have felt myself at liberty to have taken such steps as I might have felt expedient to have given that protection which he would have failed to give." *

It will be observed that there is a strange similarity between the situation in June 1894 and that which arose eighteen months later, in December 1895. If it be the case, as I venture to contend, that any estimate of the degree of guilt, legal and moral, which attaches respectively to Dr Jameson, to Mr Rhodes, and to the Transvaal Reformers, must largely depend upon the attitude of the High Commissioner and of the Imperial Government, up to the crisis, and at the time when that crisis arose, the fact that the situation was no new one—that, in fact, the drama of 1895-6 had been fully rehearsed in 1894—is one of singular significance. Incredible as it seems, the fact is there. Her Majesty's High Commissioner at Capetown and Her Majesty's Ministers in Downing Street, were

* *Times* report.

THE REVOLT OF THE UITLANDERS

familiar with the condition of the Transvaal; they knew that the Uitlanders had long been suffering from "very real and substantial grievances;" were being goaded to desperation by the insolent trifling or contemptuous indifference of President Kruger and the Volksraad; knew that Johannesburg was arming in its amateur fashion; knew, in a word, that all the materials for a conflagration had been collected; that all that was needed was to apply the match and kindle the flame—and yet they sat still and did nothing, until they were galvanized into action by the news that Dr Jameson had crossed the Transvaal border.

In the face of Lord Loch's action in 1894, it is hard to regard the explanation of this supineness which Mr Chamberlain gives as wholly sufficient; or to acquit either Lord Rosmead or the Imperial Government of all responsibility for the disasters which arose out of Dr Jameson's gallant but misjudged interference. According to this explanation the Imperial Government refrained from interference because, in the first place, "the Uitlanders and their organs had always deprecated the introduction into the dispute of what is called in South Africa the 'Imperial factor;'" and, in the second, because the "'rumours' of violent measures 'were continually falsified by the event.'"[*] It is, of course, necessary to remember that there was nothing in the actual assembling of the police forces to arouse the suspicion of the Colonial Office, or of the High Commissioner. The arrangements which had lately been made for the transfer of the Bechuanaland Protectorate (with the exception of Khama's Country) to the Chartered Company, and the consequent inspection and retention of a section of the Bechuanaland Border Police by Dr Jameson, with other circumstances, sufficiently accounted for what took place at Pitsani Pitlogo and Mafeking up to the period when the expedition set out.

It is not easy to relate the actual circumstances of the

[*] Despatch, February 4th.

revolt within the compass required for these pages. But the attempt must be made.

On the 20th November 1895, Mr Lionel Phillips, the Chairman of the Chamber of Mines at Johannesburg, delivered a speech which was marked by a note of menace. "Nothing," he said, "was further from his heart than a desire to see an upheaval, which would be disastrous from every point of view, and which would probably end in the most horrible of all possible endings—in bloodshed." At this time an understanding had been entered into between the reform leaders and Dr Jameson, that the latter should, under certain circumstances, throw a force of the Chartered Company's police into Johannesburg. On the 26th December, the Manifesto of the Transvaal National Union was issued at Johannesburg; it was signed by Mr Charles Leonard, the Chairman. It was published in the Johannesburg *Star* in full, and a summary appeared in the London *Times* of December 28th. It commenced by announcing that the meeting which was to have taken place on the 27th December was postponed until the 6th January next. It ended with the following summary of the objects of the Union :—

"We want :

1. The establishment of this Republic as a true Republic.

2. A Grondwet or constitution which shall be framed by competent persons selected by representatives of the whole people and framed on lines laid down by them, a constitution which shall be safeguarded against hasty alteration.

3. An equitable franchise law and fair representation.

4. Equality of the Dutch and English language.

5. Responsibility to the Legislature of the Heads of the great departments.

6. Removal of religious disabilities.

THE REVOLT OF THE UITLANDERS

7. Independence of the Courts of Justice with adequate and secured remuneration of the Judges.
8. Liberal and comprehensive education.
9. An efficient Civil Service, with adequate provision for pay and pension.
10. Free Trade in South African products.

This is what we want.

There now remains the question which is to be put before you at the Meeting of the 6th of January, viz.: How shall we get it? To this question I shall expect from you an answer—in plain terms according to your deliberate judgment." *

On Sunday, the 29th December, two bodies of mounted police marched respectively from Pitsani Pitlogo, and Mafeking, and effected a junction at Malmani, a point within the Transvaal border, early on the following morning. This force, which consisted of between 500 and 600 mounted troopers, was commanded by Dr Jameson, the British South Africa Company's administrator, and Major Sir John Willoughby, the company's senior military officer. Before leaving camp on Sunday afternoon the men were informed that Dr Jameson had received a letter from the principal residents in Johannesburg inviting him to proceed to that place for the purpose of protecting the lives and property of the British residents. On Wednesday, the 1st January, 1896, after disregarding two messages from the High Commissioner, Dr Jameson reached Krugersdorp, a point some ten miles west of Johannesburg, and came into conflict with the Boers. On the following day (January 2nd), after an engagement of some hours' duration, in which twenty-five men were killed on the side of the Chartered Company, the column surrendered at Doornkop, and were subsequently taken to Pretoria. There was a dispute as to the terms under which the surrender was effected. The Boers maintained that the surrender

* As it appeared in the Johannesburg *Star*.

was unconditional, alleging that Mr Cronjé, the officer who conducted the negociations, had no authority to offer any other terms than those of an unconditional surrender. Sir John Willoughby was able, however, to produce the written communications which passed between him and this officer; and on this, and other evidence which was submitted for their consideration, the War Office decided " that whatever position Mr Cronjé may hold in the Transvaal Army, he decidedly, on the occasion in question, acted as an officer in authority, and guaranteed the lives of Dr Jameson and all his men if they at once laid down their arms ; " and further, that " no subsequent discussion amongst the Transvaal officers could retract the terms of this surrender." *

Meanwhile "the Uitlander Tortoise had put out its head." On the 30th December the Transvaal police and officials were withdrawn from Johannesburg, and on the following day a Provincial Government was proclaimed. But no force advanced from Johannesburg to meet the Chartered Company's column, although Dr Jameson was so near that it was actually reported in London that he had entered the town. And it was to this circumstance that the failure of the expedition as a military enterprise was due. After the surrender of the column Johannesburg lay at the mercy of a burgher force variously estimated at from 8000 to 12,000 men.

Here two questious arise : First, what was the cause of the hitch ? and, second, what was the position of Mr Cecil Rhodes ?

Neither of these questions can be fully answered until the South Africa Committee has held its enquiry ; but sufficient facts and evidence have already been disclosed to enable us to form an approximately correct conception of what really took place.

It appears that it was arranged that on a given day—the 28th December—the Reform Committee should declare a

* C—8063.

Provisional Government, Dr Jameson should enter the Transvaal, and Mr Rhodes should start from Capetown for Johannesburg. Up to Monday, the 23rd, the three parties were in harmony, for on that day Dr Rutherfoord Harris, the Capetown secretary of the Chartered Company, telegraphed* to Dr Jameson—

"Company (*i.e.*, insurrection) will be floated next Saturday at 12 o'clock at night. They are very anxious you must not start before 9 o'clock. Secure telegraph office silence."

But on the 26th a difference of opinion had arisen. On that day Dr Jameson hears from Col. Rhodes at Johannesburg that "it is absolutely necessary to postpone flotation," and receives the same telegram through Dr Harris at Capetown, with the addition of the words, "You must not move until you hear from us again. Too awful. Very sorry." And a further telegram from his brother (Mr S. A. Jameson) at Johannesburg tells him why the "flotation" is postponed.

"It is absolutely necessary to postpone flotation through unforeseen circumstances here altogether unexpected, and until we have C. J. Rhodes's absolute pledge the authority of Imperial Government will not be insisted on. Charles Leonard left last night to interview C. J. Rhodes. We will endeavour to meet your wishes as regards December, but you must not move until you have received instructions."

So far as Mr Rhodes knew the insurrection was now indefinitely postponed. He distrusted, too, either the energy or the good faith of the Reform leaders. On the following day, Friday, the 27th, Dr Harris telegraphs to Dr Jameson—"You must wait patiently and I will do my very utmost, but am beginning to see our shareholders in Matabeleland concession were very different to those in Secheland matter." And again, in the course of further communications—communications in which Dr Jameson's objection

---

* These telegrams were in cypher; but it will be remembered that the key fell into the hands of the Transvaal Government—being found in the baggage captured at Krugersdorp.

that the Chartered Company was already compromised by the concentration of the police, was answered by the statement that the taking over of the B. B. Police was in itself a sufficient explanation of the circumstances in question—Dr Harris telegraphs on the 28th:

"You are quite right with regard to cause of delay of flotation, but Charles Leonard and Hamilton of *Star* inform us that movements not popular in Johannesburg. When you have seen Captain Maurice Heany let us know by wire what he says. We cannot have fiasco."

And later in the same day came a more decided warning

"Lionel Phillips telegraphs A. Beit the following:— 'It is absolutely necessary to delay flotation. If foreign subscribers (Chartered Company) insist on floating without delay, anticipate complete failure.'"

And on this same day, Saturday the 28th, as we know from the Blue-book,* Mr Rhodes had an interview with Sir Graham Bower, the Imperial Secretary, at Capetown, in the course of which he gave an accurate account of the situation. The Johannesburg insurrection, he said, "had fizzled out as a damp squib. The capitalists financing the movement had made the hoisting of the British flag a *sine qua non*. This the National Union rejected, and issued a manifesto declaring for a republic. The division had led to the complete collapse of the movement, and it was thought that the leaders of the National Union would now probably make the best terms they could with President Kruger."

Mr Rhodes's position, then, was this. He was prepared to assist in the insurrection, provided that the Transvaal was thereby converted into a British possession. He did actually assist the conspirators to the extent of placing the resources of the Chartered Company and of the De Beers Consolidated Mines at their disposal. But he stopped

* C—8063.

THE REVOLT OF THE UITLANDERS 235

short at the point of allowing Dr Jameson to cross the border for the purpose of supporting an insurrectionary movement which aimed solely at converting a Boer Republic into a Uitlander Republic. But in spite of the risk of failure threatened by the breach between the Reform leaders and Mr Rhodes, and in spite of the latter's orders not to move under existing circumstances, Dr Jameson resolved to enter the Transvaal on his own responsibility, and, if possible, to win the game off his own bat. More than that, carried away by the confidence of the high spirited young officers who served under him, he entertained the conception of marching directly on Pretoria if the Johannesburg auxiliaries proved efficient, and met him as had been arranged. Under this impulse he resolved to himself initiate the insurrection, and force the hands of the Reform Committee, by an appeal to the spirit of the general mass of British residents. Accordingly he telegraphed on Dec. 28th, to Mr Wolff, the Chartered Company's representative at Johannesburg, "Meet me as arranged before you leave by Tuesday night, which will enable us to decide which is best destination." And on the following day, the 29th, he telegraphed to his brother, Mr. S. A. Jameson; " Dr Wolff will understand the distant cutting (*i.e.*, that he had cut the wires which communicated with Mr Rhodes and Capetown). British Bechuanaland police have already gone forward. Guarantee (*i.e.*, of expenses of the force) given."

Mr Rhodes received the information that Dr Jameson had crossed the border on Sunday the 29th. He communicated the intelligence to Sir Graham Bower on the same day. In a telegram despatched to Mr Chamberlain on the 31st, Lord Rosmead says,* that he has "seen C. J. Rhodes, who assured him Jameson acted without his authority . . . he at once endeavoured to stop him, but found wires cut." According to Mr Schreiner's evidence,

* C—7933.

given before the Jameson Select Committee at the Cape,* Mr Rhodes made use of the following words in speaking to him of the event :—

"Yes, yes, it is true. Old Jameson has upset my apple-cart. He has ridden in. Go and write your resignation [Mr S. was Attorney-General in the Government]. I did not tell you yesterday, because I thought I had stopped him. Poor old Jameson! Twenty years friends, and now he goes in and ruins me. I cannot hinder him, and I cannot destroy him."

As regards the legality of Mr Rhodes's action, I may remark, without endeavouring to anticipate the result of the enquiries of the South Africa Committee,† that the conclusion of the Cape Committee on this question does not appear to discriminate on a point of the highest importance. This committee found that :

" . . . Mr Rhodes did not direct or approve of Dr Jameson's entering the territory of the South African Republic at the precise time when he did so, but the committee cannot find that that fact relieves Mr Rhodes from responsibility for the unfortunate occurrence which took place. Even if Dr Jameson be primarily responsible for the last fatal step, Mr Rhodes cannot escape the responsibility of a movement which had been arranged, with his concurrence, to take place at the precise time that it did, *if circumstances had been favourable at Johannesburg.*"

Surely this proviso is in matters of this kind all-important. The offence which is punishable under the Foreign Enlistment Act is that of "fitting out any . . . expedition to proceed *against* the dominions of any Friendly State." If a Provisional Government, claiming authority over the Republic, had been established and maintained at Johannesburg, and this Government had eventually been recognised as the successor of the Repub-

* Reported to the Cape Assembly on July 17th, 1896.
† Ordered July 30th, 1896.

lican Government by foreign powers, how could Dr Jameson's expedition have been shown to have committed the offence of proceeding *against* a friendly State? Moreover, in the case of this insurrection the words which Lord Palmerston used in defending his Government against the charge of allowing Englishmen to enlist in the revolutionary forces commanded by Garibaldi, have a special significance :

" It is the fault and fortune of governments when their subjects have revolted that they appeal to all friendly powers for assistance to remove the men who are the authors and instigators of the revolution. These governments forget that *they* are the real and original authors and instigators of these revolutionary movements ; and if their prayers were granted, the first, most effectual, and only necessary step would be *their own removal.*"

To return to the narrative of events. As I have already mentioned a summary of the manifesto of the National Union was published in the *Times* of December 28th, 1895 ; and before that day the *Cologne Gazette* was reported to have accused Mr Rhodes of "inspiring and fomenting the discontent of the Uitlanders for the purpose of incorporating the South African Republic with Rhodesia." Possibly in consequence of these reports, Mr Chamberlain telegraphed* at 5.30 P.M. on Sunday, the 29th, to Lord Rosmead, that it had been suggested that " some one in the service of the Company was advancing from the Bechuanaland Protectorate with police." At the same time he desired him to remind Mr Rhodes that such action was contrary to certain articles in the Charter. Early in the afternoon of the next day the reassuring statement made by Mr Rhodes† that the "movement at Johannesburg had collapsed," reached him. In reply to this, Mr Chamberlain telegraphed to Lord Rosmead, " Are you sure Jameson has not moved in consequence of collapse." He had scarcely sent off this pertinent enquiry

* C—7933. † See p. 234.

before he received a definite confirmation of his fears, with
the information that Lord Rosmead had forthwith telegraphed to Mr Newton, the Resident Commissioner at
Mafeking, to send a special mounted messenger in pursuit.*
This was the first of a series of disquieting telegrams,
including an intimation forwarded from the British Resident,
Sir Jacobus de Wet, that "President S. A. R. has asked
for the intervention of Germany and France." Late that
Monday night Mr Chamberlain desired Lord Rosmead to
"leave no stone unturned to prevent mischief." And on
the following afternoon he telegraphed directly to President
Kruger, "Can I co-operate with you further . . . bring
about . . . peaceful arrangement which is essential . . .
and which would be promoted by the concessions which I
am assured you are ready to make?" It is interesting to
note that Mr Chamberlain at once addressed himself to the
question of the Uitlanders' grievances. If there had been
supineness at the Colonial Office before the crisis, activity
and alertness was the order of the day now. Mr Chamberlain personally devoted himself to the direction of affairs
with unremitting energy. Every step which could reassure
the Republican Government, and allay the excitement of
race animosity in South Africa was taken. The Chartered
Company was ordered "to telegraph at once to their
representative in Matabeleland to stop the intended movement" of Rhodesia Horse southwards. Official notices
were published through the South African press that the
Imperial Government, the High Commissioner, and Mr
Cecil Rhodes, all alike, repudiated Dr Jameson's action.
And, at the suggestion of Mr Hofmeyr, Lord Rosmead and
the Governor of Natal issued proclamations forbidding the
British colonists to take part in the hostilities. The British
subjects in the South African Republic were by the Queen's

* Sir Graham Bower had been unable to give Lord Rosmead the
information (which Mr Rhodes had given him late on Sunday night)
until Monday morning.

command enjoined to abstain from "aiding or countenancing Dr Jameson or his force." On the evening of Thursday, the 2nd of January, Lord Rosmead, under directions from Mr Chamberlain, proceeded from Capetown to the scene of action, to act as a "peace-maker" between the insurgents and the Republican Government. He reached Pretoria on the evening of Saturday the 4th, and remained there until the 14th. As the result of his mediation, he was able to inform Mr Chamberlain on the 7th of January that the Reform Committee had sent a message to the effect that they had resolved "to comply with the demands of the South African Republic to lay down their arms; the people of Johannesburg placing themselves and their interest unreservedly in my hands in the fullest confidence that I will see justice done to them."* And on the same day he reported President Kruger's determination to hand over Dr Jameson and his men to the Imperial authorities on the

* With this statement of the understanding upon which the Reform Committee surrendered Johannesburg, the following notices which were printed in large type in the *Standard and Diggers' News* (a copy of which is before me) must be read: "We understand on the authority of Sir Sidney Shippard that, if a single shot is fired against the burghers, Dr Jameson's life will be seriously endangered." "The High Commissioner earnestly requests the people of Johannesburg to lay down their arms." And, although it is quite true that from a military point of view Johannesburg lay at the mercy of the Boer levies it must be remembered that to storm or starve Johannesburg would inevitably have led to a contest between the Dutch and British colonists in South Africa, in which the Imperial forces must have intervened. It is possible that the burghers who, as it was, were restrained with difficulty by President Kruger from resorting to extreme measures in dealing with the Jameson force, would not have recoiled before this prospect. It is possible, too, that in addition to the immediate assistance which the Free State had already offered, the Republican Government would have relied to some extent upon the assistance of Germany and France. But the temper of England being what it was—the temper in which the German Emperor's congratulatory message to President Kruger was answered by the immediate equipment of a Special Service squadron—the gravity of the situation, which the reduction of Johannesburg by force of arms would have created, must have been realised by the leaders of the Dutch nationality both within and without the Transvaal.

borders of Natal. On the 10th, he was able to add that President Kruger had issued his "forgive and forget" proclamation, and had promised to submit a law for the establishment of a municipality in Johannesburg to the Raad during the next session.

Nevertheless it is plain from the language of Mr Chamberlain's despatches that he was not at this time satisfied with the course which events had taken. On the 4th of January he instructed Lord Rosmead to remind the Republican Government "that the danger from which they had just escaped was real, and one which, if the causes which led up to it were not removed, might recur, although in a different form." And on the 15th of the same month he exhorted Lord Rosmead to "use plain language." The people of Johannesburg, he said, had surrendered "in the belief that reasonable concessions would be arranged by your intervention; and until these are granted, or are definitely promised to you by the President, the root cause of the recent troubles will remain." To this Lord Rosmead replied somewhat curtly: "The question of concession to Uitlanders has never been discussed between us." I quote these expressions of Mr Chamberlain because the opinion which they embody provides us with a test by means of which we can estimate both the extent to which Mr Chamberlain has modified his original policy of securing an immediate redress of the "admitted grievances" of the Uitlanders, and the value of the measures (note 29) which have been passed by the Raad up to the present in fulfilment of the promises made in this proclamation of the 10th of January.

It is not my intention to pursue the narrative beyond this point. The negociations which subsequently took place between the Colonial Office and the Republican Executive relative to Mr Chamberlain's invitation extended to President Kruger in his despatch of Feb. 4th, 1896, are to be found in the Blue-books. The account of Mr Cecil Rhodes's resignation of the premiership of the Cape

THE REVOLT OF THE UITLANDERS

Colony and subsequently of his directorship of the Chartered Company will be found, together with the changes already introduced in the administration of Rhodesia, in the following chapter.

There are, however, two events which arose so directly out of the Johannesburg revolt that a brief reference to them is necessary. I refer, of course, to the trial of the sixty-three members of the Reform Committee at Pretoria, and to that of Dr Jameson and his officers in London.

Sentence was pronounced on the Johannesburg Reformers by Judge Gregorowski (of the Free State) on April 28th, 1896. The four leaders, Messrs Lionel Phillips, George Farrar, J. H. Hammond, and Colonel Rhodes, pleaded guilty to the charge of having negociated with Dr Jameson; and the fifty-nine remaining members of the Committee to having assisted in furnishing the people of Johannesburg with arms. The leaders were sentenced to death, and the others to various terms of imprisonment and to fines. The death sentences were afterwards commuted by the Executive, under Article III. of the *Grondwet*, to fifteen years imprisonment, and finally to fines of £25,000, and an undertaking (on pain of banishment) not to take part for the future in any political movement in the Republic. Ultimately all the reformers,—except one who died in gaol at Pretoria, and two who refused to submit to any penalty on the ground that the Imperial Government were pledged to hold them safe under the terms of the Johannesburg surrender—were released on payment of fines varying in amount with the degree of culpability.

Dr Jameson, C.B., Major Sir John Willoughby, Captain the Hon. Robert White, Colonel Grey, Major the Hon. H. F. White, and Major the Hon. C. J. Coventry, were convicted under the Foreign Enlistment Act, 1870, on July 29th, 1896, after trial at bar before a special jury, and a court composed of the Chief Justice (Lord Russell of Killowen), Baron Pollock, and Mr Justice Hawkins.

The case of Regina *v.* Jameson and others has an importance altogether independent of the forensic interest which it has created. The story of the events which culminated in those seven dreary days in the Chief Justice's Court will live in the pages of history. With the blame which henceforth attaches to the names of Dr Leander Jameson, Sir John Willoughby, and the rest, there will be mingled a feeling of compassionate regard such as has rarely, if ever, been felt towards any convicted persons. And this feeling is natural: it is explained by the consideration that the crime of which these men have been found guilty is a conventional one. Conventional, because there is no Englishman who believes that either Dr Jameson, or any one of his associates, is one whit less worthy of regard, one whit less capable of honourably performing any of the duties or responsibilities of human life, *now*, than he was before he had been found guilty of fitting out an expedition against a friendly State—to wit, the South African Republic.

I do not say that the sentence is not in accordance with the law. It is this very fact, the irreproachable legality of the entire proceedings in this trial, which shows that the crime is itself conventional. The prisoners were convicted by what is probably the most perfect judicial procedure in the world. A strong Court—no single judge, but the Chief Justice of England supported on his right by the soundest lawyer on the Bench, and on his left by the most experienced of our criminal judges—the most able counsel of the English Bar, a jury alike intelligent and honest, afford the elements out of which must come a true verdict and a just sentence. The defence essayed to show that the violation of the Transvaal territory was by an improvised act, an act done under a sudden and generous impulse. The evidence which was brought forward by the Crown, letter after letter, telegram after telegram, showed that carefully concealed measures had been taken, and a

THE REVOLT OF THE UITLANDERS 243

deliberate and preconcerted plan eventually carried into effect. Even the approximate date of the expedition, the 26th of December, had been fixed more than a month before the two columns simultaneously marched out from Mafeking and Pitsani Pitlogo.

With such evidence before them, it was impossible for the jury to find a verdict other than "guilty"; nor could the Court—this strong and learned Court—have pronounced any lighter sentence. It would be unreasonable to expect that the verdict of history could ever reverse the verdict of this consummate tribunal.

And yet, I repeat, there is no Englishman worthy of the name who thinks the worse of Dr Jameson and his associates. He is a criminal in the eye of the law, but he is no criminal in the judgment of the nation. We have this astonishing fact before us. The verdict is universally admitted to be true, the sentence to be just, and yet these facts do not prevent the nation from feeling the fullest sympathy with these men against whom the verdict has been recorded. This feeling of sympathy is something quite different from the natural feeling of commiseration which is felt by all persons of ordinary benevolence for one who is visited even by a well-merited punishment. The feeling of sympathy for Dr Jameson is so genuine and so powerful that it amounts to nothing more nor less than a direct refusal to believe that he or his associates are in any ordinary sense criminals, although they have been convicted of crime. And the reason is not far to seek. The nation cannot dissociate itself from the crime of these men. The culpable inactivity of the Imperial Government in South Africa led directly to the state of affairs at Johannesburg which made this expedition possible, and which, according to the rider appended by the Jury to its verdict, presented great provocation to the accused. The grievances and the consequent discontent of the Uitlanders in the Transvaal were known to the British agent at Pretoria;

they were known to Her Majesty's High Commissioner at Capetown; they were known to Her Majesty's Secretary of State in Downing Street. Two years ago, Lord Loch proposed to use the very same body of troops for this very same purpose—the purpose of protecting British lives and British property in the event of an insurrection of the Uitlanders in the Transvaal. The Chief Justice, in the course of his exhaustive summing-up, very pertinently asked, "Why was not that letter of invitation addressed to the High Commissioner, or the Secretary of State?" But the Chief Justice seemed to be entirely ignorant of the significant answer which his enquiry invited. Neither of these officials were addressed because the British people in the Transvaal had learnt by bitter experience the utter futility and uselessness of making any appeal directly or indirectly to the Imperial Government. The condition of the British subjects in the Transvaal before Dr Jameson's expedition was the condition which is expressed in those burning words of Junius, "What has an Englishman now to hope for? He must turn from King, Lords, and Commons, and look up to God and himself if he means to be free."

For the incredible supineness of the Imperial Government, which left the fires of revolt to smoulder at Johannesburg for two years, the British nation is itself responsible; for the Government is its agent and servant Out of this supineness arose Dr Jameson's crime; and the British people do well to refuse to dissociate themselves from the men whom they have themselves made criminals

CHAPTER XIV.

THE INSURRECTION IN RHODESIA.

IT will be remembered that in a previous chapter,* mention was made of the partial amalgamation of the Dutch and English parties in the Cape Colony under the leadership of Mr Rhodes. The alliance between him and Mr Hofmeyr, the leader of the Africander party, was undoubtedly one of the most hopeful signs in the political situation as it appeared before the end of the year 1895; for it strengthened the prospect of a general union of the Republics and Colonies to be achieved through the unique position of Mr Rhodes as managing director of the Chartered Company and Prime Minister of the Cape Colony. But when Dr Jameson had "ridden in"—to use the expression with which Mr Rhodes is credited in his interview with Mr Hofmeyr—"the crockery was broken"; and on the 6th of January 1896 Mr Rhodes resigned the premiership, and Sir J. Gordon Sprigg was called upon to form a new ministry.

After this event Mr Rhodes returned to England, saw Mr Chamberlain, and forthwith returned, by way of the Suez Canal and Beira, to Rhodesia. Here, in the country which bore his name, he announced his intention of residing for the future, and of henceforth devoting his energies to the development of its resources.

While the negociations for the visit of President Krüger were in course of progress, the Imperial Government at once endeavoured to satisfy the Transvaal Executive that they were prepared to offer " a complete guarantee " against

* X. p. 179.

any attack upon the independence of the South African Republic "either from any part of Her Majesty's dominions or from the territory of any foreign power." For this purpose certain changes were without delay introduced into the administration of Rhodesia. The entire forces, police, volunteers, and native levies, were placed under the command of an Imperial Officer, who was styled "Commandant-General of the local forces in the Bechuanaland Protectorate and in the territories south of the Zambesi under the direct administration of the British South Africa Company, and Deputy-Commissioner of the last mentioned territories"; and Col. Sir Richard Martin was appointed to this office. Changes in the *personnel* of the Company also followed as a result of the Jameson incursion. The duties of the Company's Administrator, now purely civil, were undertaken by Lord Grey. Dr Rutherfoord Harris was removed from the Capetown Secretaryship ; and towards the end of June, the resignations of Mr Rhodes and Mr Beit from the Board of Directors were accepted, and at the same time Mr Rochfort Macguire retired as being Mr Rhodes' representative on the Board. Mr Rhodes's resignation, and the subsequent cancellation of his power of attorney to represent the Directors in South Africa, followed in awkward proximity to a strongly worded despatch, signed by Dr Leyds, the State Secretary of the Transvaal Executive, in which the Imperial Government were called upon to prosecute Mr Rhodes, Mr Beit, and Dr Rutherfoord Harris.

But before Sir Richard Martin had received his final instructions, an event had happened which compelled the Imperial Government to make further arrangements. This event—the insurrection of the natives in Rhodesia—was the disastrous sequel of Dr Jameson's expedition. It was necessary now to supplement the local by Imperial troops. And it was thought advisable to place a general officer in active service, Sir Frederick Carrington, over the combined forces, with supreme authority until the power of

THE INSURRECTION IN RHODESIA 247

the rebels should be declared to have been broken by the High Commissioner.

Two main causes are assigned for the irritation and discontent of the natives—the cattle question and the abuses committed by the native police.

The former of these causes requires some explanation.

After the war with Lobengula the proprietorship of the royal cattle passed to the Company. But only part were taken possession of by the Company's officials; the remainder, 90,000 head of cattle, were branded with the Company's mark and left to the natives to pasture and tend as before. Then the Government called up the cattle as they required from time to time. As the result of this course of procedure the natives were irritated by what seemed to them to be a continual process of confiscation. At last, in view of their discontent and on the recommendation of Mr Herbert Taylor, chief Native Commissioner, the Company decided to take two-fifths of the then remaining balance of 70,000 head, and leave the remaining three-fifths as the absolute property of the natives. Under this arrangement the indunas were summoned to Buluwayo, and after they had expressed their satisfaction at the proposal, the cattle were distributed.*

Certain causes, not under the control of the Company's government, also contributed to render the natives uneasy at the presence of the white man. In 1890 there was a plague of locusts; in 1894 and 1895 there was a partial drought; and immediately before the outbreak the prevalence of the rinderpest or cattle plague (note 31) necessitated the wholesale destruction of cattle in the infected districts with a view of arresting the spread of the disease.

But there is good ground for believing that this irritation would not have culminated in an insurrection had it not

* For particulars of cattle trouble see C—8130. (Report of Matabeleland Land Commission of 1894.)

been for the disastrous circumstance that the Jameson expedition had practically denuded the country of the white police.

The narrative which Mr F. C. Selous tells of his own experience of the outbreak in its earliest stage points significantly to this conclusion. The murder of a native policeman on the night of Tuesday, the 20th of March, was, he says, the first overt act of rebellion on the part of the Matabele against the government of the British South Africa Company. On Tuesday, the 24th of March, on reaching his homestead, Essexvale, about mid-day, he found that some natives from the neighbouring village of Intuntini had been over to borrow some axes. The request caused no surprise to Mrs Selous, as they were accustomed to render such services to their Matabele neighbours. He continues :—

"About sundown some of these same men brought the usual evening's milk, and my wife and I chatted with them for some time. We spoke about the recent murders on the Umzingwani, and the conduct of Umzobo and Umfondisi, and my wife asked me to say that she thought they had acted very foolishly, as the white men would punish them. At this they laughed, and one of them said significantly, 'How can the white men punish them? Where are the white police? There are none left in the country.'" *

What follows is equally significant, as tending to refute the allegation that the white settlers in general ill-treated the natives. Without denying that there were isolated acts of lawlessness—such acts as are found in every community, old or young—he holds that the charge is otherwise baseless. And this general conclusion (elsewhere stated) is supported by the fact that he finds himself unable to attribute the escape of his wife and himself to the circumstance that they had lived on the best of terms with the natives round the homestead. "Why no attempt was made

* "Sunshine and Storm in Rhodesia," p. 23.

THE INSURRECTION IN RHODESIA 249

to murder us on that Tuesday," he says, "will always remain a mystery to me." He thinks that the real reason was, that the natives supposed he had gone from home to fetch assistance. That their disposition was by no means benevolent was shown by the fact that they went off that night with the cattle which had been placed under their charge, and probably assisted in the murder of Messrs Foster, Eagleson, and Anderson.

But it remains for the investigations of the South Africa Committee to sift the truth of these allegations. And at this point it will be convenient to set out in full the order of the 30th July, 1896, under which this Committee was appointed by the House of Commons.

"That a Select Committee be appointed to inquire into the origin and circumstances of the incursion into the South African Republic by an armed force, and into the administration of the British South Africa Company, and to report thereon; and, further, to report what alterations are desirable in the government of the territories under the control of the Company."

Meanwhile a brief account of the actual circumstances of the rebellion may be of interest.

As already stated, March 20th is the date which marks the commencement of the insurrection. From that time onwards the settlers in the scattered homesteads or mining camps were exposed to the murderous attacks of the Matabele. On Tuesday, the 24th, news of the murder of Mr Bentley, the native Commissioner, and of the whites in the Insiza and Filabusi districts, reached Mr Duncan, the Company's administrator at Buluwayo. In order to realise the extreme gravity of the danger by which the Rhodesian settlers were thus suddenly confronted, and the consequent merit of the efforts made, both by themselves and by the Cape and Imperial authorities on their behalf, it is necessary to know the position of the government at Buluwayo, and the meagre character of the resources at its command.

At this time affairs were in a transition state. The Chartered Company were represented by the acting-administrator, Judge Vincent, at Salisbury, and by Mr Duncan, at Buluwayo. Lord Grey, the new administrator, was on his way to take up his duties; Sir Richard Martin had not left England. The Imperial Government was represented at Buluwayo by Captain Nicholson, under whose control the military forces of the Company had been placed after the Jameson incursion.

Mr Duncan and Captain Nicholson had at their disposal a few mounted police under Captain Southey, 580 rifles, about 100 horses, and fortunately a good supply of ammunition. It was obvious that under these circumstances the settlers must defend themselves. The promptitude with which they undertook this duty is shown by the fact, that within a few hours of the receipt of the news of the Insiza murders, three parties of mounted men set off to relieve and bring in the whites in the outlying districts. One example will suffice as evidence of the work achieved by these patrols. On Thursday night, Mr Maurice Gifford relieved Cumming's store, and thus rescued thirty-six men and one woman, who were in laager. The relief force themselves lost one man killed, and three wounded.

On this same Thursday, the 26th, Buluwayo went into laager; and on April 1st, the Buluwayo Field Force was constituted, and in this force practically all the able-bodied males enrolled themselves. On April the 5th, a count was taken of the population of Buluwayo as they left the laager, in the morning. It appeared that there were 1547 persons, of whom 632 were women and children, and 915 men. On the same day a parade of the Buluwayo Field Force was held. There were 500 men on parade; and this force, together with the 270 men who were outside the town, engaged in bringing in the unprotected settlers,—making a total of less than 800 men,—represented the whole available force with which the Europeans could confront the rebel

Matebele. Of this force 400 men were required to garrison Buluwayo, 130 men were despatched to keep open the Mangwe road—the line of communication with the south—and the remainder, less than 300 men, aided, however, by 150 Cape "boys," under Mr Colenbrander, were free for offensive operations.

One of the most alarming features of the situation was the defection of the armed and trained Matabele native police. Of these about one half joined the rebels in the course of the insurrection; and those who did not revolt could not be trusted to remain loyal. On March the 28th, 80 native police were for this reason disarmed at Buluwayo.

Meanwhile the news of the rebellion, and of the desperate position of the handful of Europeans, severed by 600 miles of road from the nearest railway-terminus, had been telegraphed to the High Commissioner at Capetown, and to the Colonial Office in London.

Lord Rosmead (Sir Hercules Robinson) at once placed the Imperial stores at Mafeking at the disposal of the Chartered Company, and a supply of 500 rifles and ammunition, forwarded by coach under an armed escort from this source, reached Buluwayo on April the 1st. On the 2nd of April, Colonel Plumer, of the York and Lancaster Regiment, with a staff of officers from the garrison at Capetown, was despatched to Mafeking with instructions to raise a force of 500 mounted men—eventually 720 were equipped—to relieve Buluwayo. This force was recruited at Kimberley and Johannesburg, and it included a number of Dr Jameson's troopers, who had been handed over by President Krüger to the Imperial Government, and had now returned from England to South Africa. Colonel Plumer acted with great energy. On April the 12th, the first detachment of 50 men left Mafeking; on May the 3rd, the entire force had been moved up to Macloutsie; and on the 15th, Colonel Plumer and Sir Richard Martin together reached Buluwayo.

At the same time preparations were being made at Salisbury to equip a relief column from that place. It was with this column that Mr Rhodes fought his way through the insurgents to the centre of the rebellion, eventually reaching Buluwayo on the 30th of May.

But the events of the first three weeks, indicating as they did that the whole Matabele people had risen in revolt, caused the Imperial Government to supplement these irregular and volunteer forces by drafts from the Imperial troops at Capetown and Maritzburg, and to place the combined forces, local and Imperial, under the command of a general officer, Sir Frederick Carrington. In the second week in April, Lord Grey, who was now in the Cape Colony, accepted on behalf of the Chartered Company an offer of the Imperial Government to send 300 men of the 7th Hussars and 150 mounted infantry from Natal. In a despatch to the High Commissioner, dated April 15th, Mr Chamberlain announced the intention of the Imperial Government to send reinforcements to South Africa, in order to supply the place of the drafts which would be forwarded to Matabeleland. On the 17th of April, General Carrington was recalled from Gibraltar; and on the 25th he sailed for South Africa, and reached Buluwayo on the 2nd of June. The forces placed at his disposal were stated in his instructions (April 25th) to consist of the following:—300 men of the 7th Hussars and as many mounted infantry as could be spared from the Cape and Natal regiments; 720 Colonial Volunteers raised by Colonel Plumer, D.S.O. at Mafeking; and the various police and volunteer forces, etc., serving in Matabeleland and with Colonel Plumer. In addition to these, General Carrington was authorized to use, if necessary, the police and native forces in the Bechuanaland Protectorate, and 450 mounted infantry which were being sent out from England to reinforce the Cape garrison.

To return to Buluwayo. The settlers enrolled them-

THE INSURRECTION IN RHODESIA 253

selves in the Buluwayo Field Force on April 1st. Of this force only a part could be employed outside of Buluwayo; but the few hundred men thus available succeeded in achieving two purposes. In the first place, they brought in the unprotected whites, and, in the second, they engaged and drove the enemy from the immediate neighbourhood of the town into the hills and forest recesses. In these conflicts severe losses were inflicted upon the Matabele; but it is noticeable that the settlers had to fight in exposed positions and did not rely upon the maxims but upon their rifles. On Thursday, the 16th of April, the Matabele, notwithstanding the checks which they had received, had advanced within a short distance of the town. The situation at this time was sufficiently alarming. There were 1500 men, women, and children in Buluwayo who retreated within the shelter of the laager every night. At Gwelo there was a collection of some 400 persons, including 29 women and children, in laager; and there was a lesser collection of refugees under like circumstances at Belingwe. With these exceptions the whole country was at the mercy of the Matabele rebels. Twelve miles west of Buluwayo, at Redbank on the Khami river, there was a large impi. Some thousands of Matabele under Myamanda, Lobengula's eldest son, were encamped on the banks of the Umguza; and there were two large impis on the Elibaini hills. Altogether ten thousand natives were massed in a semi-circle, stretching from the west to the north-east of the town; while large numbers were assembling to the south on the Matoppo hills. The main road to the south was, however, still open—a circumstance due, according to Mr Selous, to the orders of the M'Limo.

That under these circumstances the settlers should have been able to hold their own until the arrival of the relief force from Mafeking a month later, is an achievement which has scarcely yet been appreciated at its real value.

On the 28th of April, Lord Grey reached Buluwayo and

took up his duties as Administrator. In what spirit he entered upon those duties is apparent from the brave speech which he made on the 3rd of May. He then said that at the beginning of the outbreak the Government had only 379 rifles; but *now* "Buluwayo was as safe as London."

On the 18th of April, the Salisbury relief column, commanded by Colonel Beal, and accompanied by Mr Rhodes and Sir Charles Metcalfe, set out; and on the 3rd of May it relieved Gwelo. Meanwhile, on the 11th of May, when Colonel Plumer's force was getting within striking distance, a column was despatched from Buluwayo to meet and co-operate with the Salisbury column. The Buluwayo column consisted of 42 officers and 613 men, under Colonel Napier, who commanded the Buluwayo Field Force during the rebellion. The two columns met on the 19th of May; and a flying column, under Colonel Spreckly, was shortly afterwards despatched to attack the natives on the hills south of the Insiza River. On the 27th the Salisbury force, with Mr Rhodes, went southwards, and finally reached Buluwayo on the 30th.

Meanwhile, on the 23rd of May, Colonel Plumer's force attacked the enemy on the Umguza river, about twelve miles from Buluwayo. In this engagement the Matabele were driven from a strong position on the densely wooded hills into the open valley of the river, and then pursued for a distance of three miles.

After the arrival of General Carrington on June 2nd, offensive operations on a larger scale were commenced. By the end of the first week in that month, three considerable patrols had been despatched against the insurgents. Colonel Plumer proceeded with a force of 600 men westwards to the Khami river. Captain Macfarlane, who was accompanied by Mr Rhodes and Sir Charles Metcalfe, took 300 mounted men and 100 Colonial "boys" northwards to the Umguza. And a third force under Colonel Spreckly

THE INSURRECTION IN RHODESIA 255

was directed to co-operate with a column under Colonel Beal in dislodging a body of natives who had occupied a ford on the Umguza River, at a point six miles from Buluwayo on the main road to Salisbury. The purpose of these operations was to disperse the natives in the neighbourhood of Buluwayo before attacking the gathering masses of Matabele on the Motoppo hills.

But the insurrection was not confined to the Matabele. On the 23rd of June the disturbing intelligence reached Buluwayo that the peaceful Mashonas had also risen against the white man. The number of whites murdered in Mashonaland was comparatively small. Salisbury went into laager, and relief parties were sent out to the homesteads and mining camps. For some weeks the position of the settlers was one of extreme discomfort and no little peril; but forces were rapidly despatched from Matabeleland, and on the 23rd of July the Salisbury laager was broken up. Shortly after this date, communication between the various settlements was restored, and the insurgents were scattered and broken. But the rising of the Mashonas for a time delayed the execution of General Carrington's measures for reducing the Matabele insurgents.

On the 4th of July the Buluwayo Field Force was disbanded. From this point the task of quelling the insurrection was taken out of the hands of the settlers. The forces employed were under an Imperial Officer, General Carrington, and consisted, as has been already stated, in part of Imperial troops; but the expense was defrayed by the Chartered Company. The attitude of the Directors will appear from the reply which Lord Grey made to the offer of assistance from the Cape Government, and which was read in the Cape Assembly on the 9th of July.

"It is the ambition of the Chartered Company and of the people of this country to secure for England the peaceful possession of Rhodesia at their own cost and without calling upon the tax-payers of England or of the Cape Colony for the contribution of a single sixpence."

Without attempting to narrate the operations of General Carrington's force in detail, I shall refer to one or two significant episodes which will enable the reader to form some conception of the character of the fighting and of the subsequent course of events.

The first of these episodes is the shooting of the M'Limo by the American scout, Mr F. R. Burnham, in his cave in the Matoppo country on June 23rd. The M'Limo was the head of a priestly caste and the mouthpiece of the native god; and he, like Nongase,* had incited the natives to rebel by promises of supernatural assistance—promises which included the re-appearance of King Lobengula. Mr Burnham, who was one of the survivors of Wilson's party, has described his exploit in a report addressed to Lord Grey. He says:—

"After several attempts that were failures, on the 23rd of the month, we [*i.e.*, Mr Burnham and Mr Armstrong, a native commissioner] succeeded in catching the M'Limo in the act of going through his incantations in the cave. Our orders from General Carrington were to capture him if possible, but on no account to allow him to escape us. We were surrounded by Kaffirs in all directions. The ground is very rough—huge granite kopjes, and boulders, and dongas. We hid our horses as near the cave as it was possible, and with great difficulty got ourselves into the cave. M'Limo was going through a preparatory Indaba this day, and the women and the old men were carrying beer and utensils for the big Indaba to come off on the following day. The Impi was supposed to be behind the big granite hill. Just as M'Limo had finished his dances in the smaller crevices and pathway leading to the main entrance, and was starting into the main cavern, I shot him with a Lee-Metford rifle, killing him instantly. We left

* See Note 11.

THE INSURRECTION IN RHODESIA 257

his body at the entrance to the big cave. He is a man sixty years old, with short-cropped hair. He was not dressed with any snake skins, charms, or any of the ordinary equipment of the witch doctor, neither had he any article of white manufacture of any kind. He is not a Ringkop [*i.e.* of Zulu blood]; he is a Makalaka. His features are rather aquiline for a negro; very wide between the eyes. His skin is more red than black. Immediately after killing him we rushed down the side of the mountain. Just at the foot there is a large kraal of over one hundred huts, built on waving grass, no dagga being near it. The huts are conical, with low doors, and were used as temporary resting-places by the people coming to hold Indabas with M'Limo. We fired these huts. The winds blowing strongly against the kopje carried a huge sheet of flame and volumes of smoke far over the top. The Kaffirs saw us, and shouted and shrieked as we got to our horses. For two hours we were hotly pursued, and were nearly exhausted. Fortunately, the Kaffirs abandoned the chase after we crossed the Shashani River. We arrived at Mangwe at 6.30 p.m. I would say that all the trails leading to this cave have been worn and beaten down several inches in depth by constant travel this year. The dust on all the trails is an inch or more in depth, showing that this was the great Konza [Council] place for the whole country. The Kaffir information by which Mr Armstrong was enabled to discover the movements of the M'Limo was obtained under strict bond of secrecy never to betray their names to the white Government or anybody, as it would mean absolute and certain death to all of them."

A second episode is the storming of Secombo's stronghold in the Matoppo Hills by Colonel Plumer's column on the 5th of August. In this engagement the fighting lasted from eight o'clock in the morning to three in the afternoon. The impis under Secombo and Umlugulu, with three others, were broken up. Secombo's stronghold was stormed

by 200 infantry under Captain Beresford. This force was
then surrounded by the Matabele rebels, but kept them in
check until it was relieved by Major Kershaw. Ultimately
the rebels retreated to their caves with a loss of 300.
The column lost 5 men killed and 15 wounded. Among
the former was Major Kershaw, an officer of great promise
In this engagement the Cape "boys" fought with great
bravery; but some of the "friendlies" (*i.e.* Matabele) went
over to the enemy.

Among the measures adopted by the High Commissioner for the termination of the insurrection was the issue
of a proclamation, declaring that all natives who submitted
before the 10th of August, with the exception of persons
convicted by the civil authorities of the murder of unprotected whites, would be pardoned. The date of the expiration of the amnesty was afterwards extended; and the
third episode which I propose to bring before the reader—
the negociations conducted in person by Mr Rhodes with
the rebel chiefs—forms part of the effort thus made to
secure the peaceable surrender of the insurgent Matabele.

On the 23rd of August Mr Rhodes, with Dr Sauer and
Mr J. W. Colenbrander, rode without any escort five miles
into the heart of the Matabele position in the Matoppo
Hills, and held an indaba, or council, with Secombo and
other native chiefs. I take the following account of their
daring adventure from the columns of the *Daily Telegraph*
of August the 24th.

"About noon yesterday John Grootboom arrived in Mr
Rhodes's camp and asked to see those in command. He
then stated that six principal chiefs, two princes, Lobengula's
brothers, and thirty-four indunas and captains of the
Matabele impis were gathered in solemn council in the
hills, four miles away. The meeting was being held in
secret, as the chiefs were afraid to come into the open
owing to their distrust of the white troops. They wished,
however, to see Mr Colenbrander, whom they trusted as

THE INSURRECTION IN RHODESIA 259

a friend, and while they dared not ask such a great man as Mr Rhodes to come to the council, he would, nevertheless, be welcome if he were willing to do so.

"Thereupon Mr Rhodes promptly decided to go. The military staff at once wished to accompany him in order to ensure his safety, but Grootboom strongly advised that no such step should be taken, inasmuch as it would only defeat its object and undoubtedly involve Mr Rhodes in great personal danger.

"Accordingly, Mr Rhodes, Dr Sauer, Mr Colenbrander, and the Press representative started for the spot indicated, every man taking a revolver in each pocket, except Mr Rhodes, who went unarmed, declining to carry any weapon. John Grootboom and John Makings made up the party to the number of six, and together they moved quietly into the rugged portion of the Matoppos, the route lying over land covered with kopjes, and honeycombed with caves.

"Externally every man endeavoured to display a calm and even nonchalant air, but they all felt terribly anxious, as they feared they might be running into a trap set by the rebels to catch the great white chief, Rhodes, alive, and to murder the others. This, moreover, they could easily have accomplished.

"Just four miles from camp the six reached the foot of a huge kopje, and one hundred yards further on was the trysting-place.

"Mr Rhodes and his companions dismounted in dignified silence, and took up their position by a large ant-heap and waited. The suspense seemed interminable, and although there was the stillness of death, the six knew well enough that the place was surrounded by hundreds of armed Matabele. Any wavering sign of fear would have been fatal, but nothing of the kind was shown.

"The critical moment came when Grootboom advanced to the kopje to say the party were awaiting the appearance of the chiefs.

"Suddenly there was a gleam of dead white from the kopje, and all the chiefs filed out in a row, headed by one carrying the white flag. They drew near to the party in silence, and squatted round them in a semi-circle. The Indaba lasted for five hours, all points at issue being thoroughly discussed, and full explanations proffered by the white men to allay the uneasiness which the chiefs evidently felt at certain possible consequences of the surrender.

"Then the chiefs rose, and each threw a small stick at the feet of Mr Rhodes, indicating their willingness to surrender their guns, while another similar stick meant they were ready to hand over their assegais.

"In return Mr Rhodes, whose coolness and dignity were never at a loss, promised that the desired abolition of the native police force should be taken into serious consideration. The chiefs then solemnly declared that hostilities should cease at once, and guaranteed the safety of the roads and of the coaches."

This striking scene was the central incident in negociations of the value of which Lord Grey has thus written:—

"I cannot speak too highly of the immense services rendered by Mr Rhodes in connection with his negociations in the Matoppos. With infinite patience and characteristic tenacity of purpose, he has sat down at the base of the Matoppos in a camp unprotected by a single bayonet, which could have been perfectly well rushed any night during the last six weeks by the rebels, with absolute safety to themselves. It was entirely due to the confidence which this action on his part inspired in the minds of the rebels, who were very suspicious and alarmed as to the treatment they would receive if they surrendered, that they were at length induced to go out from the hills on the flats. In this work he has been most ably assisted by Mr Colenbrander, whose manner with the natives is perfect." *

* Letter of the 16th October, addressed to the Secretary of the Chartered Company.

But this is by no means the sum of the services rendered by Mr Rhodes during the year 1896 to the settlers in Rhodesia and to the Chartered Company.

It is scarcely necessary to assert that both the commercial development and the future peace of Rhodesia depends upon the rapid extension of the railways more than upon any other single measure. The distances to which the railways have been already carried forward, both from the Cape Colony and from the East Coast, have been already stated in a previous chapter.* To this all-important work of advancing the railways, Mr Rhodes applied himself on his return to Rhodesia at the beginning of the year (1896); and it is not too much to say that the result achieved is due to his untiring energy and great resources.

The rebellion in Rhodesia still smoulders, and the fate of the Chartered Company hangs in the balance. In view of these facts it may seem premature to discuss the remedial proposals advanced by the Chartered Company. But this account, however limited in its scope, would be incomplete without some reference to the future.

The Directors have to allay the dissatisfaction both of the natives and of the European settlers.

In respect of the former it appears from Lord Grey's letter of the 18th of October, that it is the intention of the Buluwayo Government to introduce a system of native control practically identical with that which is in force in the Colony of Natal. That is to say, the natives are to be governed through the chiefs, and the tribal divisions and organisation is to be as much as possible restored. The chiefs or *indunas* will become salaried officials of the Government, and the maintenance of order will, in the first instance, be entrusted to them. In each division, however, there will be a European official, the Native Commissioner, to whom the chief will refer in matters in

* Chap. xii. pp. 217-18.

which the interests of the white settlers are involved. Further, the native police force is to be abolished, and only European police will be employed in the future.

The requirements of the settlers have been met in a generous spirit. The Company have promised to compensate them for losses incurred in the destruction of cattle, in pursuance of the Rinderpest regulations, and for all losses caused by the insurrection. They have also undertaken to complete the railway system as speedily as possible, and to reduce the charges laid upon mining properties.

In estimating the possibilities which the future holds for Rhodesia, there is one feature of the insurrection which must not be overlooked. Although Rhodesia is distinctively an English colony, there are two considerable Dutch settlements—one in Gazaland effected towards the end of 1891, and another south of Fort Charter, established after the Matabele war. There were also at the time of the Insurrection a number of Dutch Africanders employed as carriers upon the roads, in addition to stray agricultural settlers. Part of these Dutch settlers formed the Africander Corps under Commandant Van Rensberg; and the men of this corps fought throughout the insurrection side by side with the British settlers. This union of the races in the face of a common danger is a significant and hopeful sign.

In conclusion, let me say one word as to the future.

Lord Salisbury, in a statement which he made* in the House of Lords on the subject of the Soudan Expedition, remarked that the operations of that expedition were limited by the small amount of the funds at the disposal of the Egyptian Government, and suggested that here was a field for the activities of the millionaires who had financed the "invasion" of the Transvaal. It was a humorous turn in the mouth of the Prime Minister of England, but the idea

* In June 1896.

THE INSURRECTION IN RHODESIA 263

which underlay it was serious. That private individuals should devote part of their wealth to the development of the resources of the Empire is a thought which has been brought home to the people of England by the object-lesson which they have had in South Africa; and it is one which has taken hold of the national mind. As it is, Lord Salisbury's account of what was going forward, pending the assistance of the millionaires, was not disappointing. Speaking of the responsibilities of England, the Premier said :—

We shall not have restored Egypt to the position in which we received her, we shall not have placed Egypt in that position of safety in which she deserved to stand, until the Egyptian flag floats over Khartoum.

But for the present the expedition must halt at Dongola, for the "controlling factor is the question of finance." One advantage of Dongola, he added, was "that it is on the road to Kartoum." I could suggest that Kartoum also has this advantage—that it is on the road to Uganda. And if the millionaires have not come to the assistance of the Soudan expedition, they are busy carrying forward the British flag from the South of Africa northwards. If we carry our minds forward for twenty years, and forecast the results of this simultaneous advance towards Uganda, the prospect which rises before our mental vision is inspiriting.

By that time the territory of British East Africa will unite with that of the Eastern Soudan. The Uganda railway will have done its work and brought the western highlands into communication with the coast. Uganda will be then in the position of Natal : that is to say, there will be a small European population organising and controlling the natives, and so developing the natural resources of its own and the surrounding districts. Rhodesia will be peopled with European settlers, and it will then be seen that the temperate uplands of Mashonaland and Matabeleland are the key to Central Africa; since here alone can a considerable European population live under European conditions, and so preserve the mental and physical characteristics of the parent races. Politically, Rhodesia will be the centre of a group of Colonies and Protectorates, including Nyasaland, the territories of the British South Africa Company north of the Zambesi, and the Bechuanaland Protectorate. Here will be a British group bulky enough to outweigh the Dutch Republics in a common system which includes all the States and Colonies from Lake Tanganyika to Cape Agulhas. Capetown and Cairo will be united by telegraph, and the International Congo State, traversed by the Stevenson Road, will alone obtrude between the British system stretching northwards from Uganda to Alexandria, and the consolidated and frankly British South African Federation. Johannesburg will be as populous as Sydney or Melbourne, and the Boer will have passed out of knowledge as a political force.

If this forecast be realised—if this estimate of the importance of Rhodesia be not excessive—it is fitting that Englishmen should not forget that the acquisition of Rhodesia is the work of Mr Cecil Rhodes.

NOTES.

1. Organisation of Dutch East India Company.

General Directory (or Chamber XVII.).

[This consisted of—eight representatives of Chamber (or office) of Amsterdam; four of Zeeland; two of the Maas; two of the North Quarter (Hoorn and Enkhuizen); and one sent by all these alternately except Amsterdam. It met at various places in Holland.]

Governor-General and Council of India.

[Sitting at Batavia (in Java), the centre of the Company's settlements in the East.]

Admirals, Governors, and Commanders who, with their Councils of Policy, administered the various settlements of the Company formed in pursuance of the Charter (1602), which granted a monopoly of the trade of the Netherlands "eastward of the Cape of Good Hope, or westward of the Straits of Magellan."

2. Origin of Conflict with the Natives (Hottentots).

Extract from a despatch dated July 29, 1659, of Commander Van Riebeck and Council to the Governor-General and Council, Batavia.

"The Hottentoos have been again at work . . . the fiscal Gabbema . . . took two . . . killed one . . . one taken prisoner.

"The said prisoner, who was one of the Caepmans, and spoke tolerable Dutch, being asked why they did us this injury, declared . . . because they saw that we were breaking up the best land and grass, where their cattle were accustomed to graze, trying to establish ourselves everywhere, with houses and farms, as if we were never more to remove, but designed to take for our permanent occupation more and more of this Cape Country, which had belonged to them from time immemorial. Aye, so that their cattle could not get at the water without passing over the corn land, which we would not allow them to do; that they consequently resolved (as it was their land) to dishearten us, by taking away the cattle (with which they could see that we broke up and destroyed the best land); and if that would not produce the effect —by burning our houses and corn until we were all forced to go away: that Doman had also put it into their heads that after all the houses in the country were destroyed, the fort could be easily surprised—as the earth walls were built with a slope—and then the Dutch might be forced quite to abandon the country . . . " ("The Record.")

3. Title by deed of purchase.

The form of the first of these two "agreements" was as follows:—

"Agreement entered into between the Commissioner Arnout van Overbeck with the Council at the Cabo de Boa Esperance, on the part of the General Chartered Dutch East India Company, on [of] the one part; and the Hottentoo Prince Manckhagou, alias Schacher, hereditary sovereign of the land of the Cabo de Boa Esperance, on [of] the other part.

"First the said Prince Schacher promises for himself, his heirs and descendants, to sell, cede and deliver, in full, perpetual and hereditary property, as he doth by these presents sell and deliver, to the said Company, the whole district of the Cabo de Boa Esperance, beginning from the Lion Hill and extending along the coast of Table Bay, with Hout and Saldanha Bays inclusive, with all the lands, rivers, creeks, forests and pastures, therein situated and comprised, together with their dependencies, so that the same may be everywhere cultivated and occupied, without let or hindrance from any one—with this understanding, however, that he and his Kraals and herds of cattle, may come freely and without molestation to the outermost farms of the said district and where neither the Company nor the freemen depasture their cattle, and that he shall not be expelled from the same by our nation, by force, and without cause.

[Secondly, the Prince shall not annoy, &c., the Company's servants. Thirdly and fourthly, he shall act as an ally of the Company.]

"The Honble. Company promise on [of] the other part, to give and present to the said Prince Schacher, for this surrender and sale of the whole Cape district, as is now given and presented, once for all a sum of four thousand reals of 8, in sundry goods and articles of merchandise, this day delivered to his contentment.

[Secondly, to allow him peaceable possession, &c.; and to assist and protect him against enemies, &c.]

"All which aforesaid points of agreement . . . have been read over to the said Prince . . . and the sundry wares paid . . . whereupon the contract was confirmed on both sides by shaking hands, and signed and sealed by the Company's seal.

"Done in the Fortress, the Good Hope, April 19th, 1672.

[L. S.] Aernout van Overbeke. | Thus X marked by the Prince
[L. S.] Albert van Brugel. | Schacher aforesaid.
[L. S.] Conrad van Brietenback. | Thus X marked by T. Tachou,
[L. S.] J. Coon. | chief person next to the Prince.

"In my presence—H. GRUDOP."

A similar deed of May 5, 1672, conveyed "the whole district of the land called 'Hottentoos Holland'" to the Company for goods estimated at 4000 reals: and the captain of a ship despatched to Natal was instructed (*inter alia*) to purchase from the chief "the bay of Natal and the adjoining land," to have the purchase "attested by a deed in common form," to pay the estimated price of 19 or 20,000 guilders (florins) in "beads, copper, ironmongery, &c.," and to take care "that the articles of merchandise are not noticed in the deed." The actual value of the merchandise given by the two agreements was very trivial, as appears from the following:—

Extract from despatch of Gov: Isbrand Goske and Council to Chamber XVII., 1673, May 10.

"Hottentots Holland was last year ceded, &c., for the sum of R.4000 which was paid with merchandise of the value of ƒ81 16. prime cost, ... The land of the Cape which the owners often complained had been wrongfully withheld from them, &c., was also ceded ... for a like sum of R. 4000, but which was paid with the value—in tobacco, beads, brandy, bread and other trifles—of ƒ33 17, also prime cost ..." These sums amount respectively to not quite £7, and £2, 16s. 0d. in English money. ("The Record.")

4. Conditions under which the Huguenot Refugees were permitted to settle at the Cape.

"Règlement de l'assemblée de Dix-sept ...

[i. The Company is to provide means of transport from Holland to the Cape.

ii. The Refugee must undertake to support himself by labour or trade; but implements, seed, &c., to be advanced by the Company and repaid by the Settlers.

iii. The Refugee must (except by special permission of Chamber XVII.) remain for five years at the Cape; and, if he then returns, must pay for his passage out, and further sell all his property acquired at the Cape, receiving its equivalent in letters of exchange of the Company.

iv. He must take the following oath of allegiance ;]

"Je promets et jure d'estre soumis et fidelle à leurs hautes puissances les Estats Generaux des Provinces Unies, nos souverains maistres et seigneurs, à son Altesse, monsieur le Prince d'Orange, comme Gouverneur, Capitaine et Amiral General, et au Directeurs de la Compagnie

Generale des Indes Orientales de ce pais, Pareillement au Gouveneur General des Indes, ainsi, qu'a tous les gouverneurs, commandants, et autres, qui durant le voyage par mer et en suite par terre auront commandement sur nous.

" Et que j'observeray et executeray fidellement, et de point en point, toutes les lois et ordonnances, faites ou a faire tant par Messieurs les Directeurs, par le Gouverneur General et par les Conseillers, que par le Gouverneur ou Commandant du lieu de ma residence, et de me gouverner et comporter en toutes choses comme un bon et fidelle sujet. Ainsi Dieu m'aide.

" Fait et attesté dans l'assemblée des Dix-sept le 20 Octobre, 1687." (" The Record.")

5. Origin of "trekking" or the nomadic manner of life pursued by the Dutch farmers.

In 1705 the Government issued "loan leases," or occupation licences, resumable at any period by the Company. The bad effect which this uncertainty of tenure produced upon the character of the loan-lessees was soon apparent, as appears from the following:—

Extract from a Resolution of the Council, dated Feb. 13, 1770 (passed after receiving a report from the Landdrosts (Magistrates) of Stellenbosch and Swellendam, and forbidding the issue of further loan-leases).

" And as it has further appeared by the said report to the especial displeasure of the Council that the aforesaid Commission, on their way from the Fish to the Gamtoos River, met several persons grazing considerable herds of cattle, according to their own pleasure, and without possessing there, or thereabouts, farms in loan from the Company; while others did not scruple to wander about with their cattle, hither and thither, several days' journey from their loan farms;—it was accordingly taken into consideration, that the same not only tends to the evident injury of the Honourable Company, with reference to the income derived from the rents of cattle farms, but, that it must be concluded beyond doubt, that such covetous conduct is chiefly practised in order to enable them more conveniently to carry on an illicit traffic in the bartering of cattle, whether with the Hottentots residing thereabouts, or with the so-called Kaffirs as—among other appearances noticed by the Commission—sufficiently appears from their having found a beaten waggon-road leading out of the Swellendam district to the residence of the Kaffirs: and this all notwithstanding that the said cattle barter has been from time to time prohibited on pain of bodily and capital punishment, especially by the proclamation still in force of the 8th December 1739. It is resolved, &c.

" In the Castle, the Good Hope, Feb. 13, 1770.

(*Signed*)   R. TULBAGH.
   J. V. PLETTENBURG."
(and eight others.)   (" The Record.")

Origin of the "Apprentices" of the Boers.

". . . The Dutch masters went still farther (*i.e.* than claiming the children of their slaves); for the children of Hottentots living with them as hired servants, although both father and mother belonged to that race, were yet retained as slaves till they arrived at the age of twenty-five years; and although the laws in favour of the Hottentots obliged the Dutch to register such children at the Cape, and to give them their freedom at this age; yet the period of their liberty was in reality little nearer than before, unless they deserted into the wild and uncultivated parts of the interior, far beyond the reach of their masters. Many arts were employed to retain them beyond the age of twenty-five years; it was usual to keep them in ignorance of the date of their birth, and thus make them continue to work till their strength began to fail them. When old, &c., they were discharged . . . to misery."

Dutch Government of Hottentots.

"From policy, which they have been willing to pass for a sense of justice, the Dutch have paid some marks of attention and respect to the chiefs or heads of these tribes; and have publicly nominated them captains over the rest; adding, at the same time, as a badge of office, a chain and staff, or pole, headed with silver or brass, with the arms of the Republic engraved on it. These chiefs, in return for these marks of distinction, are obliged to appear at certain periods at Capetown, before the Governor and Council, and there give an account of the people under them, and receive orders from the Dutch. After performing this duty, they are generally sent back with presents of gin, brandy, tobacco, iron and toys."

(From an account of the Colony written by Captain Robert Percival, who visited the Cape in 1796, *i.e.* the second year of the temporary British occupation.)

6. Slave Emancipation.

When the Slave Emancipation Act was passed on August 7, 1833, by the Imperial Parliament, £20,000,000 was voted as compensation to slave proprietors. The official valuation of the 35,000 slaves in the Cape was £3,000,000; but instead of this sum being paid, only £1,247,000 was apportioned to the Cape. Not only so, but the compensation money was made payable in London, and the colonists were compelled to employ agents, whose charges still further reduced the sums of money to which the claimants were entitled. Some owners refused to forward their claims at all; and in 1843 an unclaimed balance of £5906 due to the Cape proprietors of slaves was transferred from the National Debt office to the Master of the Supreme Court at Capetown, and by him invested to the credit of the Education Department on account of mission schools.

As originally passed, seven years' apprenticeship was allowed as an intermediate period; but this was shortened to five years'. August 1st,

1838, was the "day of freedom" elsewhere, but at the Cape on December 1, 1838, the former proprietors of slaves saw . . . "the whole of their farming pursuits and plans destroyed: no bribe, nor entreaty, I believe did avail in one single instance to induce any one of these now free persons to stay over that day . . ."

"In some places remunerative wages were offered . . . but in the Eastern country districts this was impossible, and the agriculturists there found themselves totally deprived of every vestige of labour to improve or cultivate their farms, or even to superintend or herd their flocks."

The above is taken from Judge Cloete's "Five Lectures on the Emigration of the Dutch Farmers," etc.

These were delivered before the Natal Society, and published at Capetown in 1856. They contain an expression of opinion rendered valuable by the fact that the writer was himself both a Dutch colonist and a high official, being in fact the Commissioner appointed to establish British authority over the emigrant farmers in Natal in 1843.

7. Origin of the Feud between the Missionaries and the Dutch Settlers.

[Circuit Courts were established by Lord Caledon in 1811.]

". . . The very first circuit which proceeded through the Colony was furnished with a calendar containing between 70 and 80 cases, of murders, aggravated assaults, and the like; which the missionaries Dr Van der Kemp and the Rev. J. Read, constituting themselves the protectors of the Hottentot race, and who had then established the first missionary school or location on the frontier (at Bethelsdorp) deliberately brought forward, and transmitted to the local government, as charges against the members of almost every respectable family on the frontier . . . it is but just to add, that of the long list of atrocious crimes thus enquired into with the utmost care and impartiality, not one single instance of murder was proved against the accused, although in a few cases acts of personal assault and transgression of some colonial law were brought home to them, and punished accordingly."

[The parties accused—there were 100 families involved and over 1000 witnesses summoned and examined—had to pay heavy expenses, because, under the then colonial law, the public prosecutor could claim costs in any event, and was himself entitled to double fees.]

. . . "all those results engendered a bitter feeling of hostility towards the administration of justice in general, and more particularly against the missionaries, who had brought forward these accumulated charges against such a number of colonists." (CLOETE.)

8. Origin of Kafir Wars.

The great Fish River was the eastern, and an imaginary line the northern, boundary of the colony as surrendered to the English. The arid deserts to the north forbade migration; on the eastern boundary the colonists were confronted by the Amakosa . . . "Who, far from allowing any inroads upon their own territories, commenced a system of aggression upon our colonists, which extended over the greatest part of the Graaf Reinet and Uitenhage districts, from which they were not finally expelled until the year 1812. But this system of aggression they have never abandoned, but on the contrary have perseveringly carried on for nearly seventy years; each succeeding war having only formed them into a more dangerous, experienced, and vindictive foe." (CLOETE.)

Kafir methods of warfare.

"The Kafir, at the first onset, is perhaps less ferocious than cunning, and more intent upon improving his own interests by theft than in taking life from the mere spirit of cruelty: but once roused, he is like the wild beast after the taste of blood, and loses all the best attributes of humanity. The movement of a body of these savages through the land may be likened to 'a rushing and mighty wind.' On, on they sweep! like a blast; filling the air with a strange *whirr*—reminding one, on a grand scale, of a flight of locusts.

"An officer [in the war of 1835] had his attention suddenly arrested by a cloud of dust; then a silent mass appeared, and lo! a multitude of beings, more resembling demons than men, rushed past. There were no noises, no sound of footsteps, nothing but the shiver of the assegais, which gleamed as they dashed onwards."

Attack on Fort Peddie.

This was an incident in the "War of the Axe" (1846-48). Fort Peddie was "a mere earthen embankment" held by a handful of soldiers. The account is that of "an eye-witness" published in a frontier paper.

"Were it not that life and death were concerned in it, I should have pronounced it [the attack] a most beautiful sight. The Kaffir commanders sent their aides-de-camp from one party to another, just as you would see it done on a field day with European troops. The main bodies were continually increasing with horse and footmen, and soon after eleven the array was truly terrific. The largest body was to the westward; finding their schemes of drawing the troops out did not succeed, small parties advanced in skirmishing order, and then the two divisions of Pato and the Gaikas moved towards each other, as if intending a combined attack on some given point. Colonel Lindsay was superintending the working of the gun himself, and, as soon as a body of Gaikas came within range, a shot was sent into the midst of them. . . . The Kaffirs now extended themselves in a line six miles in length. These advancing at the same time so filled the valley that it seemed a mass of moving Kaffirs; rockets and shells were poured rapidly on them, and presently a tremendous fire of musketry poured over our heads. The enemy, however, did not come near enough for the infantry to play upon them, and only a few shots were fired from the infantry barracks. . . . The actual fighting was between the Fingoes and the Kaffirs; the troops could not have gone out without exposing the forts to danger, as there were masses ready to pour in from all quarters." (From Mrs Harriet Ward's "Five Years in Kaffirland.")

9. Sir George Grey's Kafir Policy.

Sir George Grey (1) established schools and hospitals, (2) broke down the power of the chiefs by (a) purchasing from them by monthly stipends the right to inflict fines and punishments, and introducing European Magistrates to administer justice, (b) discrediting witch-doctors who were the instruments of the chief's cupidity, (3) substituted individual for tribal tenure of land.

The measures thus initiated have since been adopted as the basis of the native policy of the Cape Government.

"The aim of the policy of the Colonial Government since 1855 has been to establish and maintain peace, to diffuse civilisation and Christianity, and to establish society on the basis of individual property and personal industry. The agencies employed are the magistrate, the missionary, the schoolmaster, and the trader." (Noble, "History of South Africa.")

To this statement we may add a pregnant remark of Sir Langham Dale (Late Superintendent General of Education).

"Every native who owns a plot of land or a plough or a wagon and oxen is a hostage for peace."

Another measure of Sir George Grey was the introduction of a body (2000) of agricultural immigrants from Germany into the valley of the Buffalo river (East London is the port) in 1858-59. These immigrants formed a useful complement to the military settlers of the Anglo-German legion previously introduced in 1857.

Sir George Grey is also remarkable for the daring assumption of personal responsibility by which, in Lord Malmesbury's words, he "probably saved India." In September 1858, he despatched the returning troops from China to India, and "stripped the colony of troops to aid the Indian Government."

10. Sir George Grey's forecast.

The necessity for a federal union of the South African States was clearly stated by Sir George Grey in a despatch to Sir E. B. Lytton, dated November 19, 1858. It must be remembered that he (Grey) had seen the provincial governments of New Zealand successfully united by a central government. The whole despatch contains a masterly review of the conditions created by the previous policy of non-interference, and a no less masterly forecast of future dangers.

Of the general results of the non-interference policy he writes:—

"16. The defects of the system thus described [i.e. the recognition of the Dutch Republics, the separation of Natal, and the abandonment of the Native chiefs—measures which he has collectively called 'the dismemberment of South Africa'] appear to be that the country must be always at war in some direction, as some one of the several states, in pursuit of its supposed interests, will be involved in difficulties, either with some European or native state. Every such war forces all the other states into a position of an armed neutrality or of interference. For, if the state is successful in the war it is waging, a native race will be broken up, and none can tell what territories its dispersed hordes may fall upon. Nor can the other states be assured that the coloured tribes generally will not sympathise in the war, and that a general rising may not take place. Ever since South Africa has been broken up in the manner above detailed, large portions of it have always been in a state of constant anxiety and apprehension from these causes. The smallness and weakness of the states, and a knowledge that they are isolated bodies, bound by no ties of interest or common government with other states, has encouraged the natives to resist and dare them, whilst the nature of the existing treaties, and the utter abandonment of the natives by Great Britain, to whom they had hitherto looked up, has led the natives to combine for their mutual protection, and thus to acquire a sense of strength and boldness such as they have not hitherto shown; so that, whilst the Europeans have appeared to grow weak, they have felt themselves increase in strength and importance.

"17. Again, such petty states must be constant foci of intrigues and internal commotions, revolutions, or intestine wars. . . . "

Of the future attitude of the Dutch population he says :—

"14. I think there can be no doubt that, in any great public, or popular, or national question or movement, the mere fact of calling these people different nations would not make them so, nor would the fact of a mere fordable stream running between them sever their sympathies or prevent them from acting in unison. I think that many questions might arise in which, if the government on the south side of the Orange River took a different view from that on the north side of the river, it might be very doubtful which of the two governments the great mass of the people would obey."

This was the state of things which Sir Bartle Frere was, twenty years later, commissioned to remedy by giving effect to Lord Carnarvon's bill for "enabling the Union of South African Colonies and States," passed by the Imperial Parliament in 1877.

Extract from despatch of April 12, 1877 (Lord Carnarvon to Sir Bartle Frere).

"5. I request that you will lay this despatch with its enclosure (the draft bill) before the Houses of the Legislature, and [transmit copies to the Presidents of the Free State and of the Transvaal Republic]. I will only add an expression of my hope that they will perceive, in the alterations I have now made, a further evidence of my regard for the natural wish of any government or community which may propose to take advantage of the measure that no question should be prejudged which can properly be left open for subsequent consideration. [I have sent copies of the bill, &c., to the Lieutenant-Governor of Natal.]"

11. Prophecy of Nongase.

Nongase, niece of Umlakazi, prophesied that on Feb. 18, 1857, a hurricane would sweep the earth, the ancestors of the Kafirs would rise with countless herds of cattle, and that they, and the followers of the prophetess, would sweep the white men and the Fingoes from the earth. Under the influence of this promise the Kafirs destroyed their cattle and neglected to sow their corn. 50,000 died of starvation, 34,000 were brought into the Cape Colony and employed, and others were assisted in their own country. Sir George Grey had carefully watched the course of events, and made provision both for defending the frontier and assisting the starving Kafirs.

12. Annexation of the Transvaal.

The Justification for the annexation of the Transvaal (effected under instructions from Lord Carnarvon before Sir Bartle Frere commenced his period of Governorship) appears from the following :—

Extract from despatch of December 11, 1878 (Frere to Sir M. Hicks-Beach).

"32. The Zulu king and his 'dog' Sikukuni . . . were able to challenge the power that had destroyed Dingaan . . . and the English Government believed there was a very serious danger of Zulus and other native tribes driving back the white settlers in the Transvaal, and once more contesting the supremacy of race on our northern border.

"33. This danger was one main ground for the annexation of the Transvaal. . . .

"34. This is a sound argument . . . if we do really protect the Transvaal; but it will cease to secure acquiescence . . . unless [we 'let the natives know that if the English Government is non-aggressive, it is so from a sense of justice, and from no want of power ']."

13. Character of Ketshwayo.

In reply to a remonstrance from the Governor of Natal, on the subject of the murder of Zulu women, in which he was reminded of the promises he made on his coronation to the British representative then present, Ketshwayo said (1876):

"Did I ever tell Shepstone? Did he tell the white people I made such an arrangement? Because, if he did, he has deceived them. I do kill, but do not consider yet I have done anything in the way of killing. Why do the white people start at nothing? I have not yet begun. I have yet to kill; it is the custom of our nation, and I shall not depart from it. Why does the Governor of Natal speak to me about my laws? Do I go to Natal and dictate to him about his laws? I shall not agree to any laws or rules from Natal, and by so doing throw the great Kraal which I govern into the water. My people will not listen unless they are killed ; and, while wishing to be friends with the English, I do not agree to give over my people to laws sent by them. Have I not asked the English Government to allow me to wash my spears, since the death of my father Umpandi, and they have kept playing with me all this time, and treating me like a child? Go back and tell the English that I shall act on my own account, and if they wish me to agree to their laws, I shall leave and become a wanderer; but before I go it will be seen, as I shall not go without having acted. Go back and tell the white man this, and let them hear it well. The Governor of Natal and I are equal. He is governor of Natal, and I am governor here." (From despatch of Frere, December 10, 1878.)

14. Recall of Sir Bartle Frere.

The reasons for the defeat of the Colonial Government and the failure of the proposal for a Federation Conference in June 1880, appear from the following :—

Extracts from Sir Bartle Frere's despatch of August 3, 1880, replying to telegraphic announcement of his recall sent by Lord Kimberley on August 1.

In 5. he complains of the unfairness of leaving him in office "condemned to removal upon change of government" [the Liberals came in power in the spring of this year], and "weakened and discredited by the want of the full confidence of their successors, to attempt such a task as forwarding the policy of a union of South African Provinces." And continues :

"7. My ministers loyally made the attempt . . . relying on the tradition that the varying political views of parties in England did not influence the great lines of English colonial policy, and that in attempting the task undertaken at the desire of your lordship's predecessor, they would enjoy the benefit of the hearty support of Her Majesty's present Government.

"13. [The position of the Transvaal . . . was an essential element in the question of South African union. There were present in the colony at the time delegates from the disaffected party in the Transvaal], ably directed by leading members of the local opposition. They were generally believed to be in close correspondence with some leading members of the Liberal party in England, who were said to assure them of success . . . [Members of the Cape Parliament who represented Dutch constituencies were asked to postpone the Conference proposals to the question of cancelling the annexation of the Transvaal]."

Lord Kimberley says, in his reply to this despatch (addressed to the Administrator of the Cape, and dated October 14, 1884) :—

That (1) there has not been "the smallest indication of any difference of opinion between Her Majesty's Government and Sir Bartle Frere" on the question of Confederation ; (2) that it was precisely for this reason that the Government of the Colony was not taken out of Sir Bartle Frere's hands on the change of Government in England, and because they did not wish it to seem that they withdrew their support from him and his Colonial ministers "at the critical moment when the conference resolutions were about to be brought before the Cape Parliament."

The despatch concludes,

"6. Her Majesty's Government fully recognise that Sir Bartle Frere failed in carrying through that policy from no shortcoming on his own part, and they are content to accept his statements of the reason of that failure as evidence that the causes lie much deeper than any mere personal considerations."

Of these "causes," the strongest was the sympathy of the Colonists of Dutch extraction at the Cape with their kinsmen in the Transvaal. In fact, the words of Sir George Grey (written in 1858) had come true. The whole Dutch population in South Africa were "acting in unison."

15. The relationship of England to the Transvaal.

Extract from a despatch of Sir Michael Hicks-Beach to Sir Garnet Wolseley, November 20, 1879.

"4. . . . The power and authority of England have for many years been paramount there [*i.e.* in the Transvaal]; and neither by the Sand River Convention of 1852, nor at any other time, did Her Majesty's Government surrender the right and duty of requiring that the Transvaal should be governed with a view to the common safety of the various European communities. It has long been obvious that the largest measure of freedom which the country could enjoy consistently with the fulfilment of this condition, would be found in that union which seems to have been contemplated by the Volksraad in 1877, when by a resolution quoted and adopted in the memorial of the Boer Committee, dated April 16, and again in their memorandum of the same date, they declared their readiness to enter into a closer union with Her Majesty's Colonies for the benefit of South Africa.

"5. As there has never been any room for doubting that Her Majesty's power would continue to be supreme in South Africa, the union provided for by the South African Act, 1877, is practically that which the people of the Transvaal have professed to desire; and it is obvious that, as a member of a South African Confederation, the country might receive a constitution which would confer upon the people, under the paramount authority of the British Crown, the fullest independence compatible with that thorough unity of action which the common welfare demands; and would enable them practically to govern themselves according to their own views in all matters, except those as to which an independent power, unless determined to be hostile, would be obliged to co-operate with its neighbours."

16. The attitude of the Orange Free State.

Extract from telegram of President Brand, Bloemfontein, to Consul for Orange Free State, London (Feb. 15, 1881).

". . . As soon as I heard that a collision had taken place, I ordered circulars to be written to our border Landdrosts, to publish and make known to our Field Cornets and Burghers that, as their President and Friend, I requested and directed them to abstain from taking any part in the unfortunate state of affairs; that by so doing the time might perhaps come when, by our friendly offices, the Government and people of the Free State might be of real service to secure the blessings of peace, and assist in a satisfactory settlement."

Extract from Sir Evelyn Wood's despatch announcing agreement to terms (March 21, 1881):—

" Brand's presence has been invaluable." (c—2837.)

17. The attitude of the Africander party in the Cape Colony.

Telegrams from Mr Hofmeyr, the leader of the Africander party in the Cape Colony, to General Joubert.

" March 8.

" Friends have heard with great pleasure armistice, as promising of peace. Believe British Government anxious to meet wishes of Boers, but difficulty is how to grant concession either before you have desisted from opposition, or British arms victorious. We pray you help Government, by adopting conciliatory tone, and offering desist from armed opposition, on tacit understanding that no further use be made by British of such desisting than to send limited number of troops across border, and provisioning garrisons. Also hope if Commissioners proposed if either Wood or Robinson, with Brand and Villiers, you will not hesitate accept, if such commission have full power."

" March 11.

" After a thorough investigation by my friends, independence can be secure in no other way than as follows: the assembly of a Commission as proposed in my former telegram; should the Commission be appointed with full power, your conditional independence must be begged for through the people as a reclamation; but in any case, before the Commission can be appointed, either the British arms must have conquered, or the Boers must have given a tangible proof of submission in the eyes of the world; consider earnestly I pray you what is said in my previous telegram; also that, in case no agreement is come to, the armistice will give rise to great dissatisfaction among the Boers, and give occasion for fresh accusation of untrustworthiness against the Boers. God give you peace." (c—2837.)

18. The Retrocession of the Transvaal.

Letter of Sir George Colley to General Joubert before the advance upon the Boer position at Langsnek.

"Head Quarters Camp, Fort Amiel,
"January 23, 1881.

"SIR,

"I duly received the letter of December 17, signed by yourself and other leaders of the insurgents; and, simultaneously with it, the news of the attacks made at different points on Her Majesty's forces. . . .

"The men who follow you are, many of them, ignorant, and know and understand little of anything outside their own camp. But you, who are well educated and have travelled, cannot but be aware how hopeless is the struggle you have embarked upon, and how little any accidental success can affect the ultimate result. To save, therefore, the innocent lives that must be sacrificed and the blood that must be uselessly spilt in a prolonged resistance, I call upon you to dismiss your followers; and when the forces now in arms against Her Majesty have dispersed, I shall be prepared to give attention to, and to forward to Her Majesty's Government for consideration, any representations which are made to me of grievances under which any of Her Majesty's subjects in the Transvaal believe themselves to suffer.

"I have, &c."

Joubert's reply.

"Camp of Commandant General,
"January 27, 1881.

". . . We are unable to satisfy your demands in terms of your letter. So long as your Excellency addresses us as rebels, and intimates that the leaders are contemptuously misleading a multitude of ignorant people, it is utterly hopeless for us to find proper words to reply.

"But before God we would not be justified if we did not avail ourselves of this, perhaps the last opportunity, of speaking to you, as the representative of Her Majesty the Queen and the people of England, for whom we have the highest respect.

"We must emphatically repeat that we are willing to assist in respect of the wishes of the Imperial Government for the Confederation of South Africa.

[Refers to the Proclamation of the Triumvirate] . . . "We would be satisfied with the cancellation of the annexation and the restoration of the South African Republic under the patronage of Her Majesty the Queen, so that once a year the British Flag shall be hoisted, all in strict accordance with the above-mentioned claim of our first proclamation.

"If your Excellency perseveres to refute this, we shall submit ourselves to our destiny. But the Lord will provide.

"I have, &c." (c—2866.)

Colley moved out and attacked on January 28. Then followed Langsnek (Jan. 28); Ingogo Heights (Feb. 8); Majuba Hill, and death of Colley (Feb. 27).

The terms actually offered by Sir Evelyn Wood, and accepted by the Boers, were these :—

(i.) Complete amnesty to all, including leaders, except to persons who had committed acts contrary to rules of civilised warfare. (Despatch of Colonial Secretary of March 8.)

(ii.) Commission named—Sir H. Robinson, Chief Justice de Villiers, and Sir E. Wood; President Brand to be present at proceedings.

(iii.) Complete self-government under British suzerainty, with British Resident at Pretoria; provision to be made for (*a*) protection of native interests, (*b*) arrangement of frontier affairs, and (*c*) relations with Foreign Powers by the Commission.

(iv.) Complete self-government to be granted, at latest, within six months. (Despatch of Colonial Secretary of March 12, and Sir E. Wood of March 21.)

They were ratified on receipt of telegram from Colonial Secretary on March 22. (c—2837.)

19. Behaviour of British troops in action against the Boers.

The charge of the 58th at Langsnek.

"Colonel Deane, with splendid gallantry, tried to carry the hill by a rush. His horse was shot but he extricated himself, and, dashing forward on foot, fell, riddled with bullets, ten yards in front of the foremost man . . . the 58th, which had fallen back leisurely (supported by part of the 60th), without haste or confusion, reformed at the foot of the hill, and marched back into position in as good order, and with as erect and soldierly bearing, as when it marched out." (From despatch of Commander Romilly.)

Corporal Farmer and Private Murray were recommended respectively for the Victoria Cross and the Distinguished Service Medal, by General Sir Evelyn Wood, for bravery displayed at Majuba Hill.

"Corporal Farmer showed a spirit of self-abnegation, and an example of cool bravery which cannot be too highly commended. While the Boers closed with our troops near the wells, Corporal Farmer held a white flag over the wounded, and when the arm holding the flag was shot through, he called out that he had 'another.' He then raised the flag with the other arm and continued to do so until that also was pierced by a bullet.

"Private John Murray was close to the brow over our line of advance during the final forward movement of the Boers. A Scotchman in the Boer ranks called upon Private Murray to surrender. The latter replied 'I'll see you d——d first,' and jumped down, receiving a bullet-wound in the arm. Half-way down the hill his knee fell out of joint, but, obtaining the assistance of a comrade to restore it to place, he returned at six o'clock with his rifle and side-arms to camp, where he was seen by Second-Lieutenant Sinclair-Wemyss, of the 22nd Highlanders." (From despatch of General Wood to Secretary for War.)

It is noticeable that three companies of the 92nd Highlanders—the regiment which was most distinguished in the march to Candahar—were in action at Majuba. (c—2950.)

20. Mr Pearson's argument from Natal.

Natal is a case in point, and "the case of Natal is most instructive for what may be expected in Africa generally" (p. 36). In 1891 the colony had a European population of only 36,000 out of a total of 481,000 inhabitants. Moreover, "the lower races have nearly doubled since 1863, when one-seventh of the population was European."

The weak point in Mr Pearson's argument is the absence of analogy between Natal and "Africa" as a whole. Africa cannot increase by immigration, but only by natural increment.

(1) But in Natal the growth of the Native population is not due to natural increment, but mainly to immigration. The Kafirs are attracted by the leniency and security of British rule, and these immigrants have sometimes travelled 500 or 600 miles on foot from the interior. (Peace, "Our Colony of Natal," p. 44.)

(2) The growth of commerce has enhanced the value of the cow, an animal adopted by the Kafir as the general measure of wealth, and, in particular, the medium in which the bride-price is paid. The Natal Legislature, so far from fearing the increase of the natives, have actually had to pass a law, fixing the legal maximum price for a bride at *ten* cows, in order to prevent the operation of this check on marriage. (Natal Laws, 1891, No. 19.)

(3) Mr Pearson's figures do not allow for a recent increase in the white population due to immigration. The figures, as given by the Colonial Office Report (1891-92), are as follows:—

	1879.	1891.
Whites,	22,654	46,788
Indian Coolies,	16,999	41,142
Kafirs,	319,934	455,983

21. Change of opinion in the Cape Colony.

The following extract is from Mr Leonard's (late Attorney-General) speech at the meeting held on September 24, 1884, at Capetown, to protest against the abandonment of Bechuanaland (and the trade route to the interior) by England. This meeting was termed by the *Volksblad* "the most important meeting held in the colony since that held in 1849 to protest against the formation of a penal settlement at the Cape." His words indicate that a great change had taken place in the public opinion of the colony, as compared with that prevalent in 1879-1880 (the period of the Transvaal War). In fact, for the first time the question of the northward expansion of the whites was recognised to be a question of civilisation, and not one of racial jealousy.

"Certain individuals in this colony, and certain individuals in the interior states have made up their mind to trade upon the ignorance of the poor people in the Transvaal, who think the people of Great Britain have been defeated at Laings Nek and Majuba, and the object of their intrigues is to destroy the British supremacy in South Africa. . . . This has been the object of some of the people of the Transvaal, and *per fas et nefas* to make this colony a hidebound dependency of the British Crown. Their object has been . . . to cross our northern boundary, to take land down to the Indian Ocean on the East, and down to the Kalahari on the West, in order that this portion of the British Empire may for ever be shut in, and British sentiment be destroyed; that so the Transvaal, by its powers of unlimited expansion, shall become the paramount state in South Africa; and with them is to rest whether we shall be graciously allowed to guard our coasts, or whether that simple privilege shall be denied us. . . .

"It would be a disastrous thing to everyone if Great Britain should lose her supremacy here; and the withdrawal of the British flag from this country would be disastrous not only to loyal subjects of Her Majesty, but to the sedition-mongers, the traitors, and the rascals who have for years past endeavoured to break down our British supremacy. All South Africa would then be reduced to the same state as the Transvaal—a country without a Government—and I should be sorry to see this colony in the state of the South African Republic; and I should be sorry to see this country under the flag of mighty Germany or of Republican France.

"Well, gentlemen, I came to say my say, and I think I have said it. We, as loyal subjects of the Queen, as law-abiding and law-loving people, whether born subjects of Her Majesty or not, have been challenged to say our say, we have been told England durst not move hand nor foot to maintain her honour, to uphold her supremacy, because of the colonists. I am not going to speak of the colonists of Rooi Grond, who slaughter young people of five, six, seven, and eight years of age, nor of colonists who shoot women, but I claim to-night to speak for ten thousand, or one hundred thousand, in this colony, and I say that is our answer to the taunt which has been put upon us." (From the *Cape Times*, September 25, 1884.)

22. The Diamond Laws.

Under the Trade in Diamonds Consolidation Act (No. 48, 1882), (inter alia) :—

(1) It is declared unlawful for any person to have in his possession any rough or uncut diamond unless he is able to produce his proper permit for the same, or to account satisfactorily for, or prove his right to, the possession of the same. Only duly licensed dealers, etc., are permitted to buy, etc., any rough or uncut diamond. The penalty for contravention is a fine not exceeding £1000, or imprisonment up to fifteen years, or both.

(2) Persons finding diamonds on private property are required to make a declaration of the fact within fourteen days to the Resident Magistrate of the district.

(3) All persons authorised to deal, etc., in diamonds are required to keep a register of their transactions. Such record including (*a*) date of purchases, etc.; (*b*) name of consigner, cutter, seller, buyer, owner, etc.; (*c*) weight of each parcel; (*d*) number of stones of 10 carats and upwards in each parcel; (*e*) price paid or received; (*f*) weight of a single stone valued by buyer at over £100. A copy of this register must be forwarded every month to the Chief of Police, etc., and produced when required.

The operation of this Act is confined to "the district forming the late Territory of Griqualand West"; but a subsequent Act (No. 14 of 1885), extends its operation (with slight modification) to the whole of the Cape Colony.

23. The Transvaal Gold Laws.

By the law of 1872, the right to all minerals and precious stones is declared to be vested in the State. This and subsequent enactments were codified in 1885 by the "Consolidated Gold Law."

The President with the consent of the Executive Council is empowered to declare both Government and private lands to be "public diggings"; and further provisions secure an equitable distribution of the prospective mineral wealth between the government, the owner (if private land), the prospector or discoverer, and the public.

The owner is entitled to (1) a *mijnpacht* or mining lease over not more than one-tenth of the "farm" or estate; (2) "owner's claims" in proportion to the extent of the farm but not exceeding ten in number, and certain "preferent claims" for his nominees; (3) one-half of the proceeds of diggers' or prospectors' licences, and three-fourths of the "stand" (or building) licences. The mijnpacht is granted for not less than five, nor more than twenty years, and is renewable.

The prospector or discoverer is entitled to six claims free of licence so long as they remain registered in his name.

The Government provides officials for the administration of justice and the collection of licence fees and other revenue. The rent on the area covered by the mijnpacht is fixed at 10s. per morgen (two acres). Prospectors' licences are issued at 5s. per month, and entitle the licensees to hold and examine claims. Diggers' licences are issued at 15s. or 20s. (with machinery). The Government also takes one-fourth of the "stand" licences.

In extent the claims measure :—(1) 30 × 30 Dutch feet (30 Dutch are equal to 31 English feet) for precious stones; (2) 150 × 150 for alluvial mining; (3) 150 on the strike × 400 on the dip for quartz mining. Only Europeans can hold claims, and each claim must be pegged off and registered in the name of a separate person.

The Transvaal claim rights are identical with those of the Spanish "custom" in the Americas. The claim holder is only entitled to work minerals within the limits of the surface boundary carried vertically downwards. He cannot follow the reef in all its "dips, spurs, and angles," as is the case in the United States. In consequence of this limitation claims have been secured on the Randt for more than a mile southwards across the dips; and it is combinations of these claims which constitute the properties of the "deep-level" Companies.

24. The Chemical Processes in use on the Randt.

Chlorination. The concentrates obtained by the vanner from the pyritic ore are (1) roasted to rid them of sulphur, (2) charged into vats and permeated by chlorine gas for sixty hours or a sufficient period for the gold to combine with the chlorine. The chloride of gold thus formed is (3) dissolved by the introduction of water, and, after the solution has been freed from sand and iron oxides, it is run into precipitating vats, and the gold which it contains is (4) precipitated by sulphate of iron. These precipitates are (5) collected and smelted into bars of almost pure gold. By this process 95 per cent. of the gold is recovered from the concentrates, an amount which represents 9·5 of the total recovery of 90 per cent. obtained by all processes from the pyritic ore.

Cyaniding. The tailings left by the vanners are charged into vats where the gold is (1) dissolved out of the mass by successive solutions of cyanide of potassium. These auriferous solutions are carried into precipitating boxes, and the gold which they contain is (2) precipitated by the medium of zinc scrap. By this process 70 per cent. of the gold in the tailings is recovered, or 21 per cent. of the total extraction by all processes.

25. Extract from Mr Hamilton Smith's article in *Times*, February 19, 1895.

"In the report of 1892 I estimated for the length of 11 miles the average thickness of the ore to be worked was 5 ft.; I should now estimate it to be 6 ft., but I find in many mines that a good deal of poorer ore has been left standing, so that the average yield from this thickness of 6 ft., when it is all mined, will be less than the 13 dwt.

before given. My opinion, though, as given in 1892 of the quantity of gold to be extracted remains unchanged, the greater thickness compensating for the smaller yield per ton. In 1894 the value of the Randt gold bullion was £7,000,000, and this without any increase from the new deep-level mines; these latter will become fairly productive in 1897, so for that year a product of fully £10,000,000 can be fairly expected. Judging from present appearances, the *maximum* product of the Randt will be reached about the end of this century, when it will probably exceed £12,500,000 per annum. In addition to the yield which may be expected from the main reef series, I think, in a few years a considerable quantity of gold will be produced from other reefs, especially from what is called the "black reef." This reef, with perhaps one exception, thus far appears to be what in mining parlance is called "spotted," the ore varying greatly in value in the distance of a few feet. Very likely more money will be lost than made in working this deposit, but the gold from it may in time add appreciably to the bullion output of the district.

From the foregoing statement it is evident that the chances are far greater now than they were in 1892, of my conjectures of that date being realised, and to-day nearly every one conversant with the Randt considers them as being considerably under the mark. The Randt for 1894 with its product of £7,000,000 stands third in the world, the United States still remaining first with its greatly increased output of over £9,000,000, and Australasia (Australia, New Zealand, and Tasmania) being probably second with a product of about £8,000,000. In 1849 the world's product of gold was about £6,000,000, which increased to something over £30,000,000 in 1853, owing to the discovery and working of the rich placers of California and Australia; from 1853 the yield steadily declined until in 1883 it had fallen to less than £20,000,000. Since 1887 the yield has advanced by leaps and bounds, the increase being chiefly due to the new discoveries in South Africa, until for 1894 the product has most probably amounted to fully 8,600,000 ounces of fine gold, worth over £36,500,000, an output certainly much greater than that for any previous year in the history of the world. In 1853 it was evident that the great yield from both California and Australia would be short-lived, whereas the probabilities now are that this great product of £36,500,000 will be fully maintained for quite a number of years to come; and yet, in spite of this fact and this belief, the prices of commodities generally in use, such as wheat, cotton, wool, sugar, iron, copper, &c., are now lower than they have been for the past hundred years. It has been generally accepted that one of the principal causes of the rise in the price of standard articles from 1849 to 1860 was due to the influx of gold from California and Australia. Will the same rise in values measured by the ounce of gold take place in the coming five years? This is a question of vast importance to all of us, from the richest capitalist to the poorest labourer. I see that at least one authority of position seems to be of the opinion that the probable rise in prices due to this great flood of gold will have the effect of so increasing the cost of mining and reduction that many mines in the Randt will be compelled to suspend work. This, I think, is an altogether erroneous view, for should general prices recover to their level of ten or fifteen years ago, this additional cost would be fully compensated for by the increased economies which year by year will be carried into effect in operating the Randt mines; so, unless a mountain of gold should be discovered somewhere or other, the Randt will in every probability continue to increase its yield for at least five or six years to come."

26. Equality of Natives.

Baron von Hübner says :—

"Experience has shown the impossibility in the long run of governing colonies of mixed population, where the blacks form the large majority, by means of a responsible or Parliamentary Government. Thus Jamaica has asked, on its own initiative, to be made a Crown Colony. Natal, on the representation of Lord Wolseley, did the same. Cape Colony, I have been told confidentially by politicians in Capetown, will be obliged sooner or later to follow suit." ("Through the British Empire," vol. i. p. 146.)

Against this, Sir Hercules Robinson says :—

"Responsible Government . . . has been a complete success notwithstanding that the natives within the represented districts exceed the Europeans in the proportion probably of nearly two to one. Where responsible Government at the Cape has broken down has been in the attempt to govern extra-colonial native territories, such as Basutoland and the Transkei." (*Times*, March 4, 1884.)

27. The Glen Grey Act (August 1894).

The objects of the Act, as disclosed by the full title, are "to provide for the disposal of lands and for the administration of local affairs within the district of Glen Grey and other proclaimed districts."

Glen Grey (with reservations of lands owned by individuals or public bodies, etc.) is to be divided into locations, and the locations into allotments of four morgen (8 acres), to be held on perpetual quit-rent (15s.) tenure by individual natives.

Each location, with its respective commonage, is to be placed under the control of three persons, being resident holders of land within the location, "who shall be appointed by the Governor after the consideration of the wishes and recommendations of the resident holders of land in the location," and hold office for one year. These "Location Boards" can be invested with the powers, etc., of "Village Boards of Management" by the Governor's regulations. (Part I. §§ 2-16.)

The *succession* to the allotment is regulated by the provisions of §§ 24 and 25 :—"The allotment and other immovable property of every registered holder shall not be capable of being devised by will, but upon his or her decease shall devolve upon and be claimable according to the rule of primogeniture by one male person to be called the heir," and to be determined by the table given in § 24.

The *Labour tax* is treated in Part IV. §§ 33-36 :—" Every male native residing in the district, exclusive of natives in possession of lands under ordinary quit-rent titles, or in freehold, who, in the judgment of the Resident Magistrate, is fit for and capable of labour, shall pay in to the public revenue a tax of ten shillings per annum." But a native is excepted, (1) for a year, if he has been in service beyond the district for at least three months of the preceding twelve months; (2) from any further payment, if he has been in service for a total period, consecutive or otherwise, of not less than three years. Also the Resident Magistrate may exempt a native for one year on certain grounds (among them employment within the district for three months).

The powers, etc., of the *District Councils* are contained in Part V. §§ 37-59 :—These councils are to consist of twelve members, of whom six are appointed by the Governor and six are selected by the members of the Location Boards. The Resident Magistrate is an additional member of the Council ex-officio, and, when present, is to act as chairman. The Council is empowered to levy a rate not exceeding 2d. in the pound on the rateable property within the district, and a rate of not less than 5s. on every adult male native, excepting natives in possession of lands under ordinary quit-rent title or in freehold.

Liquor licences are dealt with in Part VI. §§ 60-64 :—The principle of local option is adopted, and no new licences are to be granted by the Licencing Court, except after a resolution has been passed by a majority of the members of the District Council approving of the issue of the licence. Old licences may be renewed, except they are condemned by a two-thirds majority of the District Council (§ 63).

28. The Conquest of Mashonaland by the Matabele Zulus.

"Some fifty years ago this fine country must have been thickly inhabited, as almost every valley has, at one time or another, been under cultivation. The sites of villages are also very numerous, though now only marked by a few deep pits from which the natives obtained the clay used by them for plastering their huts and making their cooking pots; and also the presence usually of a cluster of huge acacia-trees, which grow to a far greater size on the sites of old villages than anywhere else. On the summit of every hill may be found the walls, in more or less perfect preservation, of what, I think, must have been cattle kraals. These walls are very neatly built of squared stones, nicely fitted together, but uncemented with any kind of mortar. The peaceful people inhabiting this part of Africa must then have been in the zenith of their prosperity. Herds of their small but beautiful cattle lowed in every valley, and their rich and fertile country doubtless afforded them an abundance of vegetable food. About 1840, however, the Matabele Zulus, under their warlike chief, Unziligazi, settled in the country which they now inhabit, and very soon bands of these ferocious and bloodthirsty savages overran the peaceful vales of the

Mashuna country in every direction. The poor Mashunas, unskilled in war, and living, moreover, in small communities scattered all over the country, without any central government, fell an easy prey before the fierce invaders, and very soon every stream in their country ran red with their blood, whilst vultures and hyænas feasted undisturbed amidst the ruins of their devastated homes. Their cattle, sheep, and goats were driven off by their conquerors, and their children, when old enough to walk and not above ten or twelve years of age, were taken for slaves; the little children too young to walk were, of course, killed together with their mothers. In a very few years there were no more Mashunas left in the open country, the remnant that had escaped massacre having fled into the mountainous districts to the south and east of their former dwellings, where they still live. Thus, in a short time an immense extent of fertile country that had, perhaps, for ages past supported a large and thriving community, was again given back to nature; and so it remains to the present day—an utterly uninhabited country, roamed over at will by herds of elands and other antelopes." (Selous: "Travel and Adventure in Africa," pp. 80-81.)

29. Transvaal Legislation.

The Enactments of the Raad during the year 1896 include the following:—

Name of Measure.	Purpose or Effect.
Revision of the Grondwet, or Constitution.	Three months' notice of new law (by publication in the *Staats Courant*) no longer necessary.
New Press Law.	President can prohibit, entirely, or temporarily, dissemination of publications printed outside the Republic; political articles must bear name of writer, and writer, editor, printer, publisher and distributors are rendered liable to severe penalties if the matter is held to be dangerous to the interests of the Republic.
Aliens' Expulsion Law.	Any stranger dangerous to public peace and order may be expelled by order of the President within 14 days. Burghers can appeal to the High Court; but Uitlanders have no such right, being liable to six months' imprisonment if they refuse to obey (and then to be forcibly expelled).
Education Law.	Gives power to Superintendent of Education (Dr Mansvelt, a Hollander) to provide for education of non-Dutch speaking children whose parents reside on the gold-fields. This law leaves the requirements of the Uitlanders entirely in the

Name of Measure.	Purpose or Effect.
	hands of a Government official who is notoriously in favour of the policy of making the Uitlanders learn to speak Dutch. Out of £103,000 set apart for education for current year, £800 only is assigned for English schools. (See next note.)
The Johannesburg Municipality Law.	The Mayor is to be *appointed* by the Government; one half of the Members of the Municipal Council are to be elected by the *burghers*, and the remaining half by the inhabitants. In other words the control is given to the very small number of Boers and Hollanders (chiefly officials) resident in the town.
The Liquor Law.	The sale of intoxicating drinks to natives on the gold-fields is prohibited. If this law is enforced its effect will be most beneficial.
The Aliens' Admission Law.	After January 1st, 1897, all immigrants must be furnished with either (1) a regular passport, which must show that they have sufficient means to support themselves; or (2) evidence of identity and capacity to support themselves, and obtain from a Field Cornet, or other officer of the Republic, a travelling and residing passport. This latter is to be renewed every three months. But if the holder declares his intention to settle in the Republic, it need only be renewed every twelve months.

30. The Population of Johannesburg.

An official census was taken under the authority of the Sanitary Board between July 15th and Oct. 21st, 1896. It shows the total population living within a three-mile radius of the Market-square to number 102,078 persons. Of these 50,907 are Europeans, 42,533 Natives, 4,807 Asiatics, 952 Malays, and the remaining 2,879 are returned as of mixed and other races.

The *origin* of the Europeans is shown to be as follows:—

Place of Birth.

United Kingdom,	16,265.
Cape Colony	15,162.
Transvaal,	6,205.
Russia,	3,335.
Germany,	2,262.
Holland,	819.
France,	402.

With additions from Sweden and Norway, Italy, Switzerland and other countries.

The *political states* of the 25,058 European males over 16 years of age is as follows:—

    1,039 are burghers, or citizens of the Republic.
    516 are naturalised subjects.
    23,503 have no vote.

The *educational position* appears from the fact that out of 13,391 European children under 15 years of age, 6,992 are unable to read or write, and are not undergoing instruction of any kind.

The *relation of the Sexes* is shown by the fact that there are 32,387 European Males and 18,520 European females. And of 31,981 married persons, 22,968 are males and 9,013 females.

31. The Rinderpest.

The Zambesi cattle fever, or rinderpest, broke out at Buluwayo on March 5th, 1896. By High Commissioner's proclamation of March 9th, the removal of cattle without permission was forbidden, and powers were given to the Cattle Inspector to isolate and destroy affected cattle, etc. Notwithstanding the enforcement of the regulations the disease made its way to Palapye, in the Bechuanaland Protectorate; and on March 11th, the High Commissioner advised the Transvaal Government of the fact. President Krüger at once forbade the importation of cattle from Rhodesia and the Bechuanaland Protectorate. Every effort was made by Mr Newton, the Resident Commissioner at Mafeking to stay the progress of the disease in the Protectorate. On May 9th the Treasury sanctioned the expenditure of £50,000 by the Imperial authorities for the purpose of compensating the owners of sound cattle which were slaughtered, and for the distribution of food amongst the natives and the transport riders who were reduced to destitution by the loss of their cattle.

The Cape Government have attempted to stay the disease by constructing a fence across the Continent following the line of the Orange River, and guarding the fence by police. But according to a statement made by Mr F. R. Thompson, late Special Rinderpest Commissioner, to Reuter's Agency (published Nov. 19th, 1896) this measure has been undertaken too late.

"Now, after a lapse of six weeks, the fencing of the Orange River is being commenced, but as the rinderpest jumps sixty miles a day, it is too late."

"The Transvaal war, native rebellions, and the Jameson raid sink into insignificance compared with the present situation, which is undoubtedly the gravest that a British colony has ever had to face. The rinderpest will run through the whole of Cape Colony and Natal, and not 1 per cent. of the cattle in Cape Colony can be saved. I am persuaded that the pest will not stop until it reaches the dock gates at Cape Town.

To stop its course is now a matter of impossibility, and if the policy of killing cattle and compensating is pursued with the Colonial natives as in the north, my long experience of South Africa and its natives leads me to the conviction that we shall have to face one of the biggest wars Africa has ever experienced. It will be found that Zulus, Griquas, and Basutos will join hands, and, as it is a well-known fact that we could not beat the Basutos, what could be done in the case of such a combination as I have indicated ?

"Rinderpest is now in the old Cape Colony, at Bethulie, and all over the Free State. Natal is at present unaffected, but at Herschell —the great native centre which bounds the Free State—its presence may be expected at any hour."

Dr Otto Henning's account of the symptoms of the disease is as follows :—

This is a feverish disease of typical rapid course which spreads by contagion, and chiefly attacks cattle. Sheep, goats, and game are less liable ; human beings, horses, mules and donkeys do not get it.

A healthy animal which has come into contact with a sick one usually shows the first symptoms of the disease seven days after ; occasionally the period is considerably longer. General symptoms are fever, weariness, uneasiness, rough coat, failing appetite, increase of pulse and breathing, convulsive trembling of skin, rapid emaciation, and decline of strength.

Special symptoms.—One of the first and most constant is a frequent short cough, and thin slimy, afterwards mattery discharge from the inflamed and swollen mucous membrane of the nose, eyes and even mouth. On the 3rd (rarely so soon as the 2nd) day, diarrhœa sets in.

. . .

Sometimes small ulcers and sores are visible on the mucous membrane of the lips, gums and cheeks, and on those parts of the skin which can be licked.

Diseased animals rarely succumb earlier or later than from the 4th to the 7th day after the first symptoms have become manifest.

Experience has always shown that medical treatment is of no avail, but merely tends to spread the malady. It is therefore wisest and cheapest to destroy all animals affected at the earliest possible moment and all carcases, unskinned and complete, should be burnt carefully or deeply buried.

The disease does not originate through influences such as cold and fog, dew or rain, or bad food and water, but is solely due to a vegetable parasite, which is able to spread easily and rapidly. [C—8141.]

As a last resource, the Cape Government have summoned Dr Koch, the German scientist, to South Africa, and have commissioned him to investigate the disease with a view of discovering a possible remedy.

HISTORICAL SUMMARY.

B.C. 1700. Land of Punt (S.-E. Africa) conquered by the Egyptians.
1000. Solomon's Expedition to the land of Ophir (S.-E. Africa).
600. Voyage of Phœnician seamen (from Red Sea) round Africa.
A.D. 35. Sabaean King Kharabit is in possession of the E. coast of Africa.

Portuguese Period.

1486. Discovery of the Cape (Cabo Tormentoso) by Bartholomew Diaz.
1497. Vasco da Gama sails to India by the Cape.
1505. Alvarez de Cahal occupies Sofala (East Coast).
1580. Sir Francis Drake passes the Cape on his (return) voyage round the world.

Dutch Period.

1602. Netherlands East India Company chartered.
1648. Wreck of the *Haarlem* in Table Bay.
1652. Arrival of expedition under Van Riebeck.

Government by the Dutch East India Company.

1657. Nine of the Company's servants settled as "free burghers" at Rondebosch.
1679. Simon Van der Stell appointed Commander.
1688. } Huguenot emigration.
1689. }
1709. The use of French in official communications forbidden.
1714. Returns show Capetown has 300 houses, and that whole population of settlement = free burghers, 647 men, 341 women, 900 children, employing 93 men servants, and owning 1178 male, 240 female slaves.
1779. The Franco-Dutch settlers send representatives to Holland praying for reforms.
1783. Birth of Tshaka.

1786. Fish River declared limit of colony, and magistracy established at Graaf-Reinet.
1795. British Force (under Admiral Elphinstone and General Craig) take possession of the Cape.
1803. Restoration of the Cape to the Dutch after the Treaty of Amiens.
1806. Surrender of the Cape by General Janssens to Sir David Baird.

Period of British Rule.

1806. Population of Colony = 73,663, of whom 26,720 were of European descent; exports £60,000, imports £100,000.
1807. *Earl of Caledon* appointed Governor—postal communication, circuit courts, regulations for Hottentots.
1812. *Sir John Cradock*: "loan-leases" converted into perpetual quit-rent properties—public schools established in country districts.
  I. Kafir War (1811-12): Kafirs driven back to original Dutch frontier (the Fish River). Foundation of Grahamstown.
1814. *Lord Charles Somerset.*
1815. The Cape formally ceded to England by Holland. (The agreement passed the Cape and other possessions (notably Ceylon) to the British Government in return for Java and a sum of money.)
1817. ⎫ II. Kafir War: Defence of Grahamstown by Wiltshire—boundary advanced to Chumie and Keiskamma Rivers—Missionaries sent to Gaika tribe.
1819. ⎭
1820. Albany Settlement: arrival of 5000 British emigrants at Algoa Bay. Foundation of Port Elizabeth.
1826. *General Bourke*: ordinance declaring free coloured men equal in law with the whites.
  Report of Royal Commission: establishment of Executive Council, Supreme Court, Resident Magistrates (in place of Land-drosts), Schools, &c. (conversion of Dutch into English Colony). English ordered to be used as official language.
1833. Abolition Act.
1834. *Sir Benjamin D'Urban*: Slave emancipation carried out.
1834. ⎫ III. Kafir War: invasion of Colony by Kafirs—boundary advanced to Kei River: Lord Glenelg's despatch ordering evacuation of new territory, disaffection of "Boer" population.
1835. ⎭
1835. ⎫ Exodus of the "emigrant farmers."
1838. ⎭
1837. Defeat of Moselekatse by Hendrik Potgieter
1838. Massacre of Retief's party by Dingan.
  Pretorius (Andries) is Commandant-General of Boers—defeat of Dingan (Dec. 10).
1843. British government established in Natal.
1846. ⎫ IV. Kafir War (War of the Axe): war with the Gaikas—terminated by Sir Harry Smith.
1848. ⎭
1847. *Sir Henry Pottinger* first Governor and High Commissioner

HISTORICAL SUMMARY

1848. *Sir Henry Smith*: Declaration of British Sovereignty up to the Vaal River and the Drakensberg mountains.
1849. Convict agitation in Cape Colony.
1851. ⎫
1853. ⎭ V. Kafir War. Moshesh, Basuto chief, submits.
1852. Sand River Convention. Boers beyond the Vaal are absolved from their allegiance, and Pretorius is pardoned.
1853. ⎫ Boers of Orange River Sovereignty revolt. Imperial Government decide upon a policy of non-interference—withdraw
1854. ⎭ troops—acknowledge Orange Free State by convention of Bloemfontein.
1853. Representative Government (elective Council and Assembly) granted to Cape Colony.
1854. *Sir George Grey*: New Kafir Policy.
1857. Settlement of Anglo-German legion (2000) on the Buffalo River (East London founded).
1858. Agricultural German immigration (2000).
1862. *Sir Philip Wodehouse*: policy of retrenchment insisted upon by the Imperial Government.
1863. First line of railway opened—public works policy initiated.
1865. British Kaffraria incorporated into the colony.
1869. *Sir Henry Barkly*: authorised to bring in Responsible Government. Discovery of diamonds.
1871. Proclamation of British authority over the diamond fields.
1872. New constitution (Responsible Government) received royal assent: Sir John Molteno first Premier.
1873. Colony divided into legislative districts.
1874. Mr Froude's mission in favour of confederation scheme of Lord Carnarvon.
1877. *Sir Bartle Frere*: authorised to carry out confederation of South African states as Governor of the Cape Colony and High Commissioner in South Africa (April).
Annexation of the Transvaal (April 12th).
1877-8. Subjugation of Kreli and Sandele.
1879. The Zulu War.
Lord Wolseley, High Commissioner for South-East Africa (June). Administrator of Transvaal.
1880. June 29. Federation Proposals defeated in Cape Parliament.
Aug. 1. Recall of Sir Bartle Frere.
Sir Hercules Robinson succeeds.
Boers revolt under Triumvirate Kruger, Joubert, and Pretorius (Dec. 16).
1881. Convention of Pretoria (independence of South African Republic (Transvaal) recognised. Suzerain rights of British Government maintained).
1883. Imperial Government take over Basutoland.
1884. Convention of London (modification of Convention of Pretoria: Bechuanaland Protectorate (Feb. 27).

SOUTH AFRICA

1885. Sir Charles Warren's Expedition. Extension of Protectorate and formation of Crown Colony.
1886. Discovery of Gold at Witwatersrandt (Johannesburg).
1887. Zululand taken over by Imperial Government.
1888. Treaty with Lobengula and mineral concessions obtained in Mashonaland.
1889. *Sir Henry Loch* succeeds.
1889. Customs Union Convention (first step towards federation of South Africa).
Charter granted to British South Africa Company.
1890. Cecil Rhodes, Prime Minister. Pioneer Expedition to Salisbury.
1891. Anglo-Portuguese Convention.
1893. Matabele War.
1894. Matabele Settlement.
Glen Grey Act.
B.S.A. Coy. undertake administration of country north of Zambesi (Nov. 4).
Swazi Convention (Dec. 10).
1895. *Sir Hercules Robinson* re-appointed.
Annexation of Pondoland.

1895.
Dec. 26. Manifesto of Transvaal National Union issued at Johannesburg.
,, 29. Dr Jameson's force starts.
1896.
Jan. 2. Surrender of Dr Jameson's force to the Boers.
,, ,, Sir Hercules Robinson leaves Capetown for Pretoria.
,, 6. Mr Rhodes resigns Premiership of the Cape Colony.
March 5. Rinderpest appears at Buluwayo.
,, 20. Outbreak of Native insurrection in Rhodesia.
April 28. Sentence on Reformers at Pretoria.
,, ,, Lord Grey arrives at Buluwayo.
June 2. General Carrington arrives at Buluwayo.
July 17. Cape Committee report on the Raid.
,, 29. Sentence passed on Dr Jameson, Sir John Willoughby, and others.
,, 30. South Africa Committee ordered.
Aug. 21. Mr Rhodes meets rebel chiefs in Matoppos.
Oct. 18. Lord Grey addresses letter to Secretary of the Chartered Company.

STATISTICAL APPENDIX.

I. Area, population, and trade of South Africa compared with those of other countries.

	Area in Square Miles	Population			Trade £ (92-'93).
		White.	Coloured.	Total.	
South Africa	1,250,000	668,000	3,582,000	4,250,000	26,500,000
The United Kingdom	120,973	38,104,973	...	38,104,973	682,499,531
India	1,560,160	240,000	286,983,000	287,223,431	126,986,760
Australasia	3,175,119	4,185,297	100,000	4,285,297	125,339,478
Canada	3,315,647	English Speaking 3,428,265 French Speaking 1,404,974	...	4,833,239	49,596,461
United States . . .	3,501,409	54,983,890	7,470,040	62,654,302	339,486,341

II. Maritime Trade of United Kingdom in 1889.

(Based upon Sir Rawson Rawson's "Analysis.")

IMPORTS.

	per cent.		
Food	41·7	} = ⅞ths	£178,000,000
Raw Materials (with Ores)	42·5		181,400,000
Manufactured and Miscellaneous	15·8		67,800,000
		Total,	£427,200,000

EXPORTS.

Imports *Re*-exported £66,700,000

		per cent.		
British Produce	Textiles	45	} = ⅞ths.	
	Iron and Steel Manufactures,	25		
	Other Manufactures	15		
	Raw Materials	15		248,900,000
		Total	.	£315,600,000

Grand Total . . £742,800,000.

Partial Analysis of some Imports.

Grain . £52,200,000 12·2 p.c. of total Imports.
    Of which
        18,200,000 (= ⅓rd.) is from United States.
        14,000,000 is from Russia, India, Canada, Australia, &c.

Cotton . £45,800,000 10·7 p.c. of total Imports.
    Of which
        33,600,000 (= ⅔rds.) is from United States.
        5,000,000 is from India.

Wool . . £29,700,000 7 p.c. of total Imports.
    Of which
        25,400,000 (= ⅚ths) is from Australasia.
        3,000,000 (= 1/10 th) is from South Africa.

Note.—Value is only a partial measure. Bulk of goods is largely increasing. Price of goods is steadily going down.

For 1894, returns are	Imports .	.	£408,500,000
	British Exports	.	216,100,000
	Re-Exports .	.	57,900,000
	True Total .	.	£682,666,441

STATISTICAL APPENDIX

III. South African Exports in 1893.

Minerals		£10,000,000
Gold	£5,500,000	
Diamonds	4,000,000	
Copper	200,000	
Pastoral		4,000,000
Wool	2,400,000	
Ostrich Feathers	500,000	
Hides	500,000	
Hair (Angora)	500,000	
Wine		18,964
Sugar		95,943
True Total { By Durban	£1,242,169	£14,398,758
{ By Cape Ports	13,156,589	

Exports from Cape Colony only in 1892.

Wool	£2,029,093
Ostrich Feathers	517,009
Hides	478,379
Copper ore	253,681
Hair (Angora)	373,810
Wine	18,645
Grain, &c.	7,589
Diamonds	3,906,992

(From *Statesman's Yearbook*, 1894.)

IV. Gold-producing Countries.

	£ value in 1894.
North America	9,000,000
Australasia	8,000,000
Transvaal	7,000,000
Russia (1892)	4,000,000
World's Output	35,000,000

(Based on Mr Hamilton Smith's estimate.)

V. Wheat production of the Cape Colony compared with that of other Countries.

	Bushels in 1892.
Cape Colony	3,890,898
Canada	48,182,295
Australasia	41,161,057
The United Kingdom	60,775,000
France	327,000,000
The United States	315,949,000

Wheat Production of the World.

	1893. Bushels.	1892. Bushels.
Europe	1,435,666,000	1,406,933,000
Asia	345,896,000	289,944,000
Africa	35,514,000	34,464,000
Australasia	41,161,000	35,963,000
S. America	81,644,000	51,262,000
N. America	447,479,000	574,131,000
Total	2,387,360,000	2,391,697,000

(From *Statistics of American Department of Agriculture*.)

VI. Wool-exporting Countries.

	£ value in 1893.
Australasia	25,000,000
South Africa	2,400,000
Russia	1,000,000

VII. Wine exports of the Cape Colony and Victoria in 1892.

	Gallons.	£
Victoria	273,253	63,235
Cape Colony	78,836	17,964

Fertility of Vineyards in various Countries, as estimated by Baron von Babo.

Germany	24	hectolitres per hectare.
France	18¼	,, ,,
Spain	17	,, ,,
United States	14½	,, ,,
Australia	14½	,, ,,
Cape Colony—Coast Districts	86½	,, ,,
,, Inland ,,	173	,, ,,

(From *Official Handbook to the Cape Colony, &c.*, p. 271.)

VIII. Statistics of Colonies, States and Territories of South-Central Africa.

	Area in Square Miles.	Population.			Revenue. £	Expenditure. £
		White.	Coloured.	Total.		
Cape of Good Hope	222,311	376,987	1,150,237	1,527,224	6,446,149	5,734,503 ('93-'94)
Natal	20,461	42,759	512,817	555,576	1,069,678	1,099,858 ('92-'93)
Pondoland	3,869	100	200,000	200,100		
Zululand	8,900	548	145,336	145,884	45,592	43,923 ('94)
Amatongaland	5,300	...	80,000	80,000		
Basutoland	10,293	578	218,324	218,892	25,666	('93-'94)
British Bechuanaland	60,777	5,284	55,122	60,376	55,370	237,928 ('93-'94)
Bechuana Protectorate	386,200	500	110,000	110,500		
British Mashonaland (South of Zambesi)	150,000	2,500	250,000	252,500	44,489	65,766 ('93-'94)
Orange Free State	48,326	77,716	129,787	207,503	293,790	323,899 ('93-'94)
South African Republic	113,642	160,000	649,560	809,560	1,702,684	1,302,054 ('93)
Swazieland	8,000	500	63,000	63,500		
German Protectorate	322,450	1,000	116,000	117,000		
Portuguese Possessions	271,600	400	1,500,000	1,500,400		
British Central Africa and Nyassaland (North of Zambesi)	600,000	200	2,000,000	2,000,200		

This Table is from the *Official Handbook* for the Cape, &c., published in 1893; but the figures for Revenue and Expenditure have been revised from the latest returns available as noted. The Bechuanaland revenue is increased by an Imperial grant of (about) £100,000, and the expenditure as given includes the cost of the B. B. Police, £178,773 (of which £80,000 was extraordinary expenditure on account of the Matebele War). The Mashonaland expenditure does not include the cost of the Matebele War (see p. 217).

FULL TEXT OF CONVENTION OF LONDON, 1884.

A CONVENTION between HER MAJESTY THE QUEEN OF THE UNITED KINGDOM OF GREAT BRITAIN AND IRELAND and the SOUTH AFRICAN REPUBLIC.

WHEREAS the Government of the Transvaal State, through its Delegates, consisting of Stephanus Johannes Paulus Kruger, President of the said State, Stephanus Jacobus Du Toit, Superintendent of Education, and Nicholas Jacobus Smit, a member of the Volksraad, have represented that the Convention signed at Pretoria on the 3rd day of August 1881, and ratified by the Volksraad of the said State on the 25th October 1881, contains certain provisions which are inconvenient, and imposes burdens and obligations from which the said State is desirous to be relieved, and that the south-western boundaries fixed by the said Convention should be amended, with a view to promote the peace and good order of the said State, and of the countries adjacent thereto; and whereas Her Majesty the Queen of the United Kingdom of Great Britain and Ireland, has been pleased to take the said representations into consideration: Now, therefore, Her Majesty has been pleased to direct, and it is hereby declared, that the following articles of a new Convention, signed on behalf of Her Majesty by Her Majesty's High Commissioner in South Africa, the Right Honourable Sir Hercules George Robert Robinson, Knight Grand Cross of the Most Distinguished Order of Saint Michael and Saint George, Governor of the Colony of the Cape of Good Hope, and on behalf of the Transvaal State (which shall hereinafter be called the South African Republic) by the above-named Delegates, Stephanus Johannes Paulus Kruger, Stephanus Jacobus Du Toit, and Nicholas Jacobus Smit, shall, when ratified by the Volksraad of the South African Republic, be substituted for the articles embodied in the Convention of 3rd August 1881; which latter, pending such ratification, shall continue in full force and effect.

CONVENTION OF LONDON, 1884

Article I.

The territory of the South African Republic will embrace the land lying between the following boundaries, to wit :—

Beginning from the point where the north-eastern boundary line of Griqualand West meets the Vaal River, up the course of the Vaal River to the point of junction with it of the Klip River; thence up the course of Klip River to the point of junction with it of the stream called Gansvlei; thence up the Gansvlei stream to its source in the Drakensberg; thence to a beacon in the boundary of Natal, situated immediately opposite and close to the source of the Gansvlei stream; thence in a north-easterly direction along the ridge of the Drakensberg, dividing the waters flowing into the Gansvlei stream from the waters flowing into the sources of the Buffalo, to a beacon on a point where this mountain ceases to be a continuous chain; thence to a beacon on a plain to the north-east of the last described beacon; thence to the nearest source of a small stream called "Division Stream;" thence down this division stream, which forms the southern boundary of the farm Sandfontein, the property of Messrs Meek, to its junction with the Coldstream; thence down the Coldstream to its junction with the Buffalo or Umzinayti River; thence down the coast of the Buffalo River to the junction with it of the Blood River; thence up the course of the Blood River to the junction with it of Lyn Spruit or Dudusi; thence up the Dudusi to its source; thence 80 yards to Bea. I., situated on a spur of the N'Qaba-Ka hawana Mountains; thence 80 yards to the N'Sonto River; thence down the N'Sonto River to its junction with the White Umvulozi River; thence up the White Umvulozi River to a white rock where it rises; thence 800 yards to Kambula Hill (Bea. II.); thence to the source of the Pemvana River, where the road from Kambula Camp to Burgers' Lager crosses; thence down the Pemvana River to its junction with the Bivana River; thence down the Bivana River to its junction with the Pongolo River; thence down the Pongolo River to where it passes through the Libombo Range; thence along the summits of the Libombo Range to the northern point of the N'Yawos Hill in that range (Bea. XVI.); thence to the northern peak of the Inkwakweni Hills (Bea. XV.); thence to Sefunda, a rocky knoll detached from and to the north-east end of the White Koppies, and to the south of the Musana River (Bea. XIV.); thence to a point on the slope near the crest of Matanjeni, which is the name given to the south-eastern portion of the Mahamba Hills (Bea. XIII.); thence to the N'gwangwana, a double-pointed hill (one point is bare, the other wooded, the beacon being on the former), on the left bank of the Assegai River and upstream of Dadusa Spruit (Bea. XII.); thence to the southern point of Bendita, a rocky knoll in a plain between the Little Hlozane and Assegai Rivers (Bea. XI.); thence to the highest point of Suluka Hill, round the eastern slopes of which flows the Little Hlozane, also called Ludaka or Mudspruit (Bea. X.); thence to the beacon known as "Viljoen's," or N'Duko Hill; thence to a point north-east of Derby House, known as Magwazidili's Beacon; thence to the Igaba, a small knoll on the Ungwempisi River, also called "Joubert's Beacon," and known to the natives as "Piet's Beacon" (Bea. IX.); thence to the highest point of the N'Dhlovudwalili or Houtbosch, a hill on the northern bank of the Umqwempisi River (Bea. VIII.); thence to a beacon on the only flat-topped rock, about 10 feet high and about 30 yards in circumference at its base, situated on the south side of the Lamsamane range of hills, and overlooking the valley of the great Usuto River; this rock being 45 yards north of the road from Camden and Lake Banagher to the forests on the Usuto River (sometimes called Sandhlanas Beacon) (Bea. VII.); thence to the Gulungwana or Ibubulundi, four smooth bare hills, the highest in that neighbourhood, situated to the south of the Umtuli River (Bea. VI.); thence to a flat-topped rock, 8 feet high, on the crest of the Busuku, a low rocky range south-west of the Impulazi River (Bea. V.); thence to a low bare hill on the north-east of and overlooking the Impulazi River to the south of it being a tributary of the Impulazi, with a considerable waterfall, and the road from the river passing 200 yards to the north-west of the beacon (Bea. IV.); thence to the highest point of the Mapumula range, the watershed of the Little Usuto River on the north, and the Umpulazi River on the south, the hill the top of which is a bare rock, falling abruptly towards the Little Usuto (Bea. III.); thence to the western point of a doublepointed rocky hill, precipitous on all sides, called Makwana, its top being a bare rock (Bea. II.); thence to the top of a rugged hill of considerable height falling abruptly to the Komati River, this hill being the northern extremity of the Isilotwani range, and separated from the highest peak of the range Inkomokazi (a sharp cone) by a deep neck (Bea. I.). (On a ridge in the straight line between Beacons I. and II. is an intermediate beacon.) From Beacon I. the boundary runs to a hill across the Komati River, and thence along the crest of the range of hills known as the Makongwa, which runs north-east and south-west, to Kamhlubana Peak; thence in a straight line to Mananga, a point in the Libombo range, and thence to the nearest point in the Portuguese frontier on the Libombo range; thence along the summits of the Libombo range to the middle of the poort where the Komati River passes through it, called the lowest Komati Poort; thence in a north by easterly direction to Pokioens Kop, situated on the north side of the Olifant's River, where it passes through the ridges; thence about north north-west to the nearest point of Serra di Chicundo; and thence to the junction of the Pafori River with the Limpopo or Crocodile River; thence up the course of the Limpopo River to the point where the Marique River falls into it. Thence up the course of the Marique River to "Derde Poort," where it passes through a low range of hills, called Sikwane, a beacon (No. 10) being erected on the spur of said range near to, and westward of, the banks of the river; thence, in a straight line, through this beacon to a beacon (No. 9), erected on the top of the same range, about 1700 yards distant from beacon No. 10;

thence, in a straight line, to a beacon (No. 8) erected on the highest point of an isolated hill, called Dikgagong, or "Wildebeest Kop," situated south-eastward of, and about 3½ miles distant from a high hill, called Moripe ; thence, in a straight line, to a beacon (No. 7) erected on the summit of an isolated hill or "koppie" forming the eastern extremity of the range of hills called Moshweu, situated to the northward of, and about two miles distant from, a large isolated hill called Chukudu-Chochwa ; thence, in a straight line, to a beacon (No. 6) erected on the summit of a hill forming part of the same range Moshweu ; thence, in a straight line, to a beacon (No. 5) erected on the summit of a pointed hill in the same range ; thence, in a straight line, to a beacon (No. 4) erected on the summit of the western extremity of the same range; thence, in a straight line, to a beacon (No. 3) erected on the summit of the northern extremity of a low, bushy hill, or "Koppie," near to and eastward of the Notwane River ; thence, in a straight line, to the junction of the stream called Metsi Mashwane with the Notwane River (No. 2); thence up the course of the Notwane River to Sengoma, being the Poort where the river passes through the Dwarsberg range ; thence, as described in the Award given by Lieutenant-Governor Keate, dated October 17, 1871, by Pitlanganyane (narrow place), Deboaganka or Schaapkuil, Sibatoul (bare place), and Maclase, to Ramatlabama, a pool on a spruit north of the Molopo River. From Ratmalabama the boundary shall run to the summit of an isolated hill, called Leganka ; thence, in a straight line, passing north-east of a Native Station, near "Buurman's Drift," on the Molopo River, to that point on the road from Mosiega to the old drift where a road turns out through the Native Station to the new drift below ; thence to "Buurman's Old Drift ;" thence in a straight line, to a marked and isolated clump of trees near to and north-west of the dwelling-house of C. Austin, a tenant on the farm "Vleifontein," No. 117 ; thence, in a straight line, to the north-western corner beacon of the farm "Mooimeisjesfontein," No. 30 ; thence, along the western line of the said farm "Mooimeisjesfontein," and in prolongation thereof, as far as the road leading from "Ludik's Drift," on the Molopo River, past the homestead of "Mooimeisjesfontein," towards the Salt Pans near Harts River ; thence, along the said road, crossing the direct road from Polfontein to Sehuba, and until the direct road from Polfontein to Lotlakane or Pietfontein is reached ; thence along the southern edge of the last-named road towards Lotlakane, until the first garden ground of that station is reached ; thence, in a south-westerly direction, skirting Lotlakane, so as to leave it and all its garden ground in native territory, until the road from Lotlakane to Kunana is reached ; thence along the east side, and clear of that road towards Kunana, until the garden grounds of that station are reached ; thence, skirting Kunana, so as to include it and all its garden ground, but no more, in the Transvaal, until the road from Kunana to Mamusa is reached ; thence, along the eastern side and clear of the road towards Mamusa, until a road turns out towards Taungs ; thence, along the eastern side and clear of the road towards Taungs, till the line of the district known as "Stellaland" is reached, about 11 miles from Taungs; thence, along the line of the district Stellaland, to the Harts River about 24 miles below Mamusa; thence across Harts River, to the junction of the roads from Monthe and Phokwane; thence, along the western side and clear of the nearest road towards "Koppie Enkel," an isolated hill about 36 miles from Mamusa, and about 18 miles north of Christiana, and to the summit of the said hill; thence, in a straight line, to that point on the north-east boundary of Griqualand West as beaconed by Mr Surveyor Ford, where two farms, registered as Nos. 72 and 75, do meet, about midway between the Vaal and Harts Rivers, measured along the said boundary of Griqualand West; thence to the first point where the north-east boundary of Griqualand West meets the Vaal River.

Article II.

The Government of the South African Republic will strictly adhere to the boundaries defined in the first Article of this Convention, and will do its utmost to prevent any of its inhabitants from making any encroachments upon lands beyond the said boundaries. The Government of the South African Republic will appoint Commissioners upon the eastern and western borders whose duty it will be strictly to guard against irregularities and all trespassing over the boundaries. Her Majesty's Government will, if necessary, appoint Commissioners in the native territories outside the eastern and western borders of the South African Republic to maintain order and prevent encroachments.

Her Majesty's Government and the Government of the South African Republic will each appoint a person to proceed together to beacon off the amended south-west boundary as described in Article I. of this Convention; and the President of the Orange Free State shall be requested to appoint a referee to whom the said persons shall refer any questions on which they may disagree respecting the interpretation of the said Article, and the decision of such referee thereon shall be final. The arrangement already made, under the terms of Article 19 of the Convention of Pretoria of the 3rd August 1881, between the owners of the farms Grootfontein and Valleifontein on the one hand, and the Barolong authorities on the other, by which a fair share of the water supply of the said farms shall be allowed to flow undisturbed to the said Barolongs, shall continue in force.

Article III.

If a British officer is appointed to reside at Pretoria or elsewhere within the South African Republic to discharge functions analogous to those of a Consular officer he will receive the protection and assistance of the Republic.

Article IV.

The South African Republic will conclude no treaty or engagement with any State or nation other than the Orange Free State, nor with any native tribe to the eastward or westward of the Republic, until the same has been approved by Her Majesty the Queen.

Such approval shall be considered to have been granted if Her Majesty's Government shall not, within six months after receiving a copy of such treaty (which shall be delivered to them immediately upon its completion), have notified that the conclusion of such treaty is in conflict with the interests of Great Britain or of any of Her Majesty's possessions in South Africa.

Article V.

The South African Republic will be liable for any balance which may still remain due of the debts for which it was liable at the date of Annexation, to wit, the Cape Commercial Bank Loan, the Railway Loan, and the Orphan Chamber Debt, which debts will be a first charge upon the revenues of the Republic. The South African Republic will, moreover, be liable to Her Majesty's Government for £250,000, which will be a second charge upon the revenues of the Republic.

Article VI.

The debt due as aforesaid by the South African Republic to Her Majesty's Government will bear interest at the rate of three and a half per cent. from the date of the ratification of this Convention, and shall be repayable by a payment for interest and Sinking Fund of six pounds and ninepence per £100 per annum, which will extinguish the debt in twenty-five years. The said payment of six pounds and ninepence per £100 shall be payable half-yearly, in British currency, at the close of each half year from the date of such ratification: Provided always that the South African Republic shall be at liberty at the close of any half year to pay off the whole or any portion of the outstanding debt.

Interest at the rate of three and a half per cent. on the debt as standing under the Convention of Pretoria shall as heretofore be paid to the date of the ratification of this Convention.

Article VII.

All persons who held property in the Transvaal on the 8th day of August 1881, and still hold the same, will continue to enjoy the rights of property which they have enjoyed since the 12th April 1877. No person who has remained loyal to Her Majesty during the late hostilities shall suffer any molestation by reason of his loyalty; or be liable to any criminal prosecution or civil action for any part taken in connexion with such hostilities ; and all such persons will have full liberty to reside in the country, with enjoyment of all civil rights, and protection for their persons and property.

Article VIII.

The South African Republic renews the declaration made in the Sand River Convention, and in the Convention of Pretoria, that no slavery or apprenticeship partaking of slavery will be tolerated by the Government of the said Republic.

Article IX.

There will continue to be complete freedom of religion and protection from molestation for all denominations, provided the same be not inconsistent with morality and good order ; and no disability shall attach to any person in regard to rights of property by reason of the religious opinions which he holds.

Article X.

The British officer appointed to reside in the South African Republic will receive every assistance from the Government of the said Republic in making due provision for the proper care and preservation of the graves of such of Her Majesty's Forces as have died in the Transvaal ; and if need be, for the appropriation of land for the purpose.

Article XI.

All grants or titles issued at any time by the Transvaal Government in respect of land outside the boundary of the South African Republic, as defined in Article I., shall be considered invalid and of no effect, except in so far as any such grant or title relates to land that falls within the boundary of the South African Republic ; and all persons holding any such grant so considered invalid and of no effect will receive from the Government of the South African Republic such compensation, either in land or in money, as the Volksraad shall determine. In all cases in which any Native Chiefs or other authorities outside the said boundaries have received any adequate consideration from the Government of the South African Republic for land excluded from the Transvaal by the first Article of this Convention, or where permanent improvements have been made on the land, the High Commissioner will recover from the native authorities fair compensation for the loss of the land thus excluded, or of the permanent improvements thereon.

Article XII.

The independence of the Swazis, within the boundary line of Swaziland, as indicated in the first Article of this Convention, will be fully recognised.

CONVENTION OF LONDON, 1884

Article XIII.

Except in pursuance of any treaty or engagement made as provided in Article 4 of this Convention, no other or higher duties shall be imposed on the importation into the South African Republic of any article coming from any part of Her Majesty's dominions than are or may be imposed on the like article coming from any other place or country; nor will any prohibition be maintained or imposed on the importation into the South African Republic of any article coming from any part of Her Majesty's dominions which shall not equally extend to the like article coming from any other place or country. And in like manner the same treatment shall be given to any article coming to Great Britain from the South African Republic as to the like article coming from any other place or country.

These provisions do not preclude the consideration of special arrangements as to important duties and commercial relations between the South African Republic and any of Her Majesty's colonies or possessions.

Article XIV.

All persons, other than natives, conforming themselves to the laws of the South African Republic (*a*) will have full liberty, with their families, to enter, travel, or reside in any part of the South African Republic; (*b*) they will be entitled to hire or possess houses, manufactories, warehouses, shops, and premises; (*c*) they may carry on their commerce either in person or by any agents whom they may think fit to employ; (*d*) they will not be subject, in respect of their persons or property, or in respect of their commerce or industry, to any taxes, whether general or local, other than those which are or may be imposed upon citizens of the said Republic.

Article XV.

All persons, other than natives, who established their domicile in the Transvaal between the 12th day of April 1877, and the 8th August 1881, and who within 12 months after such last-mentioned date have had their names registered by the British Resident, shall be exempt from all compulsory military service whatever.

Article XVI.

Provision shall hereafter be made by a separate instrument for the mutual extradition of criminals, and also for the surrender of deserters from Her Majesty's Forces.

Article XVII.

All debts contracted between the 12th April 1877 and the 8th August 1881 will be payable in the same currency in which they may have been contracted.

Article XVIII.

No grants of land which may have been made, and no transfers or mortgages which may have been passed, between the 12th April 1877 and the 8th August 1881, will be invalidated by reason merely of their having been made or passed between such dates.

All transfers to the British Secretary for Native Affairs in trust for Natives will remain in force, an officer of the South African Republic taking the place of such Secretary for Native Affairs.

Article XIX.

The Government of the South African Republic will engage faithfully to fulfil the assurances given, in accordance with the laws of the South African Republic, to the natives at the Pretoria Pitso by the Royal Commission in the presence of the Triumvirate and with their entire assent, (1) as to the freedom of the natives to buy or otherwise acquire lands under certain conditions, (2) as to the appointment of a commission to mark out native locations, (3) as to the access of the natives to the courts of law, and (4) as to their being allowed to move freely within the country, or to leave it for any legal purpose, under a pass system.

Article XX.

This Convention will be ratified by a Volksraad of the South African Republic within the period of six months after its execution, and in default of such ratification this Convention shall be null and void.

Signed in duplicate in London this 27th day of February 1884.

(Signed)	HERCULES ROBINSON.
,,	S. J. P. KRUGER.
,,	S. J. DU TOIT.
,,	N. J. SMIT.

[C—3914.]

www.ingramcontent.com/pod-product-compliance
Lightning Source LLC
Chambersburg PA
CBHW022023240426
43667CB00042B/1065